THE WINES OF NEW ZEALAND

THE WINES OF
NEW
ZEALAND

REBECCA GIBB MW

Rebecca Gibb MW is an award-winning wine journalist and editor. Securing her first editorial role at UK wine trade magazine *Harpers* after being named UK Young Wine Writer of the Year in 2006, she has since edited several print and online publications. Rebecca contributes to prestigious titles including *Decanter*, *The World of Fine Wine*, *LUX* and *Wine Business International*, in addition to running a small business, The Drinks Project, and a puzzle company, Bamboozled.

In 2015, Rebecca became a Master of Wine. In a record class of 24 graduates, she was awarded the Outstanding Achievement Award and the Bollinger Medal in recognition of outstanding tasting ability.

Having lived in New Zealand from 2010 to 2016 with her Kiwi husband and son, Rebecca recently returned to the UK. She maintains her strong ties with the people and wines of Aotearoa.

First published in 2018 by
Infinite Ideas Limited
www.infideas.com

A CIP catalogue record for this book is available from the British Library
ISBN 978-1-906821-82-1

Maps © Igor Drecki, 2018

Front cover photo © Cephas/Kevin Judd. Back cover photo courtesy of Terence Stevens-Prior.

Page 93 courtesy of The Landing; page 98 courtesy of Terence Stevens-Prior; page 121 courtesy of Millton Vineyards & Winery; pages 144 and 164 courtesy of Craggy Range; page 184 courtesy of Auntsfield Estate; page 210 courtesy of Seifried Estate; page 224 courtesy of Kevin Judd; page 238 courtesy of Jim Jerram; page 263 © Thirst Press.

Colour plates supplied as follows: page 1 (top) courtesy of The Landing (bottom) courtesy of Destiny Bay, Auckland; page 2 (top) courtesy of Terence Stevens-Prior (bottom) courtesy of Vinoptima; page 3 (top) courtesy of Sacred Hill (bottom) courtesy of Craggy Range; page 4 (top) courtesy of Palliser (bottom) courtesy of Escarpment Vineyard; page 5 (top) courtesy of Cloudy Bay (bottom) courtesy of Brancott Estate; page 6 (top) courtesy of Chocolate Dog Studio (bottom) courtesy of Neudorf Vineyards; page 7 (top) courtesy of Black Estate (bottom) courtesy of Dean Mackenzie; page 8 (top) courtesy of Jim Jerram (bottom) courtesy of Mike Wilson, Prophet's Rock.

Printed in Britain

CONTENTS

ACKNOWLEDGEMENTS

The writing of a book is a rather solitary experience that requires more stamina than a marathon. The process of writing a book is far from solitary, however. Without the support of my other half, this book would not have been possible. Ben has experienced the ups and downs of this endeavour, which has seen us travel from the UK to the other side of the world with a three year old in tow. Life has thrown its share of obstacles en route and it is with great sadness that we said an untimely goodbye to my brother-in-law Nick and my father-in-law's new wife Heather while we were in New Zealand to research the book.

There are many people who have helped along the way in their different ways. First of all, I am greatly indebted to New Zealand Winegrowers without whom I would not have been able to visit New Zealand to conduct the additional research necessary. The UK team, Chris Stroud and Sarah Shepherd, continue to offer support and the occasional cup of tea. The regional wine bodies across New Zealand have also been instrumental in organizing visits and providing essential information.

I am greatly indebted to all those involved in grape and wine research in New Zealand who have given their time freely to talk through their work and share their knowledge. In particular, I would like to thank Dr Wendy Parr who has always been willing to help me over the years. I owe you far too many drinks. To those involved in the history of New Zealand, thanks go to Kevyn Moore, an expert on Romeo Bragato's life, Paul Mooney for providing access to the Mission Estate archives and to Graeme Cowley of Auntsfield for his work on the Marlborough pioneer David Herd.

There are too many wine producers to mention who have opened their doors, their minds and their wines to assist with the project. Occasionally they have opened their homes too and it is a privilege to be invited to share dinner with their families. There are a number of individuals and wineries that I owe particular thanks to. In the North Island, James and Annie Millton, Glenn and Jan Cunningham, the Ata Rangi team, and all at The Landing, Northland for your warm hospitality. Also to Rick Lindsay of Luna Estate who provided an excellent taxi service to Martinborough, complete with coffee and an excellent music selection. On the South Island, thank you to the Herzogs in Marlborough for their unstinting generosity, Anna Flowerday of Te Whare Ra for sourcing the Beavertown T-shirt and a huge shout out to Nick Gill of Greystone and Muddy Water and his stupendous wife Angela, who provided warmth, shelter and lots of support. And to Paul Pujol of Prophet's Rock who has always thrown open the doors to the vineyard cottage and lavished us with his insightful and humorous company. The view really is hard to beat.

I have many friends and colleagues that have provided support along the way. To the editors that have sent me on this route: Christian Davis, Stuart Peskett, Richard 'chief' Siddle, Guy Woodward, Amy Wislocki, Felicity Carter and to all those who have supported my journalistic endeavours, thank you. Writing about wine has also brought great friendships: Tina Gellie has supported me along this undulating path and always provides a great bottle from her stash, which we usually enjoy while watching *Only Connect* dressed in our pyjamas. To my mum and dad and sister who put up with me, thank you for your support. And to my son, Macaulay, you have not been a great deal of use assisting with the writing of this book, but you are a wonderful distraction and our baking sessions have provided many sweet treats to get me through the afternoon slump.

Thanks also to the Infinite Ideas team. Firstly to Sarah-Jane Evans MW, whom I met on the Eurostar on a press trip to Burgundy just days after she had received her Master of Wine. A decade later, she presented me with my Master of Wine certificate and it was she who put my name forward to author this book. To Richard Burton and Rebecca Clare at Infinite Ideas for supporting me on this journey and providing your expertise in taking this from manuscript to published work. And to Millie Hoskins of United Agents, your patience will be rewarded.

To those I have inadvertently overlooked, I offer my sincerest apologies and the promise of a decent glass of New Zealand Sauvignon Blanc, Pinot Noir – or maybe even an Albariño.

INTRODUCTION

My love affair with New Zealand wine began on a trip to Australia. In 2006, I secured a job working for a family friend's winery in the Alpine Valleys, Victoria and before starting a gruelling harvest, a three-week cycle trip around New Zealand beckoned. Leaving Sydney behind, two hours and then three hours passed, before finally touching down in Auckland four hours later. Make no mistake, New Zealand may be considered part of Australasia but it is not close to Australia. In the same time, you could take a flight from London to Moscow.

Arriving at Auckland's finest Youth Hostel Association premises in the pouring rain without luggage, the omens were not good but things soon looked up: a day trip to Waiheke, 'the island of wine', followed by a night out at a seedy backpackers' bar (wearing clothes borrowed from a girl in the same dorm) where I met my future husband shifted my Kiwi experience into gear. There was only time to visit a few wineries on the trip: I longingly pressed my nose up against the bus window as we drove through Marlborough without stopping but the wines were as bright and clear as the New Zealand skies. The unglamorous reality of my Australian harvest experience made it glaringly obvious that winemaking was not my calling and after a bit of luck and a lot of hard work I found myself in the equally unglamorous offices of wine-trade magazine *Harpers* in 2006, writing about the liquid that fills life's glass. In late 2009, New Zealand was calling again and with my other half, we moved back to his homeland. It was soon apparent that I had found a wine community where I felt comfortable. The suits and ties of the Bordelais were replaced with singlets, shorts and flip-flops – or jandals, if you want to sound like a local.

It is an exciting time to be writing about New Zealand wine. It remains a young winegrowing country but it has come of age since the 1990s and is now ripe for the equivalent of its Bar Mitzvah. And, let it be known, the New Zealand wine industry knows how to throw a great party. From wine exports of just 4 million litres in 1990, to 19.2 million litres in 2000, New Zealand has experienced a sharp ascent in its vinous fortunes: in 2010, exports had reached 142 million litres and in 2017, 253 million litres worth $1.6 billion, an increase of more than 6,000 per cent. Wine is now the country's fifth most exported good after dairy, meat, wood and fruit. Exported to all four corners of the earth, its exuberant expression of Sauvignon Blanc has made Marlborough a household name.

New Zealand and all those involved in the industry should celebrate its success but also remember it is not operating in a silo. Domestically, there are many cheerleaders, praising seemingly anything that comes out of a New Zealand winery, but this does not help the industry to improve. Those who know me will know that I do not refrain from giving an opinion but this is intended to foster debate and provide food for thought for New Zealand's wines and wineries. Constant praise does not help and becomes meaningless if doled out constantly. It is increasingly important to strive for continuous improvement and remain a world leader, with domestic consumption stagnating. Exports now represent more than 80 per cent of its annual wine sales (54 million litres sold in New Zealand in 2017 versus 253 million litres exported) and it is important for the industry to stay on its toes and understand what the competition is doing. Winemakers and wine critics must remain objective and take a world view of New Zealand's place in a wine store in New York or Tokyo: it is still a tiny drop in the world's wine lake.

New Zealand wine has reached its early adulthood with new faces, new varieties and innovative new methods appearing at breakneck speed and yet there is so much more to come. The national industry and all its many components are constantly adjusting, whether it is in the vineyard, the winery or the global marketplace. In a decade's time, the industry will be a different beast to the one we know today and this book will need to be updated to reflect those changes. It has been informative – and sometimes entertaining – to read New Zealand wine books that date from ten, twenty, thirty or even forty years ago. There are some familiar names that have survived the upheavals of oversupply and shortage, phylloxera, globalization and natural disasters to remain stalwarts of the New Zealand wine industry today. Photographs of current industry leaders in their youth, sporting outlandish hair styles and questionable clothing, have provided light relief from the long days researching and compiling this book. And yet there are many producers who have not survived the rapid evolution of New Zealand wine. This will not change.

This book is first and foremost a guide to New Zealand: its history, grape varieties, regions and contemporary themes. There is a hand-picked selection of must-try wines and wineries but this book is not a directory of producers: there were more than 670 producers in New Zealand at the last count (2017) and they cannot all be included or it would merely be a 'who's who' guide, which would quickly date and be almost as exciting as reading the phone book. It aims to be interesting, as wine is meant to be enjoyed, and all too often the fun is taken out of the glass. I am known to get excited about wine and I hope that this is reflected throughout these pages. That said, the book is designed to provide a comprehensive overview of the New Zealand wine scene: a reference for locals, international visitors and students alike.

I have poured six years of living in New Zealand, a two-month-long return visit traversing the country's vineyards and many months of research into this book. I have done my utmost, as have my editorial team, to offer an accurate picture of the current New Zealand wine landscape. I only wish I had written it sooner – it has been an incredible learning curve and given me a greater understanding of how far New Zealand wine has come in a very short time. I hope that you enjoy reading it, that it inspires you to explore New Zealand wine further, and that you will have an opportunity to enjoy first hand all the many delights of this majestic land laid out in the tourism chapter.

Note

All prices are in New Zealand dollars, unless stated otherwise. The grape varieties present in New Zealand and described in Chapter 3 are considered by colour in the order of most to least planted. Producer profiles in Parts 2 and 3 are arranged in alphabetical order, as are the suggestions for wines to try.

The growing degree day figures that are quoted from Chapter 3 onwards have been obtained from the successful applications for registration of a New Zealand Geographical Indication (GI), which are available to view on the New Zealand Intellectual Property Office's website (iponz.govt.nz). In some regions, the applications were still under review and thus the GDD figures were taken from Anderson et al. (2012).

PART 1
BACKGROUND

1

HISTORY MAKERS

On 6 April 1976, the country's recently instated Prime Minister, Robert 'Piggy' Muldoon, penned the foreword to the *New Zealand Wine Guide*. Born in 1921, the politician who became known for his love of a drink as well as sanctioning the controversial Springbok rugby tour of New Zealand in 1981, was once a teetotaller. Having developed a taste for wine while stationed on New Caledonia with the army in 1943 and 1944, it then continued to be an important part of his life. The politician had ridden a wave of populism to become the Prime Minister just a few months before his foreword was published. His successful election campaign promised 'New Zealand The Way You Want It'. 'Television commercials featured dancing cossacks, swarms of brown-faced migrants and trade unionists with Liverpool accents – all signposts to the route New Zealand might take unless "Rob's Mob" gained control,' noted one obituary. In power between 1975 and 1984, he travelled widely on official business but had time to enjoy some lighter moments: to mark the centenary of the creation of the Müller-Thurgau grape, a crossing of Riesling and Madeleine Royal and New Zealand's most planted variety at the time, he found time to attend the grape's celebration in Germany in 1982. He was also close friends with the head of the national Wine Institute, now known as New Zealand Winegrowers. The night he called a doomed snap election, nicknamed the 'schnapps election' because he looked a little inebriated when he announced it live on television, he dined with 'the executive' of the Institute and *The New Zealand Herald* reported that a fellow member of parliament had deliberately let one of the tyres down on his blue Triumph so that he would not drive home drunk.

In his foreword, Muldoon wrote 'There is no doubt that the New Zealand wine industry has come of age.' This was in 1976 and the first Sauvignon Blanc vine in Marlborough had only been planted a year earlier; Pinot Noir would not come to Central Otago for another decade and the country's most prestigious land for Merlot, Cabernet and Syrah was still being used as a drag strip, gravel quarry and army firing range. While Muldoon was a controversial politician, he got it right on his predictions for the industry. 'I am certain in my own mind,' he wrote, 'that as the years go by we will have an export surplus and moreover that properly marketed New Zealand wines will find their place in other countries as another natural product that this country produces superbly.'

More than 130 years earlier there had been similar predictions that New Zealand was destined to be a great wine-producing country and exporter. In 1845, Englishman Walter Brodie, the grandson of the founder of *The Times* newspaper who would go on to become a politician in Auckland, envisioned a bright future for Kiwi wine producers: 'New Zealand in a few years will export much wine. The vine grows very luxuriantly and the few hundred of Germans who have lately gone out, have turned their attention to the vine alone. At the Northern part of New Zealand all English fruits abound, and grow in great luxuriance.' While Brodie was ultimately proven right, it would take 150 years for local wine producers to fulfil their potential and for overseas markets to appreciate its pristine whites and elegant reds.

The recorded history of New Zealand wine is a series of stop-starts. Over the course of the past 200 years, many individuals have attempted to forge a vinous future for the land of the long white cloud. From Anglican missionary Samuel Marsden planting the first vines in New Zealand in 1819 to David Herd, a pioneering Scotsman in Marlborough in the 1870s, there have been isolated success stories. Yet a wine culture failed to take hold until the late twentieth century, with beer-swilling British settlers, temperance champions and farm animals thwarting the advance of the grapevine.

Hungry animals – including pigs and sheep – spelled trouble for the vine leaves and grapes on James Busby's vineyard, one of the earliest wine producers in New Zealand. Born in Edinburgh in 1802, he travelled to Australia in 1824 after his father had secured an important surveying role in Sydney. By this time, Busby had some experience of grape growing and winemaking, having spent some time swotting up on all things wine in France. Upon arrival in Sydney he was soon heading for the Hunter Valley, 145 kilometres north, where he taught viticulture and farming at an orphan school. The position only lasted two years, and he then took on several jobs including a stint collecting taxes before heading back to the UK.

Moving to New Zealand was not necessarily on Busby's bucket list when he left for England in February 1831 but he did have political goals, penning essays on a variety of subjects affecting colonial life from agriculture to criminal welfare. By the time he arrived back in England, his insight was welcomed by those in power. After pressing the flesh and massaging relationships, he bagged himself the role of British Resident in New Zealand, Her Majesty's representative on the ground.

Before heading back to the Southern Hemisphere to take up his new role, a trip around the wine lands of Spain and France beckoned. In his *Journal of a Tour through some of the Vineyards of Spain and France* Busby chronicles his journey around sherry country before working his way northward through France to the Côte d'Or and Champagne, making observations on grape growing and taking vine cuttings – but not from just any vineyard: he procured 570 varieties, from the Botanic Garden of Montpellier and the Royal Nursery of Luxembourg at Paris, as well as more during his travels. We know this because he penned a letter to the British principal Secretary of State for the Colonies on a cold January day in 1832, asking for permission to create an experimental garden using these cuttings in Sydney. Permission granted, the cuttings travelled via Kew Gardens to Sydney with some transported on board a convict ship. Built in 1799, the *Camden* was used twice for this purpose. On 21 September 1832, the ship set sail with the vines and 200 prisoners on board ranging from petty criminals – including one who was given a harsh seven years for stealing a handkerchief – to murderers such as Robert Bell, a man from Cumberland who had been given a life sentence for murder, according to the snappily entitled murderresearch. com website. Convicts and vines safely delivered, Busby's cuttings provided a wealth of plant material, enabling Australian grape growers to diversify their vineyards.

Busby arrived in New Zealand in May 1833, and a month later ordered vines for his property at Waitangi from the collection he had sent to Sydney. However, his political role took precedence over grapes; he played a leading role in the signing of the Treaty of Waitangi, an agreement brokered between the British Crown and 540 Māori chiefs that led to New Zealand becoming a British colony in 1840. Viewed as New Zealand's founding document, the Treaty was signed at Busby's house. A 45-metre marquee was erected on his lawn at what is now a thriving tourist attraction, the Waitangi Treaty Grounds, and the assembled party of Brits and Māori chiefs ate their way through thirty pigs and five tonnes of potatoes. However, the interpretation of the Treaty continues to be the subject of heated debate today with the anniversary of the signing – 6 February – a day of tension between Māori and Pakeha (New Zealanders of European descent). While many treat the national holiday as an excuse to go to the beach and invite their friends for a barbecue, politicians visiting Waitangi are often given a hostile reception and can expect to have something thrown at them – although the then economic development minister Steven Joyce was rather surprised in 2016 when he was hit in the face by a flying dildo.

By the time the Treaty was signed, Busby was already making wine. In 1836, he had written to his brother saying the 'vines were planted out under the most favourable of circumstances, just after a soaking rain. I think the majority of them are likely to survive.' He had a bit of trouble in the early years but in 1840 his white wine was declared 'delicious', according to the dashing French naval officer and explorer Jules Dumont d'Urville. D'Urville was born in Normandy, a region better known for its cider production, but his tasting note of Busby's wine remains one of the earliest New Zealand wine reviews. Although Busby wasn't at home to welcome d'Urville, the Frenchman rowed ashore from his ship *Astrolabe*. He spotted some 'flourishing' vines and explained in his journal, 'with great pleasure I agreed to taste the product of the vineyard that I had just seen. I was given a light white wine, very sparkling, and delicious to taste, which I enjoyed very much. Judging from this sample, I have no doubt that vines will be grown extensively all over the sandy hills of these islands, and very soon New Zealand wine may be exported to English possessions in India.'

Busby's vines – and his position as British Resident – were not to last, however. His vines were often damaged by 'the ravages of horses,

sheep, cattle and pigs. The leaves are ripped off as soon as they come out'
and, during the 1840s, it was British troops stationed at Waitangi rather
than farm animals that completed the destruction of his vineyard. It was
a rather unsuccessful start for New Zealand wine despite the glowing
endorsement of a Frenchman, but Busby's contribution to the Australian
wine scene was much more successful. In the year of his death – 1871
– his dreams of a New Zealand wine scene were barely alive. A handful
of religious men and optimistic immigrants still clung to the idea that
wine could be made at the bottom of the earth.

THE EXCITABLE INNKEEPER

On 29 December 1913 a short article appeared in *The New Zealand
Herald* saying that a man named Romeo Bragato had been found
dead in a hotel room in Vancouver. The Croatian-born, Italian-trained
viticulturist had committed suicide, marking the tragic demise of the
former New Zealand government's head of viticulture. The previous year,
Bragato had also made headlines but once again it was not for his grape-
growing prowess. The then-landlord of the Masonic Hotel, a seafront
pub that still operates in the affluent Auckland suburb of Devonport, was
charged with having permitted drunkenness on the premises but that was
thrown out in court. He was also charged with threatening behaviour at
closing time. Provoked by a customer he had refused to serve, Bragato was
reported to have threatened to kick him and shouted: 'You call yourselves
Britishers: you are hooligans, undesirables from Wollomooloo [an inner
city suburb of Sydney]; come on and I'll fight you one after another,' and
at the same time took off his coat. Bragato's lawyer told the court that
he was seriously provoked after the undesirables in question went 'to the
fowlhouse in the backyard and got some hens, which they brought into
the bar-room and threw over the counter, and they also threw some beer
into the defendant's face.' He was fined 10s and costs of £7 13s and told
that he was too 'excitable' to be in charge of the hotel.

Funnily enough, that part of Bragato's life doesn't get told very often;
threatening to kick his customers was far from his finest hour. Nevertheless,
he was a key figure in advancing wine production in New Zealand in the
face of a strong temperance movement, and his pioneering contribution

is honoured annually by the country's grape growers and winemakers at the national Romeo Bragato conference and wine awards.

Born in 1858 on an island that is now part of Croatia, Bragato was trained at the wine school in Conegliano, which is known today as the heartland of quality Prosecco. While working for the Department of Agriculture in Victoria, Australia, he was invited by the New Zealand government to visit New Zealand and write a report on the country's 'Prospects for Viticulture'. That's how he found himself in Bluff, the southernmost town in New Zealand, on 19 February 1895. For wine lovers, there's little reason to head to Bluff. In fact, this bleak and windswept port town has little to attract the tourist save for its annual oyster festival in May and its ferry links to Stewart Island. Bragato was soon on a train heading northward. His first destination was Queenstown, now the adventure capital of New Zealand. Sitting on the shore of Lake Wakatipu, the town also attracts more elderly tourists who enjoy the leisurely pace of a paddle steamer and wine tasting. Bragato also arrived on a steamer and then made his way eastward in search of wine tasting. He found his first glass of wine in Arrowtown, thanks to a local woman named Mrs Hutchison. He offered some faint praise for her efforts: 'although made after the most primitive fashion, it reflected great credit upon the producer, and need not be despised by any one'.

While Bragato visited during the New Zealand summer, he was quick to note the 'low temperature throughout the year' in this southerly part of the world. Almost a century later, when Michael Cooper published the third edition of *The Wines and Vineyards of New Zealand*, a question mark hung over the ability to ripen grapes in this cool mountainous region, which attracts ski bunnies from across New Zealand and Australia in the winter. Just 50 kilometres down the road in Cromwell, now home to a giant sculpture that bears a striking resemblance to Carmen Miranda's hat, he found grapes that were ripe as early as late February, which was 'a convincing fact to me that the summer climatic conditions here are conducive to the early ripening of the fruit. This and the Bannockburn district are pre-eminently suitable for the cultivation of the vine, both of wine-making and table varieties.' He was proven correct: these two districts are the heartland of Central Otago wine today.

A French flavour

In 1840, the same year that the Waitangi Treaty was signed, a shipload of French emigrants arrived in what would become Akaroa. The settlers included a shoemaker, a blacksmith, a gardener, a locksmith but no winemaker – although there was a grape grower's son. Nevertheless, there were vines on board the ship for them to plant. The journey was free and they were given 2 hectares of land, as long as they stuck it out for five years. Thirty years later, there is evidence that they had managed to tame their vines without any previous experience in grape growing. The Christchurch newspaper *The Press* reported on a carriage journey from Christchurch to Akaroa in 1870. Upon reaching Akaroa, the journalist could see the cottages of French settlers 'each with their little vineyard dotting the landscape, and making a pleasant feature in the landscape'.

By the time Bragato arrived – in 1895 – he was able to taste some Chasselas and Muscat of Frontignan, and noted that fine wine like a Rhine or Mosel white could be made here if people were prepared to put in the effort. He wasn't optimistic: 'It would seem that the pioneer French settlers of Akaroa failed to communicate to their offspring even a small percentage of that enthusiasm over the cultivation of the vine which they were in such a large measure possessed of, or it may be their descendants suspended work by reason of the vines becoming attacked with oidium, thus causing the disappearance of vineyards which had been to their forebears as a bit of the fatherland.'

There are other explanations why the 'Vineyard of Christchurch' didn't survive, from hungry birds eating all the grapes and the area's dense forest cover to the arrival of the British and the emergence of the temperance movement. There were also few people to sell the wine to in this difficult-to-reach part of Canterbury.

Today, there are a handful of vineyards on the Banks Peninsula overlooking Akaroa. A French vigneron, Renan Cataliotti, discovered Akaroa and his Akaroa-born wife while on holiday and set up home – and a vineyard – in the area. His Pinot Noir is named in honour of one of the first French settlers in Akaroa, Elie Bouriaud, whose father was a winegrower.

An area that did not stand the test of time was Akaroa. Within an hour's drive of Christchurch, this town on Banks Peninsula is a popular day trip. Settled by the French, Bragato thought Akaroa's wines could achieve world fame if the money and effort was put in. His advice fell on deaf ears, and today it is more famous for its dolphin- and penguin-spotting tours.

It appears that someone forgot to tell Bragato about Marlborough on his first visit, which is the country's most successful wine region today, accounting for three-quarters of New Zealand's production. There were vineyards in Marlborough at the time, including David Herd's Auntsfield and George Freeth's Mount Pleasant Wine Vaults. He headed up to the far north-west corner of New Zealand's South Island, Nelson, and believed that it was a good place to grow vines and grow oak trees for making barrels. He then sailed for the North Island. In Hawke's Bay, which is now the second largest vine-growing area in New Zealand after Marlborough, he found Pinot Noir growing and an 'exquisite' wine akin to the sweet wines of Greece: 'The Hawke's Bay Province is, in my opinion, the most suitable for vine-growing I have visited in New Zealand. It possesses thousands of acres which, by reason of the nature of the soil, natural drainage, and sufficiency of heat, will produce grapes of both table and wine-making varieties in rich abundance.'

In his conclusions, he was convinced that the Hawke's Bay and Wairarapa regions, which include Martinborough, were most suited to vine growing, as was Central Otago. However, he had found several cases of the vine louse phylloxera, which ravaged the vineyards of Europe in the late nineteenth century, and recommended 'a thorough inspection of all the vineyards'. Whether he was angling for more work or not, his recommendation was finally acted upon in 1901 when he was asked back to report on the problem of phylloxera. A year later, he was deemed the most suitable candidate for a newly created position in the Department of Agriculture: viticulturist and head of the viticultural division. He would remain in the role for seven years, spending most of his time at Te Kauwhata, the government's viticulture centre, trialling varieties and running field days for budding grape growers. He also won medals for his wines in London and found time to write a guide to viticulture in New Zealand in 1906. In this paper he suggested that the most suitable varieties for the climate were Black Hermitage (Shiraz), Cabernet Sauvignon, Cabernet Franc, Dolcetto, Pinot Noir, Mueller Burgundy, Reisling (sic), Pinot Blanc, Tokay and White Hermitage.

While many of his suggestions have become an integral part of New Zealand's wine scene over a century later, his recommendation that Shiraz should be 'at least one-half of the vineyard' has not transpired and is explored in more depth in Chapter 3.

Bragato left the employ of the New Zealand government in 1909 and, in 1912, after the judge ruled him too excitable to be running a hotel in Auckland, left New Zealand for Canada with his wife and children. He had arrived with great hopes for New Zealand wine but departed feeling disillusioned, with abstemious voices growing ever louder. He may be called a founding father of the country's wine industry but the vision and advances he brought seemed to count for little as the national temperance movement marched forward.

A WAR ON WINE

On 25 April, Australians and New Zealanders wake up before dawn, make themselves look vaguely presentable, and head for their local war memorial. The early start is in honour of Anzac Day, the annual day of commemoration across the Antipodes, which honours those who have served their country on the battlefield. Dawn services are a rite of passage for all young Kiwis.

Following the parade, elderly veterans laden with military medals on their breasts share a beer (and invariably a fried breakfast) with families, friends and anyone fancying a morning drink at the local Returned Services Association (RSA). While the bloody story of the Anzacs landing at Gallipoli on 25 April 1915, the site of New Zealand's first major battle of the First World War, has been told many times, those enjoying a drink at the RSA might be surprised to hear that they have First World War troops to thank for keeping New Zealand wet.

Without the votes of overseas soldiers, New Zealand might have trodden the same Prohibitionist path as the United States. In a close-run poll on Prohibition in 1919, it was the vote of overseas servicemen that saved New Zealand from going dry. Soldiers stationed in England, lobbied by a local brewer who travelled from New Zealand to London, voted four to one in favour of keeping the country wet (known as Continuance). Without those winning votes, it is unlikely that wineries like Corbans would have stayed in business.

The temperance movement had gained momentum in the late nineteenth century. Heavy drinking was a real issue in colonial New Zealand. In 1911, for example, there were 11,418 prosecutions for drunkenness versus 1,779 for theft. Temperance supporter William Fox, an Oxford graduate and parliamentarian, claimed that 500 people died each year from excessive drinking in New Zealand and that this cost the colony £50,000 a year. Religious sorts were strongly in favour of Prohibition but non-churchgoers were increasingly convinced by arguments that alcohol was damaging families, morals and society. Women, who had been given the right to vote in 1893, turned their campaigning zeal toward alcohol and the evils it caused. 'Prohibition has already taken firm hold of the masses,' said a clergyman in 1894 – and he wasn't wrong. In the same year, the district of Clutha in Central Otago voted to go dry. By 1910, a dozen of the country's seventy-odd electorates operated under a local form of Prohibition including the wine-producing district of Masterton and Mt Eden, which counted many of the new wineries in west Auckland.

While the no-to-Prohibition vote in 1919 shattered the hopes of many teetotallers, the threat hung over the industry until the 1980s. From 1919 until 1987, electors in every New Zealand general election – with the exception of 1931 and 1951 – were also asked to vote on national Continuance, national Prohibition and state control. The soldiers of the First World War had saved the country from going dry by a narrow margin, and yet the question continued to be asked for another seventy years.

Unlike western Europe, there was no wine culture in New Zealand and a series of puritanical licensing laws did nothing to encourage drinking in moderation or a food and wine culture. A 6 p.m. closing time on bars imposed during the war became permanent after the fighting ended. The '6 o'clock swill', as it became known, created a culture of binge drinking between the end of the working day and 'the abrupt cessation of the flow of beer' and was not lifted until 1967, when the country voted two to one in favour of closing at 10 p.m., as explained by Conrad Bollinger in *Grog's Own Country*. Women could not enter pubs, nor could they work behind the bar, unless they were members of the licensee's family. Meanwhile hotels could not serve alcohol after 8 p.m., even with meals, and were not allowed to open on a Sunday until

1989. It is not surprising, adds Bollinger, that the Māori name for New Zealand, Aotearoa, 'might have been translated as land of the "long white froth" rather than the "long white cloud", given the country's lack of respect for its customers and their drink of choice.'

In the context of this sobering legislation, it is hardly surprising that the number of vineyards sharply declined after the First World War. In 1906, Bragato counted more than 220 hectares of vines across New Zealand; by 1923 the area under vine stood at just 45 hectares and although it edged up to 150 hectares by 1938 half of those were table grapes rather than wine grapes. By the 1940s, the prospects for New Zealand wine did not look bright; it had suffered half a century of temperance-influenced legislation which did little to encourage quality wine producers. With the exception of a handful of quality-oriented winemaking families like the Corbans and Babichs, wine production was centred on making imitations of sherry, port and madeira as cheaply as possible, and lesser quality hybrid grapes were widespread. Table wine was produced for private consumption by many winemakers but there was little interest in quality dry wines in New Zealand. While the government appointed an experienced winemaker from the respected Australian wine family Lindeman as the national Vine and Wine Instructor in 1938 and provided extra funding to the government winery, Te Kauwhata, New Zealand wine was in a state of disarray by 1946. The Royal Commission on Licensing provides a telling summary of the issues facing the country's winemakers and drinkers: 'Most of this New Zealand wine, whatever its exact quantity, has been far inferior to that which could be imported. The Department of Agriculture states that more than 60 per cent of the wine made by the smaller winemakers is infected with bacterial disorders of one form or another. The Vine and Wine Instructor of the Department, Mr. B. W. Lindeman, said that over 50 per cent of the product was poor and markedly inferior. The Department also said that at the present time a considerable quantity of wine made in New Zealand would be classified as unfit for human consumption in other wine-producing countries, and that this was due mainly to the lack of knowledge on the part of the winemakers.'

The use and abuse of sugar and water to stretch grape juice, as well as the alleged production of wines from imported raisins, was also noted by the Commission. This was part of a long-standing problem for New Zealand. Assid Abraham Corban, a Lebanese immigrant, ambitious wine producer and industry pioneer had lamented 'unscrupulous' types as early as 1925 and the damaging effects they had on genuine producers. He had witnessed men 'waiting at the wharves for the next shipload of currants from the islands of the Greek Archipelago' – currants which could be soaked and made into wine. This type of adulteration was hardly novel: when phylloxera forged an insidious path across France in the second half of the nineteenth century, raisin wine was common. Dried grapes were shipped into France duty free and could be turned into a makeshift wine by adding hot water and sugar to start a fermentation, with a little colouring added for good measure. There was even a book published in 1880 called *The Art of Making Wine from Raisins*. As a result, millions of hectolitres of raisin wine are thought to have been made in the 1880s and 1890s accounting for between 10 per cent or as much as a sixth of French wine sold in 1890. New Zealand's volumes of wine produced using this method were tiny by comparison, but the use of sugar and water to stretch wines remained an insidious part of the country's culture until new regulations were introduced in 1980.

The 1950s marked a turning point for New Zealand wine that paved the way for gradual change, and formed the foundation of a successful wine-producing country whose wines now sit on the lists of Michelin-starred restaurants around the world. Firstly the government gave winemakers a much needed boost in 1955, allowing single bottle sales to individuals. Before 1955, the minimum purchase was 2 gallons, equivalent to a case of 12 bottles, thwarting private sales and landing winemakers in trouble: Joe Babich of Golden Sunset was fined £25 for selling single bottles to a police constable who was dressed in disguise while Josip Balich also ended up on the wrong side of the law on several occasions for single-bottle sales. His son Peter claimed that as much as 60 per cent of their wine had been sold after hours and 90 per cent of it was in lots of less than the permitted 2 gallons.

In the late 1950s, the finance minister Arnold Nordmeyer faced a foreign exchange crisis and responded by increasing taxes on imported wines and spirits, making local wines more attractive price-wise. In 1967, further duty hikes were imposed on imported and locally made spirits, giving wine another boost. Politicians were finally giving New Zealand wine producers a helping hand through legislation and economic measures, no doubt helped by liberal quantities of wine poured at 'field days' run by the Viticultural Association for Members of Parliament from 1952 onwards. But there was also a cultural shift occurring: former servicemen who had been stationed in Europe had returned to New Zealand with a taste for dry wines. Government figures show that annual consumption of wine increased from less than 1 litre per person per year on the eve of the Second World War to 2 litres by 1960. Wine drinking was a minority sport, however; beer remained the drink of choice at the start of the 1960s, with 100 litres of beer swilled per capita. However, domestic wines were clearly finding favour during this decade – no doubt thanks to pro-wine government legislation, higher taxes on beer and a new generation of wine shops – with four bottles of local wine consumed for every single bottle of imported wine by the late 1960s.

Yet fortified wine was still the wine of choice until the 1970s. Sir George Fistonich says: 'When I started Villa Maria in 1961 the market was mainly port and sherry. I started making dry red and white wine and people would say "what the hell is this?" because they were so used to sweet fortified wines.' But times were a-changing.

NEW ZEALAND WINE'S UNITED NATIONS

Browse the New Zealand wine section and the names on the labels read like a united nations of producers: Babich, Soljans, Schubert, Seifried, Le Brun and Kusuda offer a taste of the melting pot that is New Zealand wine. While the first wine producers recorded in New Zealand were from the not-so-famous wine-producing British Isles it was continental Europeans that have made Aotearoa the winemaking, wine-drinking nation it is today.

New Zealand has a lot of reasons to thank one nation: Dalmatia, which is now part of modern-day Croatia. Fleeing poverty or conscription into the Austro-Hungarian army to fight in the Balkan wars, more than half a million Croats migrated to America and a trickle headed for the far north of New Zealand in the late nineteenth and early twentieth centuries. Fresh off the boat and virtually penniless in a country whose language they did not speak, many dug kauri gum to earn a living and sent money back to their struggling families. Their work ethic did not go unnoticed. Less industrious diggers compared them to 'locusts' for clearing all the gum trees in sight and they were labelled 'the greatest pest of all' by the *Herald*, Auckland's daily newspaper.

In 1906, the Croatian-born viticulturist Bragato had kinder things to say about his countrymen who were switching from gum to grapes. 'Among those who are entering largely into grape growing and winemaking are the Austrian [Dalmatian] immigrants, who have formerly confined themselves to gum-digging. Many are now taking up land and planting it with grapes. They spare no pains and exercise the greatest care in the proper preparation of the land prior to planting, and take a pride in keeping the newly planted vineyard clean and well cultivated, with healthy and vigorous vines. Gum-digging provides them with sufficient income to live on while the vines are coming to bearing ...'

One of the gum diggers-turned-grape-growers was Jakov Babich. The eldest son of his family (born in 1884), he was sent to New Zealand in early 1904 at the age of nineteen in search of a better life for the family, and quickly saved enough to pay for his brothers' passage to the southern hemisphere. By 1910, Jakov had become a New Zealand citizen and was joined by four of his siblings, including Josip – who was just fourteen when he waved goodbye to his parents, never to see them again. While he was initially an errand boy, note Michael and Judith Bassett in the Babich family history *The Next Vintage*, he also planted vines and was making wine in his teens. Having saved enough to buy a piece of land in a suburb of west Auckland, Henderson, the Babich boys gradually planted vines and other crops on the land and became part of a burgeoning winegrowing community in west Auckland. Dalmatians dominated the Auckland wine scene at the start of the twentieth century but it was a challenging time to be both Dalmatian and a winegrower. Despite pledging allegiance to New Zealand, King and Country, they could not escape their past. Hailing from the fringes of the Austro-Hungarian Empire, they were labelled 'enemy aliens' following the outbreak of the First World War and suffered continued discrimination long after the Armistice was signed. It was no coincidence that many early Dalmatian wine producers chose Anglicized names for their businesses. Instead of his family name, Joe Balich, who planted his vines by candlelight after a full day's work at Corbans, called his vineyard Golden Sunset, and the Yelas family founded Pleasant Valley, but there were plenty of other immigrants who proudly printed their name on their wine labels including

George Mazuran and Bartul Soljans. These winegrowers were also bat-
tling an alien drinking culture; Brits who had settled in New Zealand advocated either abstinence or drinking beer. The new settlers from southern Europe were accustomed to growing grapes alongside other crops;
drinking wine was an essential part of a meal and provided much-needed
calories – and some light relief from an arduous existence.

Over the last century, Dalmatian immigrants and their families
have been at the forefront of change, innovation and progress in New
Zealand wine. They are too many to mention but names like Babich,
Mazuran and Selaks will forever be linked with the early development
of the industry, as will the name Yukich. Ivan Yukich made his first
'Montana' wine west of Auckland in 1944 but it was his ambitious son,
Frank, who will be best remembered for purchasing 647 hectares of land
in Marlborough in the early 1970s, when all around him – including
the board of the Montana – were convinced there was no future for
viticulture in the South Island. Clearly, the New Zealand wine industry
would look very different – and much smaller – without their vision
and diligence.

At its peak, there were as many as ninety wineries across Kumeu
and Henderson, which was referred to as Dally Valley. But the Dallys
didn't have a monopoly on west Auckland. In 1902, a Lebanese
immigrant, Assid Abraham Corban, bought a 3.9-hectare block of
land in Henderson for £320. He had landed in New Zealand ten years
earlier with no command of the English language and had forged a
living as a general dealer. Growing up, Corban had worked his family's
vineyard in Lebanon before and after a day's work as a stonemason. He
was no stranger to adversity which was just as well as the local electorate
voted in favour of local Prohibition in 1908 – the same year that he
produced his first vintage of Mt Lebanon wine. A solution was found:
the boundary between the dry and the wet community ran along the
railway line, explains Dick Scott in the Corban's family history, *A Stake
in the Country*. Corban rented the basement of a railwayman's cottage
on the wet side of the tracks close to the cellar so they could still sell
wine. The Corban family long battled against the odds – temperance,
phylloxera, and a 1943 court case in which they were charged with
selling less than the required 2 gallons of wine to a single customer, were
fined £50 and temporarily lost their licence.

Sir George Fistonich

The founder of Villa Maria has been a pillar in the evolving New Zealand wine community for more than fifty years. An early advocate of the move from fortified to table wines and an innovator in the sales and marketing of New Zealand wine, he remains forward thinking in the vineyard and the winery despite celebrating his seventy-fifth birthday in 2014. In recent years, he has advocated planting Arneis, Albariño and Verdelho in a land of Sauvignon Blanc, and declared the winery a cork-free zone in 2001, marking a switch to screwcaps for the winery's entire production. He has nurtured some of New Zealand's most respected winemakers including Alastair Maling MW, Rod McDonald, Kate Radburnd and Steve Smith MW.

Born to Dalmatian parents in Auckland in 1939, wine was a normal part of life and he was part of the winemaking community: his uncle would take him to buy wine at the Babich house and Mrs Delegat, the family behind the Oyster Bay brand, would look after the Fistonich family when his mother was ill. Beyond the Dalmatian community, there was virtually no wine culture and dining out was in its infancy. Fistonich recalls eating out in the 1950s at one of the first restaurants in Auckland and 'sly-grogging' because drinking was illegal with a meal until the law changed in 1960: 'When we were teenagers we would go to Hi Diddle Griddle and I would hide a bottle of wine under my coat and pour the wine into a teapot and drink it from teacups. It really was antiquated.'

At the same time as licensing laws were changing, Fistonich founded Villa Maria, aged only 21. His family had high hopes that he would be a tradesman (and he did complete a building apprenticeship), but he wanted to make wine. Since 1961, Villa Maria has gone from 0.2 hectares of land he leased from his father to being an internationally recognized brand, exporting to more than fifty countries. Fistonich is now Sir George and has a string of industry accolades to his name, while Villa Maria isn't backward at coming forward when it comes to its claim that it is New Zealand's most awarded winery. Yet success has not always been assured: in 1985, Fistonich's lofty ambitions were his undoing: according to his biography, *The Winemaker*, Villa Maria was $4 million in debt and profitability was low. A glut of wine had created a price war compounding the company's problems and Villa went into receivership. Through grit and determination, Fistonich rebuilt the company which includes the Vidal, Esk Valley and Te Awa brands and, in 2011, fifty years after setting up Villa Maria, he was awarded the Lifetime Achievement Award by the International Wine Challenge. Fistonich has not only built a successful and respected company for the next generation to nurture, he has created a legacy.

In the 1960s, the Corban family's enterprise grew at an unprecedented rate. Scott writes, 'It had taken A. A. Corban a quarter of a century to plant 30 acres – now more than that acreage was being put in every year.' By the end of the decade, Corban-owned vineyards accounted for a fifth of the national total, the company's winery capacity increased 50 per cent in the last half of the 1960s and the company was exporting to both the UK and Canada. But expansion required investment and its debts were the beginning of the end for family ownership. Rothmans, the company that had provided the finance to Corbans, made its move and acquired the business over the 1970s.

The brand lived on long after the family ceded control and the family's connection with the wine industry remained. Alex Corban, Assid's grandson, was the first New Zealander to study oenology at Roseworthy College in Australia in 1949 and introduced cold fermentation to New Zealand as well as the Charmat method for producing sparkling wines. After more than twenty years making Corbans wines, he became the inaugural president of the Wine Institute of New Zealand in 1976 and was pivotal in the creation of wine legislation which emphasized quality wine production. His son, Alwyn, went on to study winemaking at the University of California, Davis and co-founded Ngatarawa Wines in 1981 in Hawke's Bay, and became instrumental in developing the Bridge Pa area. Without a succession plan, he sold the brand to historic Hawke's Bay producer Mission Estate in 2017 but the Corban family's contribution to the New Zealand wine industry is irrefutable.

K Road

In 2015, wine lovers were given a good reason to head to Auckland's infamous Karangahape Road, commonly referred to by locals as K Road. In a former tattoo parlour, nestled between a store selling legal highs and a karaoke bar, a new wine bar opened offering Argentine Torrontes and South African Pinotage by the glass and sausage by the quarter-metre. Run by a French chef, Leslie Hottiaux, and her partner, Mo Koski, whose father is Finnish, the wine list reflects its international owners.

But the couple are not the first immigrants to open up a wine bar on K Road. Israel Wendel was born in Alsace-Lorraine and started a new life in central Auckland in 1872, planting a small vineyard on Greys Avenue, now home to hotels, overpriced car parks and a synagogue. He also opened up Wendel's Wine Bodega on K Road, New Zealand's first licensed wine shop. At this time, K Road was a buzzing, prosperous thoroughfare. The oldest street in Auckland was a route used by pre-European Māori. From the late nineteenth century until the 1960s, most large stores had a branch here, selling everything from clothes to furniture. Wendel's daughter continued the business after his death in 1896 and the bar moved up and down the street: 'from its origin at 128 to end up at 143, [it] became an outpost of wine intelligence. It continued as one of the only two specified wine bars permitted under New Zealand law before 1989,' notes Keith Stewart in his history of New Zealand wine, *Chancers and Visionaries*.

While K Road has recently been enjoying a renaissance with the influx of Apero and art galleries, it had become Auckland's red light district in the 1960s following the relocation of tens of thousands of nearby residents who were forced to make way for a new motorway. Unsurprisingly, the departure of the local community had a massive effect on local businesses who shut their doors, which meant that the red light district moved in. It remains an edgy and vibrant part of town today with sex shops, massage parlours and dodgy nightclubs dotting its length although there is now a revival with the art galleries and wine bars moving in.

In addition to selling his own wine at Wendel's Wine Bodega, Wendel sold wines made by the Englishman Charles Levet, who has been called New Zealand's first winemaker to make a living from his vineyard. The coppersmith from Cambridgeshire landed at Port Albert, around 88 kilometres northwest of Auckland, with some books on winemaking in his bag and ventured slightly inland where he found a property on the river. Once cleared, he and his son planted vines and made wines from less-than-noble varieties such as Isabella, an American variety that was widely planted in North America in the first half of the nineteenth century. Its foxy flavour hasn't found many fans since, although Levet found fans in eminent members of Auckland society, including David Boyle, the Earl of Glasgow and Governor of New Zealand from 1892 to 1897. A Scotsman who enjoyed a drink, Glasgow became one of Levet's regulars, explains Stewart, and allowed Levet to change the name of his winery to Lord Glasgow Vineyards.

THE BIRTH OF MODERN NEW ZEALAND WINE

By the time Prime Minister Muldoon penned his foreword to Frank Thorpy's 1976 *New Zealand Wine Guide*, New Zealanders were buying nearly 8.5 litres of wine a year – more than Brits and Americans at that time. There were '400-odd' wine shops across the country catering for a public with a growing thirst for knowledge: an Auckland wine club had 4,000 paid-up members and newspapers had started publishing weekly wine columns.

New Zealand drinkers were not the only ones waking up to the charms of the country's wines in the 1960s and 1970s. Overseas investors were entering the market from Australia including McWilliam's and Penfolds as well as the American company Seagram. This period of acquisition coincided with a shift away from Auckland to other regions – notably Gisborne, Hawke's Bay and Marlborough. This was a time of expansion with vineyards growing from 1,468 hectares in 1970 to 4,500 hectares in 1979. Wine production was just 4.1 million litres in 1960. By 1983, it had risen to 57.7 million litres and fortified wine was no longer the dominant force: three-quarters of production was now table wine.

The country's vineyards and wineries seemed to be gaining momentum and critical mass after a century of stop-start progress but its fortunes were to be checked once again in the early 1980s. Reacting to an undersupply of grapes and buoyed by a Wine Industry

Development Plan published in 1981 which predicted that New Zealanders and export markets were going to drink more and more of their wine, optimistic growers had been out in the fields planting vines and wineries had committed to long-term contracts. But Kiwis failed to drink as much as the wine industry had hoped and most wineries had not made any significant headway in overseas markets, despite a Department of Agriculture Committee recommending exporting since the early 1960s. Some producers had taken note and the newly unified industry body had created a New Zealand wine export committee, but it would not be enough for the industry to slide from its optimistic highs of the 1960s and 1970s into yet another trough of despair. The 1986 annual report of the Wine Institute of New Zealand explained that the 'bountiful 1985 harvest and the contractual obligations to take in grapes, left many wine companies with large inventories and a need for cash to meet grape payments, which were unreasonably high, and at a time of record interest rates ... Price cutting began and erupted into a full-scale discount war with two substantial family companies [Villa Maria and Delegats] being forced into receivership and others left financially shaky.' The Wine Institute wanted the government to reduce taxes on wine after a substantial hike in 1984, but the government wondered if that would fuel an even greater price war. Instead, it offered an alternative: a sponsored vine pull. For every hectare of vineyard pulled out, it would offer $6,175 to the grower. It cost the government $10 million. Unsurprisingly, other farmers had a good moan. In total 1,515 hectares were pulled out, reducing the vineyard area to 4,500 hectares. A decent chunk of unwanted hybrids, which had been steadily on the wane, disappeared as a result of the vine pull yet Müller-Thurgau remained the country's biggest producer of wine until 1996.

Phylloxera in New Zealand

Phylloxera vastatrix is an aphid that feeds on the roots of vines, reducing carbohydrate reserves and allowing bacteria to enter the wounds left by the feeding frenzy. The vines lose vigour and may eventually die, as European grape growers discovered in the mid to late nineteenth century. It has been estimated that 2.5 million hectares of vines were uprooted in France between

1868 and 1900 and while the solution to the problem came in the form of American rootstocks, these weren't cheap in New Zealand. According to the viticulturist behind Montana's first plantings in Marlborough in 1973, Wayne Thomas, own-rooted vines cost 15 to 50 cents per plant while grafted vines cost between $4 and $5; and, what's more, they were not a tax-deductible expense.

While phylloxera had first been detected in Auckland in 1885, viticulture had failed to flourish in New Zealand, and so had the aphid. The pioneers of Marlborough in the 1970s and early 1980s hoped they would get away with ungrafted vines for at least a couple of decades. They didn't – and with 92 per cent of vines planted on their own roots and 50 per cent of those vines under two years old, according to a Ministry of Agriculture vineyard survey in 1980, the potential for damage was huge. In 1984, two years after showing up in Gisborne, the aphid was identified in a vineyard close to Blenheim. 'It has always been considered probable that this pest would eventually spread to Marlborough,' the local spokesman for the Ministry of Agriculture and Fisheries told the *Marlborough Express*. 'Because of this growers have been advised to establish vines on resistant rootstocks. However, to date, most of the Marlborough crop is grown on susceptible roots.' In combination with the government-sponsored vine-pull scheme, phylloxera's arrival in Marlborough led to a wholesale replanting of the region. There was a silver lining: out came the hybrids and in came *Vitis vinifera*. Müller-Thurgau was on borrowed time, with Sauvignon Blanc and Chardonnay becoming the two new shining lights. It wasn't until 2001 that phylloxera was identified in Central Otago and close to half of all its vineyards were on own roots at that time, reported the American publication *Wine Spectator*. In 2007, it finally made its way to Martinborough, which had a quarter of its plants on own roots. While phylloxera has not gone away, there is a more worrying problem that growers are discussing amongst themselves today: trunk diseases. They are 'insidious … slowly spreading until it may be too late to treat,' reports viticultural expert Dr Richard Smart. There are different types of trunk disease but they are all caused by fungi. They access the vine through pruning wounds so the more times you prune – i.e., the older the vine becomes – the more opportunities the disease has to enter the vine. It is a global problem but as New Zealand's vine stock becomes older, it is becoming more common.

Other 'international varieties' such as Chardonnay and Sauvignon Blanc had been on the rise in the years preceding the vine pull and took on an even greater importance boosted by high-profile successes abroad. Marlborough Sauvignon Blanc became the new darling of the UK wine trade in the mid 1980s. Ernie Hunter made headlines at the 1986 Sunday Times Wine Club Vintage Festival that year when Hunter's Fumé Blanc topped the popular vote. No doubt he gained some votes by giving away free oysters – and by being 'a loveable rogue'. While Ernie passed away far too young in a car accident in 1988, his widow Jane recounts the story: 'He thought that it would draw people to the Hunter's stand and then he could get them to try the wines – as New Zealand wines weren't really top of people's minds back in 1986. And it worked; the wines ran out and people just loved them – an Irish accent and a good story along with the oysters helped. I'm sure he told people the oysters had been air freighted in from Bluff! [Turns out they were from nearby Colchester in Essex.] When I went to the Festival the year after Ernie died, people kept coming up to the stand asking where the guy was with the oysters.'

The idiosyncratic Marlborough Sauvignon Blanc style was flamboyant and bold and people loved it. British wine writer Hugh Johnson remembers his first tasting at London's New Zealand House in 1984 in his memoir *Wine: A Life Uncorked*: 'This was Sauvignon Blanc with the volume turned up. I remember the surge of scent, the snap on the tongue, the hundred-amp shock through the system. Like Sauvignon or not, here it was in primary colours.' New Zealand wine's new colour was gold, winning international award after international award in the 1990s. Sauvignon Blanc put New Zealand on the wine-producing map, yet many of the country's wine regions were still embryonic. For example, in the 1993 edition of *The Wines and Vineyards of New Zealand*, author Michael Cooper asked the following about Central Otago: 'The crunch question is whether this region is sufficiently warm to support commercial wineries.' Today, there are 137 wineries in the region and vines cover nearly 2,000 hectares of its dramatic landscape. Marlborough, while emerging as the leading wine region in the country in the early 1990s, had just 2,000 hectares under vine. In 2017 there were more than 25,000 hectares – equivalent to two-thirds of the country's vineyards (see Table 1 in the Appendix).

Change has been rapid and dramatic but its adolescence has not been without its share of growing pains. The twenty-first century ushered in a period of growing sales and recognition overseas. In 2005, for the first time in its history, the country exported more wine than it sold at home: Australians, Brits and Americans had gone gaga for Kiwi wines and the industry responded by planting more vines. Between 2000 and 2010, the New Zealand vineyard area tripled to 30,000 hectares. In the four years to 2009, Sauvignon Blanc plantings alone doubled but a bumper harvest in 2008 coupled with the global financial crisis dished out a harsh dose of reality for growers and winemakers alike. The industry's expansion was temporarily halted.

While many blamed the reality check that hit New Zealand after 2008 as a case of an oversupply of grapes exacerbated by the global financial crisis, Nicolas Lewis, an economic geographer at the University of Auckland, argues in an essay published in *Social, Cultural and Economic Impacts in New Zealand Wine* that the forces at play were far more complex. 'A deeper explanation would point to an overdue adjustment in wine, grape, and land prices after a long period of investment in production capacity locally and globally driven by an explosion of cultural interest in wine, intense merger and acquisition activity, a long boom of credit creation, the entry of supermarkets into wine sales and the development of new brands, supply chain management, and wine production technologies … Like all capitalist growth bonanzas, it had to come to an end.'

Bulk wine, which represented just 5 per cent of all wine sales in 2008, has since become a much more important part of the industry: around a third of all wine leaving New Zealand is now encased in large bladders holding up to 24,000 litres of liquid, which sit inside shipping containers. While some argue that this is detrimental to the image of New Zealand wine, lowering price points and allowing supermarkets to make own-label wines that are bottled on industrial parks in foreign lands and labelled with imaginary coves and bays, it is a reality of the modern New Zealand wine industry. (Next time you are in the supermarket, check the back label which will state where the wine was bottled. If it is not New Zealand, it was bulk shipped.) There are some sizeable wineries in New Zealand with millions of litres to sell in bulk and there are profits to be made. A successful bulk Marlborough Sauvignon Blanc business can support the production – and promotion – of lesser-known varietals or regions in a winery's portfolio. What's more, the quality of bottling offshore can be high and the carbon footprint of bulk shipping is far lower than shipping in bottle – a tick for sustainable businesses. The issue comes when wineries that have failed to sell or bottle their wines from the previous vintage need to empty their tanks, and quickly, before the next harvest is picked. This results in one-off, cut-price deals that overseas companies are just waiting to pounce on – no matter the quality. In a bid to gain authenticity and provenance points there have been sporadic murmurings about creating a 'bottled in Marlborough' seal of approval, but this has yet to materialize.

Despite market forces, nature is ultimately in control of the fortunes of the country's vineyards. Sitting in the middle of the Roaring Forties in the South Pacific, the country's cool, maritime climate comes with special effects; growers regularly contend with cyclones as well as not-infrequent earthquakes. Faced with the power of nature, it is a small miracle that a successful wine industry managed to emerge. It took a bunch of tenacious New Zealanders and determined migrants to overcome the barriers that stood in their way.

2

CLIMATE: AN
UMBRELLA VIEW

Vines have worked their way from the upper reaches of New Zealand to the mountainous landscapes of Central Otago, more than 1,600 kilometres to the south. At 45° S, the vineyards of Central Otago lay claim to the world's most southerly wine region while Northland sits at 35° S, positioning it on a similar latitude to Canberra and Adelaide. These huge distances alone mean that the climatic conditions of the wine regions of New Zealand are far from homogeneous.

If you superimposed New Zealand's wine regions on a map of Europe, which a cartographer first attempted in the *New Zealand Official Year Book 1919*, the far north of the country would sit close to the sherry capital of Jerez in terms of latitude while the more southerly reaches would nudge the Bordeaux area. So why isn't Central Otago making claret and Auckland concentrating on hot-climate varieties? The answer lies in its isolated position on earth. The narrow strip of islands that make up New Zealand sit in the middle of a lot of water, and this means that New Zealand has a maritime climate. Moderated by the cool Pacific Ocean on its east coast – next stop Chile – and the rough waters of the Tasman Sea to the west, its summers are cooler than its latitude would suggest and its winters are milder. Extensive work has been undertaken by a team led by the Southern Oregon University's Jon D. Anderson into the climate classification of New Zealand's wine regions. Entitled 'Analysis of viticulture region climate structure and suitability in New Zealand', it noted: 'The maritime influence is accentuated by the proximity of the vineyard areas to the east coast, with approximately

95 per cent of the vineyards in these areas planted within about 50 kilometres of the coast, the exception being Central Otago.'

The vineyards of New Zealand occupy the east coast of the country with good reason – the west coast is a wet place. Westerly winds coming off the Tasman Sea dump rain on the west coast: the website of the town of Hokitika, for instance, makes light of having the highest average rainfall in New Zealand at 14,100 mm per year (that's a little skewed due to their weather station being up in the mountains, it claims) and encourages you to get out in nature 'whatever the weather'. Wine-producing regions sit to the east, protected by mountain ranges. As a result, rainfall in most of New Zealand's wine regions is less than 1,000 mm annually. However, as the cracked lips of tourists and craggy skin of Central Otago natives attest, this comparatively continental region is far drier than most: it is considered semi-arid, receiving just 400 mm each year, and that's half the rainfall that Napier or Bordeaux attracts.

Classifying New Zealand's vineyard climates as simply 'cool' is a broad brushstroke for the time poor. There are actually large swathes of the country that are too cool for growing grapes, inland and at altitude. While slivers of New Zealand are suitable for varieties that flourish in cool climates like Sauvignon Blanc, Pinot Noir and Riesling, the country can also ripen warm-climate varieties successfully, like Cabernet Sauvignon and Viognier – particularly on the North Island. Detailed climate research gives us some answers.

Anderson and his team used a quartet of complex measurements including the growing degree day (GDD) formula, the Huglin Index (HI), and biologically effective degree-day (BEDD) index to create a comprehensive overview of New Zealand's wine climate. They could have used one or two of the indices but each has its limitations. The first measurement Anderson used was the growing season average temperature (GST). The results indicated that 'large areas of New Zealand are too cool to effectively sustain commercial viticulture, but substantial areas were classed as being suitable for cool, intermediate, and warm climate winegrape cultivars'. Meanwhile the Huglin Index calculations found that 57 per cent of the wine regions in New Zealand were classed as cool climate, two regions were temperate and six (29 per cent) very cool. The warmest region without any doubt is the Bay of Islands, home to the first European settlers and the first vineyards of New Zealand, while large swathes of Otago, home to some of the country's most coveted Pinot Noirs, were consistently found to be too cool for growing grapes due to its high mountains. This is winemaking on the edge: snow can, and has, fallen during harvest; frost can wipe out crops late in the spring.

Comparing climate data from New Zealand with other winemaking regions can be a useful tool and helps contextualize the climate. Otago, for example, compares climatically with the cool Riesling lands of the Mosel and Rhine Valleys in Germany as well as Champagne. Nelson and the Wairau Valley in Marlborough aren't too dissimilar to Oregon's Willamette Valley or Burgundy, while Hawke's Bay and Gisborne on the North Island are in a similar league to Rioja, Bordeaux and Australia's Yarra Valley. Finally, the Bay of Islands compares with Italy's Vinho Verde and Chianti regions. (Table 2 in the Appendix gives a more detailed comparison.) What makes New Zealand stand apart from its European counterparts, however, are the country's cool nights, which produce grapes that are almost always higher in acidity than comparable European regions, according to the late Dr David Jackson.

Latitude also has a large role to play in the viability of New Zealand's climate. There are some sites in New Zealand that really shouldn't be able to grow grapes, but the seemingly interminable daylight gives them the opportunity to reach full ripeness in its cooler reaches. Being so far from the Equator, at a latitude of 45° S, Central Otago should not receive as much radiation as it does but Dr John Harris, an academic and co-founder of Māori Point Vineyard, says that the South Island receives around 40 per cent more UV radiation than a comparable region in the northern hemisphere. 'This is in part due to the ozone hole, but is mostly a result of exceptionally clean air, in particular relative lack of the aerosols which absorb UV in the high atmosphere in other regions of the world,' he explains. Various studies have shown that UV helps red grapes to develop flavonoids, which are responsible for colour and also have antioxidant effects. In white grapes, phenolics are less desirable, bringing a hard edge to the wine, and thus grapes need some protection from the ferocity of the afternoon sun. That's why you'll see north–south vineyards that allow greater fruit exposure on the eastern side and more leaf cover on the western side. New Zealand isn't the only wine-producing country in the southern hemisphere to experience high UV radiation but, as Dr Damian Martin explained in *New Zealand Winegrower*: 'One of the unique things about New Zealand is that we have very high energy from the sun but with a cool ambient temperature. Most places in the world where they experienced the equivalent energy that we get, would be 45 degrees outside. Your vines wouldn't produce quality in that.'

A cautionary tale

The Tongariro Crossing is deservedly one of the most popular day walks in New Zealand. Tourists of all shapes and sizes attempt the 19-kilometre walk, traversing the moonscape-like route, climbing volcanoes, and taking inane selfies with the brilliant Emerald and Blue Lakes. On the day I took on the crossing, the weather was true to Crowded House's track 'Four Seasons in One Day' and, while I had slathered on the factor 50, I failed to acquaint the back of my neck with the Ambre Solaire. It resulted in my normally pale white skin taking on a red lobster-like shade and it became painful to turn my head. Never again, I vowed, and have been caked in sun lotion and a large-brimmed hat ever since. Many tourists learn about the ferocity of New Zealand's sun in a similarly painful way, and the high levels of UV radiation are the reason behind the lobster look. New Zealand's low air-pollution levels and the depleted ozone layer above its two islands lead to increased UV radiation and that's not just a problem for human skin, but for grape skins too. While it's important for grapes, particularly red grapes, to have exposure to the sun to develop phenolic compounds, which are conducive to higher-quality wines, the timing of exposure to the sun is all important: if you suddenly expose the bunches, without them having built a base tan, they burn. It is necessary to build up the grape's natural sun protection gradually. For white grapes, sun burn is less desirable, producing bitter phenolics and potentially reducing quality.

An unusual feature of New Zealand's South Island, in particular, is the wide diurnal temperature ranges. The difference between day and night-time temperatures can be as much as 30°C in some extreme cases. Those visiting Central Otago for a summer camping holiday, for example, would need to pack their shorts and sun-tan lotion for the days and a fleece and hat for the nights. Fascinating climate classification work by Jorge Tonietto and Alain Carbonneau suggests that night-time temperatures are crucial in the last phase of ripening: September in the northern hemisphere and March in the southern hemisphere. Hot minimum night-time temperatures (above 18°C) lead to a loss of aroma and light colour in red wines. The authors highlight that cool nights are conducive to intense aromatics and deep colour in reds, which are commonly found in Central Otago's Pinot Noirs. The very cool night category requires a mean minimum temperature of less than 12°C in September to March, which includes some of Europe's finest white wine and Pinot Noir-producing regions, including Burgundy, Champagne and Alsace, France and the Rheingau and Baden in Germany. New Zealand's most important wine-producing region, Marlborough, also sits in the very cool category (data shows that the mean daily minimum temperature in Blenheim between 1990 and 2016 was 10.5°C) as do large swathes of the South Island, while the cool night (12 to 14°C) regions include Bordeaux and Hawke's Bay.

Climate is a central pillar in determining the success of growing grapes for fine wine with a sense of place. It determines the grape varieties chosen, the viticultural practices used and the composition of the grapes harvested. There are many indices – none of which are perfect – that classify wine regions. This book predominantly uses the growing degree day (GDD) classification, which is the most widely available form of climate data for comparing New Zealand viticulture regions. This system was devised by Albert Winkler and Maynard Amerine of the University of California, Davis (UCD) in the 1940s and while it fails to tell the whole story of a place, it remains a useful tool. It is a heat summation index of the growing season, which is October to April in the southern hemisphere. It takes the daily high temperature and subtracts the daily minimum temperature, divides that sum in half and then subtracts 10°C, which is considered the 'base temperature' for vines to grow. The daily figures from the growing season are then multiplied by the number of days in the growing season to give a final number. Winkler created a scale which categorized regions in five bands based on their GDD calculations: Region I being the coolest and Region V being the warmest. The range for Region I was 1,111 to 1,390 growing degree days, which means that parts of New Zealand, including the Waitaki

Valley and Gibbston, would not attain the lowest limit of the scale. As a result, Gregory V. Jones, an Oregon-based expert on wine and climate, introduced a lower threshold of 850 GDD and divided Region I into two parts to provide greater differentiation within a cool climate. The particular conditions found throughout the country's wine lands will be discussed in greater detail in the regional chapters.

3

NEW ZEALAND'S LEADING GRAPES

WHITE GRAPES

Sauvignon Blanc

It was a bottle of Villa Maria Sauvignon Blanc that did it. In the late 1990s my parents, not known for their love of fine wine, opened a bottle of New Zealand Sauvignon Blanc. My family had spent most of the previous two decades drinking my father's potent home brew and Liebfraumilch at Christmas, and I had never smelled anything like this before. Wine tasted of wine to my teenage palate, but this smelled like a tropical-fruit party. I picked out passionfruit and mango, gooseberries and lemons. It reminded me of Um Bongo, a soft drink that many who grew up in the UK in the 1980s and 1990s supped with their packed lunches while singing the catchy theme song, which claimed the drink was produced by a fruit-picking rhino, hippo, python and marmoset before being consumed 'deep down in the middle of the Congo'.

I wasn't the only one attracted by New Zealand Sauvignon Blanc's exuberant and distinctive fruity flavours. A decade before the Villa Maria Sauvignon Blanc grabbed my attention as a teenager, wine writer Hugh Johnson had been startled by New Zealand's flamboyant offering at a London tasting in 1984, as already noted. Wine writer Oz Clarke was equally startled by the flamboyant Sauvignon Blancs that emerged from New Zealand in the 1980s. In his *Wine Atlas* he says 'No previous wine had shocked, thrilled, entertained the world before with such brash, unexpected flavours of gooseberries, passionfruit and lime, or crunchy green asparagus spears, an entirely new, brilliantly successful wine style that the rest of the world has been attempting to copy ever since.'

It wasn't just the wine glitterati who had their palates awoken to New Zealand Sauvignon's vibrancy. In 1986, guests at The Sunday Times Wine Club Vintage Festival in London tasted Hunter's 1985 oak-aged Sauvignon Blanc and the long white clouds parted: they realized that this rugby-playing, sheep-farming country at the bottom of the world was making wine, and it was bloody good. Hunter's wasn't the only Marlborough Sauvignon Blanc producer turning heads: an Australian, David Hohnen, had made the journey from his Cape Mentelle winery in Australia to Marlborough, after tasting a few bottles of Sauvignon Blanc and being impressed with the contents: 'It was a bit sugary sweet but the aromatics were amazing.' He established Cloudy Bay with Kevin Judd, an English-born winemaker who doesn't appear to enjoy the limelight, preferring the company of his dog and standing behind the lens of his camera to being the front man of what would quickly become New Zealand's most successful wine brand. Cloudy Bay's second vintage – 1986 – landed on UK shores to rave reviews, and so began the fame of New Zealand Sauvignon Blanc.

It was hardly the most opportune time to be starting a winery. The government was offering generous grants to growers to pull out their vines due to an oversupply situation, phylloxera was discovered in Marlborough in 1984, and discount wars were raging in wine stores. Wineries were in dire financial straits and interest rates were at a record high. In 1986, the vineyard area had fallen to just 4,500 hectares from 5,000 hectares in 1985 following the vine-pull scheme. Across the country, around 2,000 tonnes of Sauvignon Blanc grapes were harvested. This aromatic variety was still a drop in an ocean of Müller-Thurgau. However, with the wholesale replanting of Marlborough following the incursion of phylloxera, the hybrid's ascendancy was soon to end. A decade later, in 1995, the prolific Müller-Thurgau remained the biggest producer of wine in New Zealand by volume, but Chardonnay and Sauvignon Blanc had surpassed Müller in terms of plantings. And two decades later – or thirty years after The Sunday Times Festival put New Zealand wines on the map – Sauvignon Blanc represented 3 in 5 hectares of vines planted. Its verdant vines ripen around 300,000 tonnes of fruit each season, a 2,400 per cent increase in three decades. The current agricultural landscape of Marlborough, the home of Sauvignon Blanc, would be unrecognizable to Marty McFly if he jumped in the DeLorean time machine and went back to Marlborough's capital, Blenheim, in the early 1980s.

A long time coming

It took New Zealand a while to cotton on to the joy of Sauvignon Blanc. There was a clone in the country before 1960 at the country's national viticultural research centre, Te Kauwhata, but no one knows how long it had been there. There is a hypothesis that Romeo Bragato, the government viticulturist in the first decade of the twentieth century, had imported it, but the details are hazy. It wasn't until New Zealander Ross Spence crossed the Pacific to study winemaking in California that Sauvignon Blanc was on the radar. Spence liked the variety's aromatics and its tenacity, and thought it could ripen well in New Zealand's cool climate. 'In the mid-1960s I managed to obtain some plant material that was labelled Sauvignon Blanc from the Te Kauwhata Viticultural Research Centre and grafted this on to 1202 rootstock in my small nursery that I operated together with my wife Adrienne. It was sufficient to plant about 250 vines in our Matua Road vineyard in 1968,' he explained in the local industry journal, *New Zealand Winegrower*. But the vines were severely infected with leaf-roll virus, the fruit didn't set and the crops were very small at less than one and a half tonnes an acre. Nevertheless, the fruit that did manage to make it to ripeness went into the winery; the resulting wine was aromatic and flavoursome and could knock Müller-Thurgau off its rather unexciting perch. But Spence needed better plant material if he was to make any headway. He had heard that a newer clone had been imported into New Zealand from the University of California, Davis. After a bit of asking around, Spence got his hands on some cuttings from a trial block, in which the Ministry of Agriculture had lost interest, and which was destroyed just weeks later. Spence continued: 'Wayne Thomas, a viticulturist with Montana Wines [now known as Brancott Estate], had heard that I had found this clone and managed to convince me to part with a couple of cuttings which he was going to use for bulking up and growing in Marlborough. Wayne was operating a substantial grapevine green-tip propagation plant in Avondale for Montana and over the next few years he turned the few cuttings into thousands of plants which were trucked to Marlborough and planted.' In 1979, the first Montana Sauvignon Blanc was made in Marlborough. Released in 1980, few would have dared to imagine the success Sauvignon Blanc would experience.

The science block

What is it about New Zealand Sauvignon Blanc that has won over wine lovers from Melbourne to Melton Mowbray? The answer lies in its extrovert personality. The cacophony of flamboyant fruit flavours accompanied by a high note of acidity sets Kiwi Sauvignon Blanc apart from the more subtle expressions in Sancerre and Pouilly Fumé in the Loire and the dry whites of Bordeaux. 'Brightness of fruit and acidity is the signature of Marlborough Sauvignon Blanc,' says Brancott Estate's winemaker Patrick Materman.

It is the brightness of fruit – and its idiosyncratic spectrum of flavours – that has been of interest to wine scientists in New Zealand since the turn of the century. Dr Wendy Parr, a former nurse, is one of those scientists. She has been at the forefront of research on New Zealand Sauvignon Blanc flavour profiling. The first attempt at 'Deconstructing the concept of Marlborough Sauvignon Blanc' by Parr and a team of boffins took place in 2004. The tasting panel results showed a 'sweaty, passionfruit, more-complex style is closer to their concept of a good Marlborough Sauvignon Blanc than the green, leaner style' associated with the Awatere Valley. However, a bit of green is essential to New Zealand Sauvignon Blanc, later studies by Parr show (2007). It appears that a typical Marlborough Sauvignon requires a combination of both tropical fruit and green flavours (grassy, green capsicum) in moderate quantities with a bit of cat's pee thrown in. A Sauvignon Blanc that is really green but not very fruity, or really fruity and not very green isn't considered to be typical.

These aromas have their origin in compounds known as methoxypyrazines and thiols. Methoxyprazines give us the green capsicum and grassy aromas and New Zealand Sauvignon Blanc has no shortage of them, particularly isobutyl methoxypyrazine (MIBP). Formed in the grapes, they are relatively stable during fermentation and throughout the maturation process. In addition to this group of compounds, Marlborough Sauvignon Blanc also contains high levels of sulphur-containing compounds known as thiols, in particular 3-mercaptohexanol (3MH), 3-mercaptohexyl acetate (3MHA) and

4-mercapto-4-methylpentan-2-one (4MMP). Formed by yeasts during fermentation, each thiol has a distinctive character: 3MH often smells of passionfruit, grapefruit and gooseberry; 3MHA might also be described as sweaty passionfruit and grapefruit as well as herbaceous characters and boxwood, while 4MMP brings boxwood, passionfruit, and even blackcurrant characters to a wine. In New Zealand, Sauvignon Blanc has naturally high levels of 3MH and 3MHA, which are responsible for a large part of its exuberant and distinctive style.

The chemical analysis of Sauvignon Blanc from Marlborough translates into a white wine style which sits apart from the rest of the world. A major piece of research by Cynthia Lund (2009) compared Sauvignon Blancs from New Zealand with examples from France, Australia, South Africa, Spain and the United States. The results were clear: Marlborough and Wairarapa Sauvignon Blancs are easy to pick out in an international line-up. The wines from these regions exuded far more aromatic intensity when it came to characteristics like fresh asparagus, sweet sweaty passionfruit, capsicum, passionfruit skin/stalk, tropical, stone fruit and apple. When it came to the wines from South Africa, France, Australia and the United States, the Sauvignon Blancs were more typically described as having bourbon, flinty/mineral and canned-asparagus flavours.

Lund's findings that New Zealand Sauvignon is sufficiently different from styles made around the world have been corroborated by further papers. In a study comparing Sauvignons from Marlborough, France and Austria by J. A. Green et al. (2011), tasters were able to pick out the Kiwi wines from the Europeans without too much difficulty. The French wines lacked the overt fruity and green character found in Marlborough and were more commonly described as mineral while the Austrian wines were fruity but didn't have that all-important green character. 'These results are in keeping with those of Lund et al. (2009) who reported relatively high concentrations of volatile thiols 3MH and 3MHA and of MIBP in New Zealand wines in comparison with Sauvignon wines from Australia, France, Spain, United States and South Africa. 'This overall result is in keeping with prior research that has argued that the combination of fruity and green perceived characters is the hallmark or distinguishing feature of New Zealand's Marlborough Sauvignon Blanc wine,' Green concluded.

While Marlborough has been the focal point of most Sauvignon Blanc research in New Zealand, it is important to note that New

Zealand Sauvignon is not homogeneous. Heading north from the capital of Marlborough, Blenheim, to the town of Picton, camper vans and bus loads of tourists line up alongside lorries to catch the ferry across the Cook Strait to Wellington on the North Island. Once there, it's just over an hour's drive to Martinborough. While there's only about 130 kilometres between Blenheim and Martinborough as the crow flies, the road and sea journey takes around five hours. The Sauvignon styles aren't a world apart but Wairarapa offers more grass and green asparagus notes rather than a tropical fruit bowl. Heading to the warmer climes of Hawke's Bay, it has been found that Hawke's Bay Sauvignon has a far lower concentration of 3MHA, 3MH and MIBP than Marlborough and Martinborough, and doesn't scream 'NEW ZEEEEAAALAND'.

Heading back to the Marlborough region, the style of Sauvignon Blanc is not monolithic. Plant and Food Research scientist Dr Mike Trought and his team studied subregional differences within Marlborough (2010). Trials took place across five sites, which included four in the Wairau Valley and one in the cooler Lower Awatere, around 24 kilometres south of Blenheim. The Awatere block ripened later than the Wairau Valley, and displayed higher herbaceous characters due to higher concentrations of methoxypyrazines. Following the five-year study, the team concluded that there were marked differences in temperature and soil texture between sites within the Wairau Valley, and yet these seemed to make little difference to the final product in terms of chemical and sensory properties. In 2012, another study by Jouanneau et al. looked at the chemical composition of wines from across Marlborough's subregions over two vintages. They found that some subregions, including the Awatere Valley, Rapaura and Waihopai, tended to show lower levels of a pyrazine responsible for green and capsicum (MIBP), isoamyl acetate – an ester formed during fermentation, which gives off fruity and banana aromas, as well as higher C6 alcohols, which give off grassy notes. Meanwhile the more inland subregions, including the Southern Valleys and Central and Upper Wairau, showed higher concentration of methoxypyrazines but lower levels of the thiols responsible for the passionfruit, sweaty, boxwood aromas, 3MH and 3MHA. Despite this early work, the subregional story remains a work in progress that we will understand more fully in time.

Man versus machine

It is harvest in Marlborough and hundreds of machine harvesters straddle rows of vines, shaking the plants as they move inexorably through the vineyard, encouraging plump bunches to lose their attachment and head towards their destiny. These machines are a bit of a pain for motorists trying to get anywhere fast during harvest and they're also a no-no in some parts of the Old World; you'd think that machine harvesting was the Devil from reading the back of wine labels, which boast that the grapes were lovingly 'hand picked' in an attempt to extract your cash. Yet studies by scientists at the University of Auckland have suggested that machine picking might actually be a better option for Sauvignon Blanc producers. Professor Paul Kilmartin, a chemist and wine scientist at the university, found compelling evidence that machine harvesting is actually conducive to making what would be seen as a typical Marlborough Sauvignon. The mechanized process enhances aroma-generating thiols – 3-mercaptohexanol (3MH) and 3-mercaptohexyl acetate (3MHA) – which together are responsible for its characteristic passionfruit characters, green aromas and sweaty notes.

'This has broken the traditional view that we can get the best wines from hand harvesting,' explains Kilmartin. 'Machine harvesting seems to be quite important in obtaining thiols. In France, particularly in Sancerre, and in South Africa, grapes tend to be hand picked, generating a different style of wine.' Sancerre and its fellow Loire producers are renowned for producing restrained styles of Sauvignon Blanc, with descriptors of gooseberry, elderflower and wet stone commonly used, while South Africa makes grassy examples of the variety.

While Kilmartin is not claiming that mechanized harvesting is better than hand picking, the team at the School of Chemical Sciences are saying that levels of thiols are five to ten times higher when grapes are machine harvested. Winemakers looking to create a highly aromatic style of Sauvignon filled with passionfruit and green capsicum should stick with their machine harvesters. It's not just the machine harvesting that's responsible for Marlborough's 'Sauvignon on steroids' flavours, though. New Zealand also has a greater propensity of these thiols naturally. Why, Kilmartin isn't sure: it could be the soil, the intense sunlight, or the temperature swings between day and night that are found in Marlborough. 'The experiments have not yet been done,' he says.

The changing face of Sauvignon Blanc

When it comes to making Sauvignon Blanc, there's usually no funny business: pick it, stick it in a tank, ferment it at relatively cool temperatures to preserve the fruit, prevent malolactic fermentation, and bottle it. Patrick Materman of Brancott Estate says 'Marlborough Sauvignon Blanc has been about clean fermentation, hands off [winemaking], stainless steel, cultured yeast, with very little winemaker influence'.

Inevitably the majority of production will continue to be the exuberant thiol-driven style that the world now believes is 'typical'. However, Kiwi producers have been experimenting with different techniques in both the vineyard and winery in an effort to retain our interest in the longer term. Doomsayers have predicted the imminent demise of 'Kiwi Savvy' and even industry members are doing their best to trip up their best export, nicknaming it 'Bitch Diesel'. Despite the criticism, the variety has stubbornly defied its critics and has become a must-have by-the-glass option in every bar and restaurant in the land.

Nevertheless, there has been a realization that some wine drinkers do want more than a wham-bam, fruity white wine, and winemakers also want to keep their lives interesting and produce more than a straightforward Sauvignon Blanc – and that's why there is growing experimentation with Sauvignon Blanc behind winery doors. For instance, larger wineries use commercial yeasts (sold in foil packets that bear a striking resemblance to ground coffee) to get the fermentations off and running smoothly, However, wild fermentations are now adding extra layers of savoury complexity to a growing number of Sauvignon Blancs. There is also growing interest in the mouthfeel of Sauvignon Blanc: Greywacke's Kevin Judd allows two-thirds of his Wild Sauvignon to undergo malolactic conversion, which can also play a large role stylistically on the final wine, making it more gentle and less flamboyantly fruity. Extended contact with lees (dead yeast cells) and lees stirring is also widely adopted to bring additional interest, texture and richness on the palate. 'The movement in the last few years has been how do we add extra elements of interest, including palate weight, a textural element, complex sulphides,' explains Materman.

The use of oak has been on the increase since the early 1990s. Sacred Hill launched Sauvage in 1992, a barrel-fermented Sauvignon inspired by a trip to Bordeaux with the late Denis Dubordieu, a respected university professor, consultant and owner of estates including Clos Floridene and Doisy-Daëne. Tony Bish, Sacred Hill founding winemaker, has been banging the drum for wooded Sauvignon ever since: 'Marlborough Sauvignon suits a time and a place, and it's not sophisticated, whereas barrel-fermented Sauvignon suits fine dining. It has the potential to go nuts but it needs to achieve a higher profile.'

A few years after the birth of Sauvage came Cloudy Bay's Te Koko. Producers started with small barrels – and many continue to do so – but larger formats including puncheons and older oak seem to be more compatible with this aromatic variety. The best are moving in the right direction, nodding to a wooded Sancerre or a Graves-like style with nutty, vanilla oak playing a supporting role to flavours on the riper end of the Sauvignon spectrum.

For those that are successful, there are as many (or more) that are heavy-handed. The barrel-derived flavours of wood and vanilla seem to fight with the bold fruity aromas that are synonymous with New Zealand Sauvignon Blanc. Barrel fermentation is meant to allow better integration of oak flavours compared to tank fermentation followed by barrel maturation yet there are relatively few success stories. Tim Heath, senior winemaker at Cloudy Bay, who makes Te Koko, says 'Barrel-fermented Sauvignon Blanc styles are not as easy to make as you think and can easily become overblown. It becomes quite disjointed with oak and overpowers the fruit. It's a difficult balance to strike.'

In a bid to produce a more integrated style, viticulture and winemaking has evolved. The grapes destined for Te Koko are hand picked and whole-bunch pressed to minimize skin contact and minimize the level of thiols, which are partly responsible for the green capsicum, passionfruit and sweaty-armpit aromas in Marlborough Sauvignon Blanc. The proportion of new oak has steadily fallen in recent years and now stands at less than 10 per cent; malolactic fermentation, which Heath says 'can be a killer of varietal flavours', is now down to 10 to 20 per cent (from 100 per cent in 1996). A better balance has been struck between the natural fruitiness of New Zealand Sauvignon Blanc and oak through a better understanding of Sauvignon Blanc's chemical make-up and two decades of experience. Nevertheless, the variety's idiosyncratic aromatics when fermented in barrel remain a question of taste. And the price of an oaked Sauvignon Blanc can also be difficult to swallow. A new 225-litre French oak barrel costs around $1,500 and you will pay a premium for Sauvignon Blanc that has grown up in oak.

The clone zone

It is no coincidence that New Zealand wine's biggest export became the focus of intense scientific research in the noughties: chemical and sensory research have helped the industry understand the science behind flamboyant Sauvignon and how vineyard management and winemaking can affect its expression. Yet there has been remarkably little research and diversity in planting material until recently. The clone that has singlehandedly made New Zealand famous is referred to as Sauvignon Blanc MS or Mass Selection. It is so-called because it is difficult to trace the material back to its original mother vine. The industry relied on imports of UCD 1, which were then propagated again and again by nurseries from established vineyards. Nick Hoskins of Riversun, one of the country's leading nurseries, explains: 'In some respects, the process resembles French "selection massale" – with the important exception that it has relied on an extremely limited gene pool.' However, it produced a style of wine that put the country on the world map. Three clones were imported from Bordeaux and were available from the early 1990s but two (316 and 317) were found to be virused and the other had tight bunches and little intensity of flavour, which were hardly selling points. Hoskins adds 'It's fair to say that none of them has ever come close to supplanting Savvy MS as the "favourite". And so, as the area planted to Sauvignon Blanc increased at a breathtaking pace, the New Zealand wine industry continued to rely almost exclusively on MS – a monoculture in every sense.'

In recent times, new clones have become available, originating from the Loire, Bordeaux and Italy, which may add a new dimension to Marlborough Sauvignon Blanc. There are plenty of producers looking to make wines that are less exuberantly aromatic with a greater sensation of minerality. While techniques such as hand harvesting and whole-bunch pressing can reduce its ebullience, clonal material could also help in their quest. There's nothing wrong with New Zealand Sauvignon Blanc but it is both natural and wise to explore the capabilities of the country's dominant grape variety further.

10 must-try New Zealand Sauvignon Blancs

- Auntsfield Single Vineyard Sauvignon Blanc, Marlborough
- Churton Wines Sauvignon Blanc, Marlborough
- Cloudy Bay Vineyards Sauvignon Blanc, Marlborough
- Craggy Range Te Muna Road Sauvignon Blanc, Martinborough
- Dog Point Vineyard Sauvignon Blanc, Marlborough
- Eradus Awatere Valley Sauvignon Blanc, Marlborough
- Greywacke Wild Sauvignon, Marlborough
- Man O'War Gravestone Sauvignon Semillon, Waiheke Island
- Seresin Estate Sauvignon Blanc, Marlborough
- Supernatural Wine Co. The Supernatural Sauvignon Blanc, Hawke's Bay

Chardonnay

On the same day that Bordeaux first-growth Château Margaux released its 2014 vintage en primeur, a tasting with the great and the good of the London wine trade pitted a New Zealand winery's Chardonnays against some of Burgundy's finest whites. World-famous names like Domaines Leflaive, des Comtes Lafon and Joseph Drouhin were in the Burgundy corner while Auckland's Kumeu River agreed to the David and Goliath challenge.

It takes *cojones* to take on Burgundy at its own game and there are surely few New World producers who would be confident of competing at this level but Stephen Browett, director of Kumeu River's UK importer Farr Vintners, knows a thing or two about balls: he is one of the owners of south London football club, Crystal Palace. Having travelled to New Zealand in 1990 and tasted the 1989 vintage from barrel, Browett placed an order on the spot and has been shipping the wines ever since. Over the last quarter of a century, Browett has poured the wine to unsuspecting French winemakers who have guessed they were drinking grand cru Burgundies.

Kumeu River came out on top, winning three out of the four rounds, outperforming wines that were two or three times the price. It was a great moment for New Zealand Chardonnay. Master of Wine, OBE and unofficial HRH of wine, Jancis Robinson, was part of the tasting and in her post-match analysis noted: 'I was presented with proof that the white wine grape of which New Zealanders should be most proud is not Sauvignon Blanc but Chardonnay.'

Kumeu River is no Crystal Palace in the New Zealand Chardonnay stakes; it is rather the equivalent of Manchester United or Chelsea. It doesn't have the same salary budget, that's for sure, but it is consistently worthy of a place in the Champions League. The serious and thoughtful winemaker behind the Chardonnay is Michael Brajkovich who heads up the family business with his siblings and his mother, Melba, who still greets all visitors to the winery with incredible warmth. Her husband and the founder of Kumeu River Wines, Maté, passed away in 1992, but was able to see his son graduate top of his class at Roseworthy College, Australia and become New Zealand's first Master of Wine in 1989. The family has named its flagship wine in his honour. Michael is a thoughtful, intelligent gentle giant and an authority on all things Chardonnay, which makes up two-thirds of Kumeu's production. He explains why New Zealand can make such elegant Chardonnay: 'The one big difference between the traditional Chardonnay wines of Burgundy and those of most New World countries was that Burgundy is cool climate, where most of California and Australia are warm to hot regions, with a few notable exceptions. However, all of the Chardonnay-growing regions in New Zealand can be classified as cool climate, and this fact is a huge advantage in producing a style of Chardonnay wine that is closer to the original (white Burgundy) style that has excited drinkers for centuries.'

Despite having a climate suited to Chardonnay production, it wasn't until the 1990s that the variety took off in New Zealand. From producing around 2,000 tonnes in the mid 1980s, the national Chardonnay crush had tripled by 1992 to 6,172 tonnes of grapes. By the millennium, just eight years later, there were 23,593 tonnes processed.

But trouble was brewing: at the same time as Chardonnay vineyards were sprouting across New Zealand and many other parts of the wine-producing world, there were a growing number of Chardonnay critics. In August 1995, *New York Times* wine writer Frank J. Prial reported that Chardonnay, 'the cornerstone of America's wine culture', was being challenged by those who were bored of the grape and sought out Anything But Chardonnay (ABC). He reported that 'the chances of dislodging Chardonnay from its eminence soon are nil'. He was right: Chardonnay is still the most-consumed grape variety in the US (Nielsen, 2017). However, there was a very real backlash against the oaky, buttery

Chardonnays that Australia and other warm-climate producing countries were crafting. Despite its cooler climate, New Zealand was not immune from this Chardonnay style. Jim White, vineyard manager at Cloudy Bay, says 'I used to see my Chardonnay grapes disappear into the winery and it used to come back looking nothing like the fruit I sent!'

Brajkovich, who was trained in the hotter climes of South Australia, explains how the butteriness emerged. 'The malolactic fermentation (MLF) to reduce acidity in cool climates was ... much less suitable in warmer regions where it reduced the acidity too much. But, the butteriness that came hand in hand with MLF began to be appreciated by many, and the technique became very fashionable in many warmer regions because it introduced a distinctive character, where perhaps previously there had been none.' Chardonnay is, after all, a non-aromatic variety that can tempt winemakers to use all the tools in their box. In New Zealand, it is common to hear winemakers talk of allowing 'partial malolactic': some parcels of fruit in the blend have completed the malolactic fermentation while others have not.

Revolution to evolution

While Robert Mondavi and other ambitious Chardonnay producers in California were shipping French oak across the Atlantic as early as the 1960s in an attempt to emulate Burgundy, oaked whites took a while to catch on in New Zealand. Tim Finn, co-founder of Nelson's Neudorf Vineyards, another iconic Chardonnay producer, planted the first vines in the late 1970s and remembers 'buying our first Burgundy barrels, which I was very proud of: we had two for our first vintage and I used to bring people around to see them'.

French oak barrels were first shipped to New Zealand in the 1980s, and at first they were used for maturation rather than fermentation, which created wines that tasted oaky and were sometimes oxidized. Thankfully there has been a shift toward barrel fermentation, which Brajkovich calls a 'revolution' in the country's Chardonnay production. Fermenting in barrel moderated the oakiness and integrated it, and in this reductive environment the wine was better protected from oxidation. Finn adds: 'The big changes have been made. It's more about fine tuning than large steps now. Barrel fermentation and barrel maturation are pretty well adopted throughout New Zealand.'

Another major step forward in the quality of New Zealand Chardonnay has been the reduction in buttery flavours. Producers have wised up to the fact that leaving wine on its lees (dead yeast cells) decreases the amount of diacetyl, the compound behind the butteriness: it 'helps remove the mask of "diacetyl" and reveals many more of the inherently attractive fruit qualities of Chardonnay, which in many cases were hitherto hidden,' Brajkovich says.

There are many decisions for winemakers to take along the Chardonnay path. For instance, should they allow their juice to settle and by how much? After pressing the grapes the resulting juice is cloudy and the settling process allows the particles or solids suspended in the juice to fall to the bottom of the tank, giving a clearer and cleaner liquid. The more solids you leave in the juice, the more nutrients the yeast will have during the fermentation. However, solids also risk reduction so it's a balancing act to find a level that suits the intended wine style. A little bit of reduction, adding a hint of flint to the fruit and nut flavours of a barrel-fermented Chardonnay, acts like salt or pepper seasoning. However, there are far too many examples of Chardonnay that are dominated by struck-match flavours, overpowering the fine fruit beneath.

Staying with wine refinement, phenolics, a group of compounds which include tannins and are important in red wine for colour and structure, are also an important consideration for New Zealand Chardonnay producers. Coming from the pulp and the skins, the smaller the berries, the more phenolics; the harder winemakers press their grapes, the higher the phenolics, which can lead to bitterness and astringency. I am yet to meet anyone who wants to drink an astringent Chardonnay, so in a season with small berries, winemakers might introduce more oxygen to the fermentation. Finn notes: 'We don't want to have too many phenolics so after two or three days of fermentation, we do a bit of a "splashy turnover" of juice to introduce oxygen. It tends to oxidize some of the phenolics plus it gets the yeast population going.' As a result, many of the top New Zealand Chardonnay producers are now friends with oxygen whereas, just two or three decades ago, oxygen was the enemy. The previous result? 'We tended to end up with a lot of fruit but quite hard wines,' says Finn.

The science block

The majority of New Zealand's best Chardonnays hail from the Mendoza clone. Imported into New Zealand from Australia in 1971, it is low yielding with small bunches and good tolerance to disease. But it does suffer from millerandage, also known as hen and chicken. This means that there can be berries of differing sizes on the same bunch. It also means that picking decisions are made harder, as the smaller berries tend to ripen before the larger ones, but this can also mean that a winemaker has a greater array of flavours and acidities to create a more complex wine. Unfortunately, all genuine Mendoza in New Zealand has leafroll virus, according to Gisborne-based nursery Riversun.

New Zealand's Chardonnay stock has been based on Mendoza and three other clones: the imaginatively titled B95, UCD 6 and 15 (the letters UCD stand for University of California, Davis, the source of these clones). Riversun's Nick Hoskins notes that 'Clone 6 might be termed a "workhorse" in that it consistently produces moderate to large crops with good fruit characters, although sometimes lacking in intensity.' UCD 15, like Mendoza, displays hen and chicken tendencies but some winemakers 'prefer this clone, and believe it is richer and more intense than UCD clone 6 or Mendoza'.

In the vineyard, there are minor adjustments being made to refine the fruit heading into the winery. New Zealand's climate can produce perfectly ripe Chardonnays, which offer richness with natural freshness. On the north island, Hawke's Bay, home to iconic Chardonnays like Sacred Hill's Riflemans and Villa Maria's Keltern, offers a warmer expression of New Zealand Chardonnay than you would find in Marlborough. The warmer climate brings greater ripeness but just because ripe is good, it doesn't mean very ripe is better. Lessons have been learned through experience. Producers are moving towards earlier picking, notes Nick Piccone, group chief winemaker at Villa Maria: 'Picking dates are seasonally dependent and are also influenced by vine age and health. Young vines will generally be harvested ahead of mature vines particularly if there is any virus. All things being equal, however, I believe we now choose to pick the grapes at lower sugar levels and with higher levels of natural acidity and are perhaps more confident with our perception of flavour at an earlier harvest date than we were ten years ago.'

There has also been a slight shift in terms of canopy management. Instead of removing most of the leaves around the bunches, there is greater leaf area now, providing some shade around the fruit. This dappled light, rather than full exposure to the New Zealand sun, affords some protection to the grape skin from the powerful UV rays which can lead to sun burn, thicker skins and phenolics, which is undesirable in Chardonnay.

What is desirable in Chardonnay is a matter of taste. Whether or not you like oak or struck-match flavours in your glass, the ever-improving quality of New Zealand Chardonnay is undeniable. It is ideally placed to make Chardonnays that offer elegance, complexity and freshness and it is up to the winemakers to nurture its subtle characteristics to a nuanced conclusion.

10 must-try New Zealand Chardonnays

• Ata Rangi Craighall Chardonnay, Martinborough
• Dog Point Vineyard Chardonnay, Marlborough
• Felton Road Block 2 Chardonnay, Central Otago
• Greystone Wines Erin's Reserve Chardonnay, North Canterbury
• Kumeu River Maté's Vineyard, Auckland
• Mahi Wines Twin Valleys Chardonnay, Marlborough
• Neudorf Vineyards Moutere Chardonnay, Nelson
• Sacred Hill Riflemans Chardonnay, Hawke's Bay
• Vidal Estate Legacy Chardonnay, Hawke's Bay
• Villa Maria Keltern Chardonnay, Hawke's Bay

Aromatic whites

In New Zealand, the term 'aromatic whites' is used to embrace varieties including Gewürztraminer, Riesling and Pinot Gris.

Pinot Gris

Pinot Gris seems to be gatecrashing the aromatic party. It is far from attaining the aromatic heights of Gewürztraminer, Torrontes or the Muscat family – varieties that are naturally fragrant and contain high levels of compounds called terpenes. Pinot Gris has a rather subtle scent, particularly when overcropped, yet it is grouped in the 'aromatic' white section in New Zealand. It might be better to classify it as semiaromatic at best, watery at worst. The University of California, Davis has provided a definition of aromatic varieties based on terpenes, a class of fragrant organic compounds, which are produced by plants and stored in the grape skins. Grape varieties can be divided into Muscats with free volatile terpene concentrations of 6 mg/l, non-Muscat aromatic varieties with concentrations of 1 to 4 mg/l, and neutral varieties that aren't dependent on terpenes for aroma containing less than 1 mg/l. Some studies have found that Chardonnay and Pinot Gris show little or no terpene content. Others have found that Pinot Gris does contain terpenes but in relatively small amounts compared with truly aromatic varieties. In a recent study of monoterpenes in white grape varieties by Song et al. (2018), varieties were classified into three groups – group one included the most aromatic varieties: Torrontes and Muscat. The monoterpene concentration of these two varieties was four times greater than Gewürztraminer, which was classified in group two, six times greater than Riesling and Viognier, and more than thirty times greater than Chardonnay and Pinot Gris. Based on the results, it is somewhat unsurprising that Pinot Gris and Chardonnay were grouped into category three: 'the less aromatic varietal wines'. The position of Pinot Gris in the aromatic whites category might be convenient but these scientific studies suggests it is incongruous.

Considered one of Alsace's four noble varieties, plantings of Pinot Gris have blossomed. In 1997, there were just 32 hectares planted; ten years later that stood at 1,146 hectares – and by 2017 Pinot Gris covered 2,369 hectares, making it the third most-planted white variety in the country. Its recent appearance means that many of the vines are still in their adolescence and more time is needed for them to show their true potential. The dominant style is Pinot Gris rather than Grigio, offering a fuller bodied, off-dry style with baked apple, pear and spice flavours. The warmer North Island tends to offer more lush, sometimes waxy Pinot Gris, while the cooler climes of the South Island bring more tension to the wine. It has become a huge commercial success, producing bucketloads of inoffensive off-dry white wine. Fermented in stainless steel at cool temperatures to retain fruit purity and left with a touch of residual sugar, it has widespread appeal. The variety yields a national average 8 tonnes to the hectare but quality-oriented producers go as low as 5 tonnes to encourage greater concentration. Winemaking techniques including wild yeast, fermentation in used barrels and lees are also employed to bring additional complexity and textural interest – there is even a producer taking a leaf out of the sherry manual and making Pinot Gris aged under flor (Bellbird Spring Sous Voile). The finest offer purity of fruit, subtle nuance and carefully handled phenolics, which bring structure and drive to this low-in-acid variety.

The variety ripens early, which is useful in New Zealand when autumn rainfall can mean grapes swelling and splitting, leading to botrytis. Certain clones are prone to tight bunches, exacerbating this problem. According to Riversun, the 'workhorse' Pinot Gris clones in New Zealand were imported from the 1960s to the 1980s from Switzerland, South Africa, Germany and some cuttings from old vines taken at Mission Vineyards in Hawke's Bay dating back to the 1880s. The older clones including Barrie and Lincoln Berrysmith tend to produce tight bunches and this is a recipe for rot. If it rains late in the season, berries swell and split. Andrew Hull, viticulturist at The Landing in Northland, explains 'Barrie is a staple up here and it gives tight bunches and can crop heavily. If it rains post-veraison, the grapes swell and the skins split.' However, they are trialling a clone called 457, which has impressed Todd Stevens, winemaker at Nelson's Neudorf Vineyards: 'It's the new kid on the block, it's chalk and cheese compared to the other whoppers.' It's not just 457; there is a wide variety of clones that has been imported since the millennium. The Italian clone M2, for example, has a fan club and seems to be better suited to a Grigio rather than a Gris style.

Buyer beware: there are a number of producers labelling what is a Pinot Gris-style wine as Pinot Grigio, trading off the greater awareness and popularity of northern Italy's interpretation of the grape. The Ned Pinot Grigio, for example, has an almost pink hue and is far richer than you'd expect from a Grigio from the Veneto.

Ten must-try New Zealand Pinot Gris

- Bellbird Spring Wines Sous Voile, North Canterbury
- Dry River Wines Pinot Gris, Martinborough
- Greystone Wines Sand Dollar Pinot Gris, North Canterbury
- Greywacke Pinot Gris, Marlborough
- Misha's Vineyard Dress Circle Pinot Gris, Central Otago
- Neudorf Vineyards Moutere Pinot Gris, Nelson

- Prophet's Rock Pinot Gris, Central Otago
- Supernatural Wine Co. Spook Light Pinot Gris, Hawke's Bay
- Valli Vineyards Gibbston Vineyard Pinot Gris, Central Otago
- Valli Vineyards The Real McCoy Pinot Gris, Central Otago

Riesling

New Zealand's cool climate provides the perfect setting for scintillating Riesling and it has a hardcore of loyalists among the wine community who profess their love of the grape through temporary tattoos and T-shirts. There are even competitions for best T-shirt: if you donned a 'Jesus drinks Riesling' T-shirt in the normal world, most people would think you were one sandwich short of a picnic but among other Riesling freaks in New Zealand, it doesn't make the grade. At a Riesling-only symposium in New Zealand in 2011, a gentleman wearing an 'Auslese ist beste' T-shirt won the day – but it wasn't the 'beste' T-shirt that stole the show but the generously proportioned man wearing it. He was so keen to win that he turned it into a wet T-shirt competition and no one else would go that extra mile.

Riesling clearly drives some to madness, but it is those who don't drink Riesling that are insane – and there are plenty of them, which explains why there are so few vines in the ground. From a high of 993 hectares in 2011, there were just 721 hectares of Riesling in the ground by 2017, and that figure was predicted to fall further. In comparison, there were more than 22,000 hectares of Sauvignon Blanc across New Zealand in 2017. The cool climes of New Zealand's South Island represent 90 per cent of all Riesling plantings, and there are very few vines further north than the Wairarapa. In terms of exports, shed a tear: Riesling accounted for just 0.1 per cent of all wine leaving New Zealand ports in 2015.

Despite Riesling's lack of popularity and its minority status in New Zealand's vineyards, there is a wide range of successful Riesling styles produced from dry to unctuous. It is a late-ripening variety and is prone to botrytis, particularly in humid and wet years. If the autumn is dry, bunches can be left on the vine to achieve riper phenolics, which contribute to the wine's structure. If the weather doesn't allow the luxury of leaving the grapes on the vine, the phenolic impression can be ameliorated by leaving some residual sugar in the wine as well as reducing skin contact by hand harvesting and whole-bunch pressing. The wines tend to be fermented in stainless steel to preserve the pristine fruit and provide a clear expression of place while others ferment a proportion in old barrels, bringing an additional layer of textural complexity and rounding out Riesling's angular frame.

Styles vary from region to region, winery to winery, with some producers making multiple styles – Marlborough's Framingham is renowned for its range of Rieslings from its organic vineyards, first planted in 1981. Under the stewardship of Dr Andrew Hedley of Gateshead, England, you'll find everything a Riesling lover could ever want in terms of styles and sweetness levels. When it comes to plantings, Marlborough leads the Riesling race but only just – North Canterbury is close behind. Both produce crisp, citrussy Rieslings but North Canterbury often shows a savouriness and orange-zest character not found in other parts of the country. In Waitaki and Central Otago, the most southerly wine region in the world, the Rieslings display intense purity of citrus fruit and an acidity akin to a harpist plucking a very high note. In Nelson, the wines are crisp and fresh with pure varietal character but do not share the wide diurnal differences of Central Otago, giving a more subtle impression in the glass. On the North Island, the wind-beaten, low-yielding vineyards of Martinborough produce an intense expression with piercing aromas and striking precision.

10 must-try New Zealand Rieslings
- Black Estate Damsteep Riesling, North Canterbury
- Felton Road Block 1 Riesling, Central Otago
- Framingham Wines Noble Riesling, Marlborough
- Greystone Wines Sea Star Riesling, North Canterbury
- Kusuda Wines Riesling, Martinborough
- Pegasus Bay Bel Canto Riesling, North Canterbury
- Prophet's Rock Dry Riesling, Central Otago
- Rippon 'Rippon' Mature Vine Riesling, Central Otago
- Seifried Sweet Agnes Riesling, Nelson
- Tongue in Groove Riesling, North Canterbury

Alternative whites
Beyond the big four whites (Sauvignon Blanc, Chardonnay, Pinot Gris and Riesling), there is increasing diversity in the vineyards of

New Zealand. From Chenin Blanc and Gewürztraminer, which have a relatively long history in the country's soils, to Albariño and Grüner Veltliner, the white wine scene is more exciting than ever before. The rats and mice are yet to take over the ship but it isn't a big step for drinkers to move fluidly from the country's fresh, fruity, unoaked Sauvignons to the fresh, fruity, unoaked Albariños and Grüners. New Zealand's cool, maritime climate is perfectly suited to whites sporting vibrant fruit flavours, moderate alcohol and juicy acidity beyond Sauvignon Blanc.

10 must-try New Zealand alternative whites
- Black Estate Home Chenin Blanc, North Canterbury
- Coopers Creek The Bellringer Albariño, Gisborne
- Esk Valley Estate Verdelho, Hawke's Bay
- Hans Herzog Viognier, Marlborough
- Johanneshof Cellars Gewürztraminer, Marlborough
- Millton Estate Clos de Ste. Anne Chenin Blanc, Gisborne
- Millton Estate Clos Monique Les Trois Enfants, Gisborne*
- Misha's Vineyard Gallery Gewürztraminer, Central Otago
- Te Whare Ra SV5182 Toru, Marlborough*
- Yealands Estate Single Vineyards P.G.R, Marlborough*

RED GRAPES

Pinot Noir

The early history of the country's most-planted red variety is wonderfully hazy. Pinot Noir may have first graced New Zealand soils as early as 1819 when missionary Samuel Marsden planted grapevines in Northland. Marsden shipped his vines from Sydney, Australia, and at that time Pinot Noir was one of the more common varieties so it is possible that Pinot Noir was among the cuttings. It is also possible that it was not. Similarly, when James Busby planted his vineyard at Waitangi in the early 1830s, it is not unlikely that Pinot Noir was among his selection. What is certain is that in 1883, William Beetham and his French wife Marie Zelie Hermance Frere planted Pinot Noir on their Wairarapa property along with Pinot Meunier, Hermitage and several other

---

* Blends

varieties. Over lunch with Henry Tiffen, a surveyor and landowner in Hawke's Bay, a taste of Beetham's wine convinced him to take cuttings and plant his own vineyard – Greenmeadows – with Pinot Noir, Pinot Blanc, Pinot Meunier and Black Hermitage (Syrah). Bernard Chambers also planted Pinot varieties on Te Mata Station. There is mention of Pinot Noir being planted by French missionaries in its earliest days and there were clearly a few vines in the ground, as Chambers took cuttings from the Mission Vineyards in 1892 to start his vineyard.

By the time viticulture expert Romeo Bragato conducted his tour of New Zealand, Pinot Noir and Pinot Meunier were thriving in Hawke's Bay. Bragato's report to the New Zealand government on the 'Prospects of Viticulture' stated that Pinot Noir was one of the most suitable red varieties for the country as well as Black Hermitage, Cabernet Sauvignon, Cabernet Franc, Dolcetto and 'Mueller Burgundy'.

The modern history of Pinot Noir begins in the mid 1970s in what now seems like an unlikely place for the variety: Auckland. The grape has since moved southward to the cooler climes of Wairarapa and the South Island but west Auckland was the early setting for its success. Nobilo's Huapai Pinot Noir 1976 has been singled out as the first quality Pinot Noir of the modern era while Babich's Henderson Valley Pinot Noir 1981 won the variety its first gold medal in a wine competition. Meanwhile, on the South Island, St Helena planted the first Pinot vines in the frosty Canterbury region: planting in this cool climate raised a few eyebrows but they were soon lowered when the 1982 vintage won a gold medal at the Air New Zealand Wine Awards, suggesting that both Pinot Noir and the soils of Canterbury might be a combination worth exploring.

Vineyards were also appearing in Martinborough in the early 1980s following the publication of a report by soil scientist Derek Milne which concluded that Martinborough, Marlborough and Waipara were well suited to viticulture. Dr Neil McCallum first took the plunge in 1979, planting grapes on Puruatanga Road, an avenue that is now lined with some of New Zealand's finest Pinot Noir vineyards. In Central Otago, home to more than 1,500 hectares of Pinot Noir (2017) or a quarter of New Zealand's Pinot vineyards, the variety was just one of many at that time, as its pioneers tried to figure out what would grow best in this arid, rocky land inhabited by sheep and rabbits.

Despite its fragility and fickle nature, Pinot Noir has thus far proven to be a winning variety for New Zealand's cool climate. From less than 500 hectares planted in 1997, that figure has increased eleven fold to more than 5,500 hectares two decades later. This early ripening variety needs a cool climate to slow its race to ripeness, allowing it to develop complexity and finesse while preserving its acidity. Its early budding nature means it can be susceptible to spring frosts, which are common on the South Island, and its thin skin means it is prone to fungal disease, which can cause difficulties in wet vintages.

In the early days, the wines lacked some colour and heft, as the Pinot Noir clones available were destined for sparkling rather than red wine. With the arrival of the Abel clone (see the Gumboot Clone box), a greater availability of improved plant material, increased vine age and a better understanding of the vines and the wines they produce, New Zealand Pinot Noir is becoming increasingly complex. There is also a growing confidence in the New Zealand Pinot Noir-growing community; a sense of self and an attitude that says 'this is who we are, this is what we do, and if you don't like it, plenty of other people do'. This confidence and pride wasn't in evidence in 2010, when I first attended the country's Pinot Noir NZ conference. Held every three years, there were frequent comparisons to Burgundy, the historic homeland of Pinot Noir, at the event. It was put on a pedestal. Yes, the French region makes the world's finest examples that most of us can't afford unless we forgo several mortgage payments, and it is inevitable that any Pinot Noir producer would like to achieve the heady heights of Domaine de la Romanée-Conti or Henri Jayer. But, let's face it, Burgundy also makes a lot of crap wine: opt for the *prix fixe* lunch at a bistro in Beaune and you'll be able to taste wines that aren't worthy of salad dressing.

Today, the pendulum has swung: there appears to be an aversion to comparing New Zealand to Burgundy because the only thing they have in common when it comes to Pinot Noir is the grape. Ted Lemon of Littorai Wines in Sonoma and Burn Cottage Vineyard in Central Otago made it clear that he thought comparisons to Burgundy were unhealthy for New World producers in a speech at the Mornington Peninsula International Pinot Noir conference in 2013. 'Look inward,' he implored. 'Do not measure all things against the Old World. And above all do not see Burgundy as a measuring stick. We must be like Odysseus, lashing ourselves to the mast of the ship in order to resist the siren song of the maidens of Burgundy.' Benchmarking against other Pinot Noir regions is hardly the root of all evil, but when trying to communicate wine styles in New Zealand comparisons with Burgundy are occurring less and less frequently.

Regionality

New Zealand Pinot Noir made from young vines is fruity, fresh and fun. It would be impossible to find a reasonably priced Pinot Noir from Burgundy that offered such attractive juicy fruit. However, there are growing numbers of New Zealand Pinot Noir producers making increasingly serious wines from Martinborough at the bottom of the North Island (latitude 40° S) to Central Otago (45° S), the world's most southerly wine region.

The styles of wine produced across New Zealand's regions are varied and distinctive. In very simple terms, Martinborough Pinot Noir is often described as savoury while Marlborough's Wairau Valley offers joyful fruitiness; Central Otago is naturally bold and black cherry-filled while Waipara's best can be brooding. The existence of regionality in New Zealand Pinot Noir had been discussed anecdotally but there was little research in comparison to the swathe of studies of New Zealand Sauvignon Blanc. In an attempt to remedy the lack of scientific evidence, Elizabeth Tomasino, a former PhD student at Lincoln University, set out to determine whether or not the Pinot Noir styles from the regions of Martinborough, Marlborough, Waipara and Central Otago were distinctive. Her results showed that there were clear and consistent differences. The Pinot Noirs from Marlborough were characterized by 'red cherry and raspberry aromas, greater red fruit in-mouth flavour, and greater balance' while Waipara's wines offered 'greater intensity of barnyard, herbal, and violet aromas and greater fruit density/concentration in-mouth flavour'. Martinborough's wines are typically described as savoury but Tomasino's research panels found 'greater intensity of black cherry, oak, and spice aromas' and Central Otago wines had 'fuller body'.

Tomasino's work seemed to demonstrate that regionality did exist in New Zealand. Since she completed her thesis in 2011, New Zealand has rapidly evolved. Marlborough's reputation as a producer of simple red-fruited Pinot Noir needs to be revised. Yes, it still produces high volumes of juicy, fruity Pinot Noir for entry-level price points but, with an irrigation scheme opening up the clay-loam hillsides of Southern Valleys in the early 2000s, there is a band of producers making increasingly serious wines with depth and richness. Better sites, better plant material and rising vine age means Marlborough's image as a producer of fruity Pinot Noir is outdated. Producers report that they are reducing their use of new French oak as older vines are producing grapes with tannins that ooze and resolve with extended post-fermentation maceration providing natural structure.

Martinborough has a longer track record of making Pinot Noir than Marlborough and serious drinkers have looked to producers like Ata Rangi and Dry River for complex, nuanced examples. The frost-prone, windy region typically produces small bunches with small berries (producers also report thicker skins), and these factors imbue the wines with rich colour, fruit concentration and naturally abundant tannins. Typical aromas include damson, violets and spice as well as a savoury character. Naturally low yields and quality-oriented producers mean that the general standard of wine in Martinborough is high.

The Pinot Noirs of Nelson differ in style depending on their site: the alluvial Waimea Plains typically offer light-bodied, finely fruited examples for early drinking, while the clays of the Moutere Hills provide fuller, weightier expressions with cocoa-powder tannins. The Nelson region's gentle maritime climate is expressed in the glass: the bright fruit reflects the area's high sunlight hours and yet the wines retain a gentleness, which might be related to a narrower diurnal temperature range than other South Island Pinot Noir-producing regions.

The Pinot Noirs of North Canterbury are site dependent. In the Waipara area, those on the Awapuni clay loams and Omihi offer a seriousness, broody character and often display a chalky sinew in their tannin structure. The Pinot Noirs sourced from the Glasnevin Gravels are lighter in body, juicy and full of bright red fruit. The two isolated producers on limestone further inland at Waikari – Bell Hill and Pyramid Valley – have shown glimmers of greatness, with the Pinot Noirs going beyond fruit, offering a rare transparency and other worldly sensation. It is mind blowing to think that North Canterbury's finest

Pinot Noir producers did not exist at the turn of the century, and its continued evolution will be one to watch with great expectations.

Between Canterbury and Central Otago, there's a five-hour drive almost devoid of vineyards. That is, except for Waitaki. Centred around the tiny town of Kurow, there is a handful of producers defying the marginal climate to produce aromatic whites and Pinot Noir. Yields are low, in part due to hostile weather: frost, wind and rain make ripening grapes here a risky business. The wines – particularly those grown on limestone – are elegant with a line of acid that provides dart-like precision and chalky tannins. Beyond Waitaki, most Kiwis south of Christchurch realize that growing grapes at the bottom of the earth is a recipe for high blood pressure. It is only in the semi-continental climate of Central Otago, surrounded by mountains, that Pinot Noir can flourish. The variety accounts for around 70 per cent of the region's plantings and, since making a big impression on the world stage with its bold, big and ballsy 2002 vintage, it is now trying to convince the world that it does finesse. The region's dry, sunny climate with huge fluctuations between day and night-time temperatures and high levels of UV light imbues the Pinot Noirs of Central Otago with deep colour, a wealth of fruit, rich tannins and potentially high alcohol levels (14–14.5% abv is common). There are moves to pick a little earlier to retain greater freshness and rein in the region's natural flamboyance: winemaking has evolved with much gentler extraction, experimentation with whole bunches, longer post-fermentation macerations and more judicious use of new French oak.

The willingness to evolve winemaking processes and trial techniques is not just occurring in Central Otago. It is a countrywide phenomenon with the use of cold soak – which extracts both colour and perfume – common. The use of whole bunches and stems in the fermentation vat is a winery-by-winery decision: some wineries destem all the fruit and there are no stems in sight whereas Nelson-based Michael Glover produces his Mammoth Pinot Noir with 100 per cent whole-bunch fermentation. There once used to be a fear that the technique would make the wines tannic and green but even some of the biggest wine producers in the country have experimented with it and use a small proportion today in their blends. It brings spice and drive, plus the berries aren't crushed pre-fermentation. This means you get a lovely lifted perfume from a little bit of carbonic maceration but it should not dominate the wine, overpowering the sense of place with a winemaking decision. There is a greater willingness to extend post-fermentation maceration time as the vines become older, producing wines that are less fruity and allowing the tannins to resolve.

The objective of New Zealand's finest Pinot Noir makers is to make the truest expression of their place and the season. Each winemaker chooses to guide the grapes to the glass in their own way but maturity has brought greater knowledge, skills and humility: winemakers are increasingly hands off, aiming to guide the wines rather than shape them. That is why it is increasingly difficult to say what New Zealand or Central Otago or Bendigo Pinot Noir is. Individual sites, individual producers and unique seasons make it wonderfully difficult to generalize.

The clone zone

There are forty-three clones of Pinot Noir according to the Catalogue of Grapevine Varieties and Clones and experts believe that as many as 1,000 genetic variants might exist. In the early 1960s, according to Riversun, Pinot Noir clones first began to be imported. It started with a clone from Switzerland called AM 10/5 (Ten Bar Five) and became the source of Central Otago, Martinborough and Canterbury's first vineyards. Somewhere along the line, however, 10/5 got a little confused, and what producers in Central Otago call 10/5 is very different to the 10/5 in Martinborough. What they do share in common is medium to high vigour, medium to large bunches and a tendency to produce inconsistent yields. It was widely used as a sparkling wine base and has fallen out of favour but there are growers who have a soft spot for it: Dry River's success has been based on 10/5 and clone 5. 'I think a lot of people walked away from 10/5,' says Dry River winemaker Wilco Lam. 'Early producers put it in their vineyards but people are not keen on it because it ripens late – but that's vineyard management. We are able to harvest it pretty early.' Similarly, Clive Dougall, a Marlborough-based consultant who was winemaker at Seresin Estate for twelve years says, 'I'm actually starting to like 10/5. You used to be a bit embarrassed to say that your Pinot was made from 10/5 when everyone was jumping on the Burgundy clone bandwagon. It retains acidity, has a little bit of green character, it is gently tannic.'

The gumboot clone

The story of the gumboot clone has become a rural legend. The truth is a little fuzzy but the story starts with a cutting allegedly snipped from the hallowed vineyards of Domaine de la Romanée-Conti in Burgundy. Smuggled into New Zealand in a gumboot, the plant was intercepted at Auckland airport but Malcolm Abel, a local winemaker then working as a customs officer, clocked how important this grapevine was and sent it to the government viticultural research station to wait it out in quarantine. Having served its time, the first cuttings were released and Abel planted them. The Abel vineyard no longer exists, but Clive Paton of Ata Rangi had taken some cuttings and planted them in his Martinborough vineyard. The Abel clone is the foundation of many of New Zealand's greatest Pinot Noirs and represents close to half of all Pinot plantings at Ata Rangi today. It flowers a little later than other clones which is useful in Martinborough, missing some of the tumultuous cold southerlies that blow through the region in spring, which can lead to poor set and low yields. It does tend to produce a large crop so yields need to be managed through crop thinning – and cutting off wings on the bunches – to ensure the grapes ripen fully and produce wines with intensity. Ben Cowley, viticulturist at Auntsfield in Marlborough, says 'Abel has a very different character from the Dijon clones. It has a sense of the earth, savouriness, spice. It's fruitful and sets big clusters so as a quality grower you have to spend a lot more effort to tame it, but the rewards are huge.'

In the 1970s the University of California, Davis (UCD) clones were imported into New Zealand, and the most popular became Clone 5. Riversun explains that the yields are 'typically on the medium to high end of the scale and they're regular – Clone 5 normally sets well. The bunches are medium to large, and often tight, which makes it a bit more susceptible to botrytis than either 10/5 or the Dijon clones. Fruit thinning is required to achieve top-tier wines.' In the late 1980s, the first Dijon clones were imported, eventually being released from quarantine in 1992. There were hiccups early on with some proving to be virused but the clones that are sexily entitled 667, 777, 114 and 115 have become an important part of the Pinot Noir landscape of New Zealand. Each clone has its own personality and each viticulturist has their personal preferences. The most common approach is to plant several – or many – clones in the vineyard. There are some single clone Pinot Noirs produced but each clone brings its own shade to draw a multicoloured artwork. For example, Felton Road has eleven clones planted, and at its Cornish Point vineyard there are twenty-five different clone and rootstock combinations.

In search of quantity and quality

After years of funding for Sauvignon Blanc research, it is time for New Zealand to better understand Pinot Noir. In 2017, the New Zealand government agreed to grant the wine industry more than $9 million to research different aspects of Pinot Noir production and marketing, but the theme which embraces the project is how to increase production of Pinot Noir while retaining quality. It is hoped that researchers will be able to find a way to produce 10 tonnes of grapes to the hectare (around 70 hl/ha) while maintaining the quality currently achieved with 6 tonnes to the hectare (42 hl/ha). Inevitably, industry insiders have been quick to dismiss this ambition: you can't make high quality Pinot Noir with high yields; why would we want to make cheap Pinot Noir? But Damian Martin, science group leader, viticulture and oenology for Plant and Food Research explains: 'Why is it that there is a glass ceiling on yield in relation to quality perception? There's no particular reason for it from a scientific perspective.' In a bid to unravel the relationship between yield and wine quality, chemists will be hard at work in the laboratory deconstructing the components of Pinot Noir from colour to aroma compounds and phenolics while sensory experts will be working alongside them to understand what quality actually means. 'The market for $50 Pinot Noir is pretty small so if New Zealand wants to be a force we have to make the economics of Pinot Noir a little more favourable,' adds Martin.

10 must-try New Zealand Pinot Noirs

- Ata Rangi Pinot Noir, Martinborough
- Bell Hill Vineyard Pinot Noir, North Canterbury
- Burn Cottage Vineyard Pinot Noir, Central Otago
- Craggy Range Aroha Pinot Noir, Martinborough
- Escarpment Vineyard Kupe Pinot Noir, Martinborough

- Felton Road Block 3 Pinot Noir, Central Otago
- Fromm Clayvin Vineyard Pinot Noir, Marlborough
- Kusuda Wines Pinot Noir, Martinborough
- Pyramid Valley Vineyards Earth Smoke Pinot Noir, North Canterbury
- Rippon Tinker's Field Pinot Noir, Central Otago

Syrah

The first New Zealand head of viticulture, Romeo Bragato, envisioned a wine-filled future for the regions of Central Otago and the Wairarapa. He was bang on with this prediction. He also suggested that Black Hermitage, better known as Syrah or Shiraz today, should be 'at least one-half of the vineyard'. Well, that certainly hasn't happened: Syrah remains a sideshow in the New Zealand wine carnival. In the past ten years, plantings have increased more than 50 per cent, and yet it represents just 1 per cent of the country's total vineyard area.

But Syrah has come a long way since 1984. At that time the only Syrah to be found in New Zealand was a lonely 'experimental' block at the now-shuttered government research station, Te Kauwhata. Enter Alan Limmer, a soil scientist, who not only took a risk on buying a piece of land that seemed undesirable in the early 1980s – now known as the Gimblett Gravels – but also decided to give an untried variety, Syrah, a chance. It proved to be a magical combination.

It is thought that the vines that ended up at Alan Limmer's wine operation Stonecroft, which produced New Zealand's first Syrah in 1989, were brought to New Zealand by Romeo Bragato, though some believe that New Zealand's Syrah plants could have arrived with James Busby, the man who introduced Shiraz to Australia. Research by Dr Gerald Atkinson, published on Stonecroft's website, suggests that to be codswallop: '… claims that the Te Kauwhata "Hermitage" Syrah vines somehow derive from plantings at James Busby's residence at the Bay of Islands are utterly without foundation. There had been private imports of the same vine material from Australia (New South Wales and/or Victoria) before … but all of these were wiped out as phylloxera spread through the north between 1890 and 1910.'

The few Syrah vines that resided at Te Kauwhata were left unloved for most of the next eighty years. In the 1960s, the national research station had worked on eliminating virus in some of the old vine stock, creating virus-free Syrah but still no one wanted to plant it beyond the station's grounds. 'However,' explains Atkinson, 'in the middle 1980s Alan Limmer became interested in experimentally growing Syrah and happened to be working at Te Kauwhata at the same time. A small row of some of the several and dispersed plantings of the DSIR heat-treated "Hermitage" Syrah at Te Kauwhata had been listed for pulling out (doubtless to make way for something much more popular), and Alan decided to save material from each vine.'

That material would be the origin of many of New Zealand's now-iconic Syrah wines and the MS clone (Mass Selection) is the industry standard. You'll also find the loose-hanging Chave clone commonly used, which was imported from the northern Rhône, as well as a handful of other clones that have unmemorable numbers for names like 174, 470 and 524. Without Alan Limmer and his clones from Te Kauwhata, the joy of New Zealand Syrah might not have been discovered.

Memories of Côte-Rôtie

Born in the northern Rhône village of Condrieu, now famed for its production of Viognier, Brother Elie-Regis saw traces of his homeland when he planted vines on a new mission site in New Zealand in 1839.

The newly arrived Brother was part of a second wave of Marists to travel to New Zealand with the intention of converting Māori to the Catholic faith. But the missionaries weren't given a warm welcome by fellow Christians. Michael King's *Penguin History of New Zealand* describes how one Church of England missionary told his congregation that Bishop Pompallier (spearheading the Catholic effort) and his priests represented 'the Great Whore of Babylon', and sent them across the harbour to sack the first Catholic station. The new arrivals were protected by local Māori and the Marists were quickly able to prove that not all Catholics were 'given to drink and fornication' – unlike the handful of Irish Catholics living in the area at the time.

Within five years of arriving in New Zealand, there were a reported twelve mission stations around the country. Elie-Regis had planted vineyards at several sites but it was in Whangaroa, more than 320 kilometres north of Auckland, that he found a spot that reminded him of his homeland. He described a steep slope overlooking the waters of the harbour in a letter of 1841: 'I am busy just now preparing to plant vines for this year on the slope near the sea on the Aucoura [Okura] side. You know the place. It gets a lot of sun but it is very difficult to cultivate since it slopes so much. We will have to cut down the palms and level the ground to get a workable area. Further, we need a breakwater or a wall two feet by two and a half feet along the edge of the sea so I can let the soil slide down without any worry. I will then have the prettiest vineyard in New Zealand, God willing. It will be a Côte-Rôtie wine because of the position and the quality of the soil.'

Côte-Rôtie is renowned for its production of red wines made from the Syrah grape. The vertiginous terraces above Ampuis produce the Rhône's most collectible wines including Guigal's 'LaLas' – three bottlings from the vineyards of La Mouline, La Landonne and La Turque. Its steep slopes can rise at gradients of up to 60 per cent and the Okura site, Elie-Regis thought, was not dissimilar. Not long after planting vines that reminded him of his native Rhône Valley, he was transferred to Wanganui and never experienced the fruits of his labour. Was it Syrah? Some have speculated it would have produced the first Syrah in New Zealand but there are others who want to spoil a good story.

The style police

The New Zealand style of Syrah is distinctive and characterful. With its deep cherry purple-pink hue that stains your glass, it exudes a perfume of blackberries, violets, cracked black pepper, sometimes a hint of smoky bacon, and it takes kindly to oak. In terms of structure, it offers a mid-weight elegant expression of Syrah with bright acidity providing freshness. These wines are far from warm-climate Shiraz blockbusters: they are not thick in texture, nor high in alcohol or rich in chunky oak.

For this very reason, wine critics have predicted that Syrah will be New Zealand's next big thing, certain to overhaul the more capricious Pinot Noir grape, but sporadic flurries of media attention extolling the greatness of Syrah have failed to have any influence on sales. When it comes to New Zealand red wine, everyone wants Pinot Noir. Juicy, fresh with low tannins, New Zealand Pinot Noir is the by-the-glass go-to for most drinkers on the domestic scene. Men's men, who have enjoyed drinking old-school Barossa Shiraz for the past twenty years, don't give New Zealand Syrah a second glance. Local retailers also have to take some of the responsibility for allowing Syrah to languish. In a respectable Auckland supermarket, Stone's Green Ginger Wine occupies a treasured slot in the designated Kiwi Syrah section. The lonely Syrahs have been relegated to an unloved corner next to the fire exit while Shiraz, predominantly from South Australia, occupies a prominent section and has more than double the shelf space. There's a price issue, of course. There is a host of South Australian Shiraz-based wines that are significantly cheaper than the New Zealand Syrahs on offer. But it might also be semantics. In the UK, Villa Maria has adopted the moniker Shiraz rather than Syrah for its entry level Private Bin range in the hope that it will boost sales.

New Zealand Syrah: the best red wine in the world

Rod McDonald had made the journey from Hawke's Bay to London to collect a slew of certificates at the annual International Wine Challenge awards dinner in 2017. His Quarter Acre Syrah 2015 had been named the best Hawke's Bay Syrah, the best New Zealand Syrah, the best New Zealand red and the best Syrah in show. He didn't know he was about to take the top prize: the best red wine in show. Earlier in the day he'd been out 'for a boozy – no, sorry, work – lunch in London'. It was one of those rare London days when the sun shines and the temperatures on the Underground are stifling. It was so hot and sweaty, McDonald had to stop between sales calls to buy a fresh shirt. When he finally arrived at the awards, he was 'handed a shopping bag' containing his certificates. When the Champion Red Trophy was announced, the words that followed 'And the winner is …' were the Quarter Acre Syrah. McDonald's heart raced. 'I had just bought an Apple watch that showed my heart rate. I was doing 167 beats per minute – that's close to capacity if you are a 48-year-old man!' The party continued long into the night and needless to say, the wine sold out in record time.

In short, Syrah drinkers are a rare breed, or perhaps the Australians have sewn up the market. Gordon Russell, senior winemaker at Esk Valley, says 'We do have something different with Syrah and it can find a niche in the global wine market. Maybe we will get there with Syrah, but the Americans don't like it – they want Cabernet [Sauvignon]. In Australia they are always going to drink their Shiraz, so that just leaves us with New Zealand and the UK.'

It's not a problem that's confined to New Zealand. On the other side of the Pacific, the long-haired, bespectacled Randall Grahm, a founding member of Californian wine group The Rhône Rangers, recalled an old joke with some sadness about the state of Syrah's popularity: 'What's the difference between a case of Syrah and a case of the clap? Answer: Eventually the clap will go away.'

The science block

Cracked black pepper is one of the appetizing scents of a cooler climate Syrah but it isn't universally appreciated. Fresh off the boat, I attended my first-ever trade tasting in Auckland in early 2010. Peter Cowley, the long-serving winemaker at Te Mata Estate in Hawke's Bay, which makes one of the most coveted Syrahs in the country, Bullnose, admitted: 'We used to call it fly spray in the winery but with vine age it's less overtly peppery. We are probably at the lower end of where you can ripen Syrah. We don't like too much pepper.'

The source of the pepper aroma is rotundone and one drop of the stuff is enough to make an Olympic-size swimming pool smell peppery. That is, if you can smell rotundone: around one in five can't detect this naturally occurring compound, known as a sesquiterpene. For those who can, rotundone is a huge part of the New Zealand Syrah story and it is a story that has only just started to be explored. Dr Gerard Logan, also known as @NZSyrah on social media platform Twitter, is an expert on rotundone in New Zealand Syrah, after spending six years researching the compound for his PhD thesis at the University of Auckland. He had been set on a career in aviation, making his first solo flight at sixteen but had taken on a job at a local vineyard near his home in Marlborough to fund the flying. Wine won the day – just as well for Kiwi Syrah. When he started his research in 2009 there wasn't much reading to swot up on rotundone in wine. Instead the academic literature centred on nutgrass (*Cyperus rotundas*) a prolific weed that is used in traditional Chinese medicine and contains rotundone in its oil.

The research that has since been undertaken in Hawke's Bay has found that of all the major Syrah-producing countries, rotundone concentration is highest in Syrah wines from New Zealand, followed by France, the US and Australia. This might be due to the cooler climes of New Zealand; it also seems that rotundone levels are higher in cooler vintages, such as 2012. There's no black pepper aroma to speak of until veraison (the period when the berries change colour) but close to a month after veraison, according to Logan, the concentration of rotundone soars over a two-week period and remains steady until harvest. His results also found a relationship between rotundone and clone selection. The clone Dijon 470 produces the highest level 'and was nearly double the concentration of other clones' like Chave, which had previously been considered the most peppery, while the MS clone, now found widely across New Zealand Syrah vineyards thanks to Alan Limmer, was the lowest rotundone producer. His extensive work also looked at fermentation techniques and it has been tentatively suggested that stainless steel open-top fermenters produce higher levels of rotundone versus oak cuves. Yet Syrah doesn't have a monopoly on rotundone. There has been extensive work in Italy on the rotundone-rich Vespolina grape, and that peppery character in Austrian Grüner Veltliner? That's not your imagination; it's rotundone. And in Hawke's Bay, the centre of Logan's research, Syrah wasn't the most peppery of all cultivars. Cabernet Franc out-rotundoned Syrah in many cases – offering 243 ng/kg in his tests, with Syrah offering a range between 13 and 300 ng/kg. Even the local Zinfandel, Merlot and Sangiovese offered rotundone levels at or above the sensory threshold of 16 ng/kg, suggesting Hawke's Bay has a close affinity with this sesquiterpene.

Where it's grown

Syrah's New Zealand home spreads beyond the shores of Hawke's Bay to Waiheke Island, and even the cooler climes of Marlborough.

While Syrah is a mid-ripening variety, in cooler regions it can be tricky to ripen. Kai Schubert of Schubert Wines and Wilco Lam of Dry River make Syrah in Martinborough (there's just 10 hectares of Syrah planted in Wairarapa). It is still hanging in the vineyard up to a month after the Pinot Noir has been harvested, which makes for lots of nail biting. 'It's the last [variety] that we pick. We are usually lucky with the weather and we will harvest in May but by that time the berries have become soft and it's not like Cabernet Sauvignon, which can resist everything thrown at it,' says Schubert. In cool or wet seasons, the variety might not make it to the winery. Despite hanging out in the vineyard for longer than most other varieties, the cool autumn temperatures mean that alcohol levels in the Syrah here don't stray far beyond 12% abv. The result is an elegant and lively blue- and red-fruited Syrah with peppery spice.

Across the Cook Strait in Marlborough there is a similarly small band of cool-climate Syrah fans, doing their best to make this variety ripen. It's hard work: Syrah is a naturally vigorous variety and large crops take a long time to ripen so crop thinning and taking shoulders off bunches is a must, and fruit exposure needs to be carefully managed. A warm site in a warm, dry vintage are also ingredients for making successful Syrah in Marlborough. The best examples such as Fromm Winery and Te Whare Ra offer a floral and spicy spectrum of aromas; concentration without heaviness.

Syrah has made Hawke's Bay its New Zealand home since Alan Limmer first planted the vines in 1984. The climate in Hawke's Bay is mild and maritime. It is a lot warmer than Martinborough, nearly 275 kilometres further south: Martinborough records 1,280 growing degree days annually while Hastings in Hawke's Bay basks in more than 1,600. Syrah can ripen fully here but it rarely becomes jammy, thanks to the relatively cool nights in the crucial ripening period, compared with Australia and even the northern Rhône. The style is medium bodied and elegant but with masses of substance. Aromatically, Hawke's Bay Syrah delivers juicy blackberry fruit with a lightly savoury and peppery edge that is given gentle support from French oak. The styles are subtly different across Hawke's Bay, whether it's the ripe, often polished, fruit of the warm Gimblett Gravels with a mass of stonelicking tannins, the more supple Syrahs of Bridge Pa, or the examples from the later-ripening coastal vineyards. John Hancock, the founding winemaker of Trinity Hill, one of the region's leading Syrah producers, compares the variety with Pinot Noir. 'It's very transparent so it shows where it is grown very well. That's why I believe it will be the grape that makes Hawke's Bay's name. Like Marlborough Sauvignon Blanc or Central Otago Pinot Noir, you can't reproduce Hawke's Bay Syrah.'

Heading further north to Waiheke Island, a forty-minute ferry ride from Auckland's central business district (CBD), Syrah shakes its fist at rival Bordeaux blends. In cooler years when Cabernet Sauvignon fails to ripen, Syrah still performs but it benefits from a sheltered spot to get to the ripening finish line. The warm island climate with a modest diurnal temperature range allows Syrah to ripen to become a medium-bodied, richly fruited and often savoury style without losing New Zealand's distinctive twist of pepper. And, if you are feeling adventurous, there are also some intriguing and sumptuous Syrahs to be discovered further north in Matakana and Northland.

10 must-try New Zealand Syrahs

- Bilancia La Collina Syrah, Hawke's Bay
- Dry River Lovat Vineyard Syrah, Martinborough
- Fromm, Fromm Vineyard Syrah, Marlborough
- Kusuda Wines Syrah, Martinborough
- Man O'War Dreadnought Syrah, Waiheke Island
- Rod McDonald Quarter Acre Syrah, Hawke's Bay
- Sacred Hill Deerstalkers Syrah, Hawke's Bay
- Te Mata Bullnose Syrah, Hawke's Bay
- Te Whare Ra SV5182 Syrah, Marlborough
- Trinity Hill Homage Syrah, Hawke's Bay

Bordeaux reds

Cabernet Sauvignon/Merlot blends from New Zealand don't have the cachet of Pinot Noir. Instead, they are tarnished with an outdated perception that they are pale, thin and acidic attempts at emulating Bordeaux. Admittedly many wines were once lacklustre, unripe imitations, particularly from those who attempted to grow it in Marlborough, but times have changed. Whether it's global warming, better clones, better vineyard management or better winemaking, or likely a combination of all the above, New Zealand red blends can be excellent.

And Kiwi claret's pedigree was acknowledged in 2017 at the annual Cape Mentelle event where twenty of the world's Cabernet Sauvignons go head-to-head in a blind tasting. Established in 1982, 2017 marked the debut appearance for a New Zealand Cabernet Sauvignon-based blend. It lined up against a seven-long flight of wines from Margaret River, Bordeaux and Napa Valley. The Kiwi wine – Destiny Bay's Magna Praemia 2013 – was named best of flight by the then managing editor of US-based *Wine Enthusiast* magazine, being confused with a top Californian Cabernet.

Mike Spratt, owner of Destiny Bay Vineyards, recalls getting the telephone call to participate after being recommended by Auckland-based Master of Wine, Bob Campbell. He sent his winemaking son, Sean, over to Western Australia to attend the tasting and recounts his experience. 'Sean went to the tasting and was sick to his stomach but after the reveal he was inundated with people coming up to him – one guy came up and admitted he had [wrongly] thought we would be lambs to the slaughter,' he says. 'How could one of the Cabernet blends come from New Zealand – the place that makes Sauvignon Blanc? The reason we can do it is because we are totally different to the rest of New Zealand. We are in a climate that is more suited to making Cabernet.'

The exclusive Waiheke Island winery sits in one of the rare parts of New Zealand that can ripen Cabernet Sauvignon. Approximately forty minutes by ferry from Auckland's CBD, Waiheke sits on the same latitude as Australia's Cabernet capital, Coonawarra. While Coonawarra boasts higher maximum temperatures than Waiheke, Waiheke's mean temperatures are higher due to the maritime influence. Nevertheless Cabernet Sauvignon is not always a success story. In dry and warm years Bordeaux blends are great on Waiheke, but Syrah performs much more consistently. In 2001 and 2003, for example, it was too cold to ripen Cabernet, and in 2017, it was too wet – Destiny Bay didn't pick a grape. Site selection is also crucial, particularly when it comes to Cabernet Sauvignon, requiring a sheltered spot away from the incoming winds.

However, Waiheke Island is far from being the country's most prolific producer of red blends – that honour goes to Hawke's Bay. The temperate maritime region on the east coast of the North Island accounts for more than 80 per cent of Cabernet/Merlot production in New Zealand. It has an average mean temperature of 19 to 20°C, just shy of Bordeaux's 20.3°C, and sits on the equivalent southern hemisphere latitude to Ibiza and Sardinia (39°). And when it comes to the crucial month of March, night-time temperatures are categorized as cool, allowing aromatic and colour development in its reds, and retention of acidity.

Nevertheless, there are some years when the late-ripening Cabernet Sauvignon doesn't quite make it to full maturation in Hawke's Bay, especially in those vineyards outside the stony, heat-retentive soils of the Gimblett Gravels. The German-owned winery Elephant Hill sits in Te Awanga, a coastal village, and having originally planted Bordeaux varieties, soon realized the temperatures just weren't high enough to ripen them. It was a rapid case of *auf wiedersehen* to the Cabernet Sauvignon, Merlot and Malbec vines.

In the warmer, inland sites on Hawke's Bay's Heretaunga Plains, ripening of Cabernet Sauvignon is not assured and, as a result, blending is key to producing a balanced wine. Merlot-based blends dominate here for both its earlier ripening and more fleshy structure. However, it is early days for Hawke's Bay red blends: the region's modern era began in the 1980s and, based on the experience of some of the region's leading viticulturists, there is still room for improvement.

Master of Wine Steve Smith has been changing his attitude toward Cabernet Sauvignon in recent years. Yes, it needs the warmest spots in Hawke's Bay but he believes that planting the right clonal material on the right rootstock could be instrumental in changing Cabernet's prospects here. 'It might not necessarily be the climate, it might be the clones and rootstock. I think Cabernet Sauvignon is as reliable [as Merlot] but with the older rootstocks and clones we were picking at the end of April; now we are picking in the first ten days of April, and the Merlot last week of March and/or first few days of April so there's not that much difference – and you are not getting the green capsicum and minty green flavours.' Could there be an even brighter future for Cabernet Sauvignon in New Zealand?

Meanwhile Merlot seems to do what it says on the tin: provide flesh to Cabernet's bones. The variety can sometimes be on the lean side when it is sourced off the boniest parts of the Gimblett Gravels. It's not altogether unsurprising: the Bordelais have had hundreds of years of winemaking experience which has led them to the conclusion that gravels and Merlot aren't the best match. In general, New Zealand Merlot is typically more sweetly fruited than in south-west France and offers a medium bodied, juicy style that is fresh and gently tannic. As with Cabernet Sauvignon, planting the right clone on the right rootstock in the right place is crucial to its future success in New Zealand (see Chapter 7 for more details).

Cabernet Franc

In the North Island, Cabernet Franc is planted mainly in Hawke's Bay as a bit part in a Cabernet Sauvignon/Merlot blends. It imbues a wine with floral and lifted aromas, providing the soprano voice to enliven the alto section that is Cabernet Sauvignon and Merlot. However, it doesn't have to be a part of the choir. It can be a soloist, and there are successful varietal examples worth seeking out, which offer aroma, density and structure such as Black Barn Vineyards.

Heading south and over the Cook Strait, Cabernet Franc is also finding a new home in the cooler climes of North Canterbury. Sitting in the Omihi sub-district of the Waipara Valley, Black Estate's Cabernet Franc was first produced in 2015 – all thirty-seven cases of it – from its Home Vineyard. The style has more in common with the Cabernet Francs of the Loire than Bordeaux with its pale appearance, scintillating aromas, delicate palate and refreshing finish. There's absolutely no reason why other South Island producers couldn't make a similarly good fist of this variety and, unlike Cabernet Sauvignon and Merlot, the whole wine world isn't making varietal Cabernet Franc.

Malbec

More commonly associated with the arid climes of Mendoza, Argentina, Malbec has been experiencing a slow but steady rise in popularity in the vineyards of New Zealand. It now accounts for – drum roll – 0.3 per cent of the country's vineyard with a fairly niche 120 hectares, but that represents a 100-hectare increase in twenty years. When it comes to colour, Argentinean Malbec is not in short supply and neither is New Zealand's interpretation, flushed with a bright purple blush.

10 (OK, 12) must-try New Zealand Bordeaux blends
- Church Road 'TOM', Hawke's Bay
- Craggy Range Sophia, Hawke's Bay
- Destiny Bay's trio of Bordeaux-inspired cuvées: Destinae, Mystae, Magna Praemia, Waiheke Island
- Esk Valley Estate The Terraces, Hawke's Bay
- Sacred Hill Helmsman, Hawke's Bay
- Stonyridge Vineyard Larose, Waiheke Island
- Te Mata Estate Awatea, Hawke's Bay

- Te Mata Estate Coleraine, Hawke's Bay
- Trinity Hill The Gimblett, Hawke's Bay
- Villa Maria Ngakirikiri, Hawke's Bay

SPARKLING WINE

New Zealand sparkling wine has great potential: Cloudy Bay's vintage Pelorus and No. 1 Family Estate show that when it is good it is very, very good. But if New Zealand is such a perfect place to make sparkling wine, why haven't more major Champagne wine houses arrived? Admittedly, Louis Vuitton Moët Hennessy (LVMH) are behind sparkling wine Pelorus, but beyond that where are the New World arms of Taittinger, Roederer, Mumm? They're in California (and England). It's not that New Zealand doesn't have a climate and soils conducive to making sparkling wines but it is at the end of the earth with a population of less than 5 million, making the domestic market nowhere near as attractive as the United States, home to 325 million people.

The climate in New Zealand's South Island is well suited to making sparkling wines: a comparison of climate data between New Zealand and other viticultural regions by Jon D. Anderson et al. (see Appendix) suggests that Marlborough's Wairau Valley sits between Champagne and Burgundy in terms of climate. Marlborough has similar annual rainfall to Champagne but it is a little warmer and a lot sunnier in New Zealand: the average annual sunshine is just 1,630 hours in Épernay, according to the Comité Champagne, while Marlborough basks in more than 2,400 hours. 'Marlborough is a perfect district to make a fantastic sparkling wine. The ripening conditions of late summer are the conditions that Champagne craves, because they only happen in Champagne once in a blue moon,' says Daniel Le Brun of No. 1 Family Estate, who left his native Champagne for New Zealand in 1975, and has been producing sparkling wine in Marlborough since the early 1980s. While the fruit hangs close to the ground in Champagne to capture reflected light and heat to achieve ripeness, the warmer, sunnier conditions in Marlborough allow higher fruiting zones, saving the backs of many vineyard workers. 'Champagne has to add sugar but we don't have to here because the fruit is sufficiently ripe. But because the fruit is riper, the acidity level is a bit lower,' he adds.

The runaway success of Sauvignon Blanc, a wine that is typically drunk between six and twenty-four months after the grapes are picked, has thwarted New Zealand's sparkling wine potential. There has thus far been little reason for producers to focus their attention on sparkling wine, which is capital intensive and, in the most ambitious instances, the wines must spend years on lees in the cellar before release. As a result, bubbles play a tiny role in the New Zealand wine scene, accounting for just 0.5 per cent of exports in 2017.

The history of sparkling wine in New Zealand is relatively short. While Dom Pérignon supposedly claimed he was 'drinking the stars' to the members of his monastery in the late 1600s, it would take another three centuries before fellow monks would produce sparkling wines in New Zealand: Mission Vineyards released the country's first-ever bottle-fermented fizz, named Fontanella, in the 1960s. At about the same time, Croatian immigrant Mate Selak was experimenting with sparkling wine production in west Auckland. In 1971, he finally released a bottle-fermented sparkling wine after many failed attempts. In the early 1980s, sparkling wine gained some momentum with the launch of Lindauer, a 'traditional method' sparkling wine sourced from grapes in Gisborne and Hawke's Bay. Over time, many of the wines were made sparkling using the cheaper and less qualitative carbonation method but the Special Reserve tier still undergoes second fermentation in bottle. Despite a change of ownership (Australian brewer Lion purchased the brand from Pernod Ricard in 2011), Lindauer continues to make affordable sparkling wine although the wines with fruit essences have more in common with an alcopop than a real wine.

In 1988, Champagne house Deutz arrived in New Zealand as part of a decade-long partnership with Montana, now the Pernod Ricard-owned brand known as Brancott Estate. The Champenois came with lofty ambitions, investing heavily, bringing their equipment and expertise, and early wines showed great promise. The Cuvée Brut accounts for most of its production and is an affordable 'traditional method' example that Kiwis view as a more sophisticated step up from the likes of Lindauer, while its finest offering, Prestige Cuvée, is a ripe yet fresh Chardonnay–Pinot Noir blend aged on lees for three years, bringing autolysis-derived brioche characters. The 1980s also brought another new sparkling wine entrant: Cloudy Bay made its first vintage of Pelorus, a blend of Pinot Noir, Chardonnay and Pinot Blanc, which was finally released in 1992. Purchased by Champagne house Veuve Clicquot in 1990 and now part of LVMH's wine arm, it is expected that its sparkling wines should be reaching for the stars. The non-vintage Pelorus is a lively, easy-drinking style with a light autolytic character whereas the vintage Pelorus is eminently more serious and noteworthy: a blend of around 60 per cent Pinot Noir and 40 per cent Chardonnay, it spends between four and seven years on lees, depending on the vintage.

There are efforts to increase the importance of sparkling wine in New Zealand. Established in 2013, Methode Marlborough brings together a group of producers with the aim of promoting 'traditional method' sparkling wine from the region. Members must make their wines from the three Champagne varieties – Chardonnay, Pinot Noir and Pinot Meunier – before spending a minimum of eighteen months on lees. However, there are no tasting panel criteria nor a minimum quality standard, so the quality of wine within the group differs widely. However, it is well intentioned and a good starting point at promoting a little known wine style in New Zealand. No. 1 Family Estate is a founding member along with Nautilus Estate. Its Cuvée Marlborough Brut has been made since 1991. It is a Pinot Noir-dominant blend that spends a minimum three years on lees, giving autolytic, savoury characters to counteract Marlborough's natural fruit expression. While the wine is fermented in stainless steel, reserve wines are aged in oak barrels and account for up to 15 per cent of the blend, making this a non-vintage expression.

Beyond Marlborough, there are some notable sparkling wines produced. In Central Otago, for example, Akarua, Amisfield and Quartz Reef are producing fresh and elegant sparkling wines made by the 'traditional method'. The region's cool and dry continental climate is well suited to the production of sparkling wines with crisp acidity. There is also no shortage of Pinot Noir for base wine. Akarua hired consultant Dr Tony Jordan, a sparkling wine specialist who spent more than twenty years with Moët Hennessy, to help them with their first sparkling wines which were released in 2011. The non-vintage Brut is a blend of one-third Pinot Noir and two-thirds Chardonnay while the vintage cuvée relies more heavily on the Pinot Noir component. Extra complexity and mouthfeel is brought through fermenting some of the base wines in old oak barrels and incorporating some older, 'reserve' wines to the blend. Meanwhile Rudi Bauer's Demeter-certified biodynamic estate, Quartz Reef, makes one of the go-to sparkling wines of Central Otago and New Zealand. It produces a non-vintage white and rosé but fine wine lovers will find the vintage cuvée of most interest. A high proportion of Chardonnay gives a fine line to the wine while forty-six months on lees brings complexity and depth. Meanwhile, Amisfield's vintage Brut is almost exclusively Pinot Noir, bringing structure and red fruit to the glass.

Daniel Le Brun

Born only a few kilometres south of Épernay, Daniel Le Brun hails from a Champagne family which can trace its involvement in the local wine industry back to 1750. Continuing the family line of sparkling winemakers, Le Brun graduated from winemaking school in nearby Avize on Champagne's Côte des Blancs, before going in search of a new, more liberal region to make wine, free of the constraints imposed by French appellation laws. He moved to New Zealand in 1975, after visiting the country earlier that year and, in 1980, bought land in Marlborough. Today, Mahi Wines sits on what was the home of Le Brun's original winery, complete with Le Brun's underground cellar hewn from the Renwick hillside, an attempt to replicate the subterranean caves found in his native Champagne. He planted the three Champagne varieties – Chardonnay, Pinot Noir and Pinot Meunier – and released his first wine in 1985, a *blanc de blancs*. Success quickly followed, winning awards and critical acclaim, but the world of business meant that, in 1996, Le Brun was bought out by the company's major shareholder. He lost his winery and his name. Today, Australian brewers Lion own the Daniel Le Brun brand, whose star has lost some of its sparkle since his departure.

But Marlborough was now his home: he had two children, Virginie and Remy, with his wife Adele, and bubbles were in his blood. As soon as his anti-competition clause expired he launched a new brand: No. 1 Family Estate. It remains the only New Zealand winery dedicated exclusively to sparkling wine. The wines are whole-bunch pressed; only the first press – the highest quality, most delicate juice – is used. The juice is inoculated with a yeast he imported from Champagne and the first fermentation takes place at a not-too-cool 17°C. The second fermentation takes place in bottle and the wines are riddled using a gyropallet rather than by hand, a technology that Le Brun first introduced to New Zealand in the 1980s. The wines include several non-vintage wines: the Cuvée No. 1 is an elegant, crisp *blanc de blancs*; the Reserve is also 100 per cent Chardonnay but it is left on lees for more than five years, bringing a rich and complex autolytic character. The vintage wines include Cuvée Virginie, a Chardonnay-dominant blend spending four years on lees while Cuvée Remy is a more structured, red-fruit filled Pinot Noir-based sparkling wine.

Daniel Le Brun has consistently shown that Marlborough can produce world-class sparkling wine when made with expertise and care. His wines suggest that, as a nation, New Zealand has yet to truly fulfil its sparkling wine potential.

Sparkling Sauvignon Blanc

I first moved to New Zealand in December 2009 and sparkling Sauvignon Blanc was the Christmas drink of choice. At $8.99 on offer, everyone seemed to love the price and fruity Sauvignon with bubbles. I hated it: carbonated and with a touch of residual sugar, it tasted unloved. But there were rosé versions and oak-influenced examples produced; even Pinot Gris had the carbonation treatment. My tasting notes for an article on sparkling Sauvignon Blanc included comments like 'a nothing wine', 'sweet and sour' and 'almost gagged'.

The rise of this style followed the 2008 vintage (285,000 tonnes), the then-biggest harvest on record. The larger-than-expected crop – up 39 per cent on the previous vintage and an increase of 100 per cent since 2005 – led to a rise in bulk wine exports and a decline in average prices; grape grower contracts were cancelled, some vineyards were pulled out and there were several receiverships. While some call it a crash, others label it a consolidation and adjustment after a period of rapid and continuous growth. In this environment, Sauvignon Blanc needed a home and making it sparkling was a natural brand extension of New Zealand's most popular variety at a time when another fruit-driven sparkling wine, Prosecco, was enjoying burgeoning sales. The global financial crisis marked a new era for sparkling wine: cheaper alternatives – Prosecco, Cava and New World sparkling wines – became the celebratory drink of choice for those who could no longer afford to drink Champagne or were self-conscious about doing so. While there was a brief flurry of excitement about sparkling Sauvignon Blanc, Prosecco has been a juggernaut whose momentum could not be slowed: it had both an appealing taste and price point, attaining sales of 25.2 million cases in 2016 (IWSR). Meanwhile sparkling Sauvignon Blanc exports peaked at a paltry 360,000-litre cases in 2013 (although it may have been higher between 2009 and 2012, there is no data available), and has since gone flat, accounting for less than 60,000 litres in 2017. George Fistonich, founder of Villa Maria, which continues to make a lightly sparkling Sauvignon Blanc, admits he is unsure about the category's future but says: 'It could be successful. A year ago we took it to America and let people help themselves to our wines. The wine they kept going back to was the sparkling Sauvignon.'

Since 2008, the wine industry has woken up to the new realities of a new New Zealand wine scene. Its producers have realized that if they are going to make wine, they need to be confident that it has a home, whether in bottle or in the increasingly important bulk wine sector. They heeded the advice of Steve Green, the chair of New Zealand Winegrowers in 2013: 'Optimism should never be unbridled but rather should be market led and fact based.' Fluctuating crop sizes (the 2012 vintage yielded just 269,000 tonnes while the 2014 harvest cropped at 445,000 tonnes) in this cool, maritime climate have created different supply challenges but the figures suggest there is no pressing need to carbonate New Zealand Sauvignon Blanc.

PART 2
NORTH ISLAND

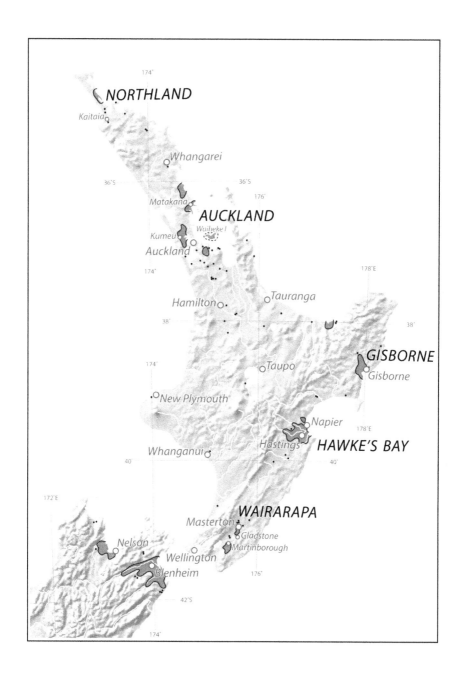

4

NORTHLAND

Grapevines first made their home in the soils of Northland in the early nineteenth century but, 200 years later, it is a region that is largely overlooked when it comes to wine. It is perhaps better to call Northland a region that makes wine rather than a wine region but there are a handful of ambitious, quality-oriented producers defying the humid climate and making pleasurable Chardonnay and savoury Syrah.

The story of how vines came to be here starts along a gravel road, north-west of the town of Kerikeri. On the day I visited, a single black trainer sat on top of the gate post marking the start of the half-hour walk to Marsden Cross, the site of the first mission settlement and Christian service in New Zealand. How anyone managed to lose a single trainer, I'm not sure but it is a very long walk back to the nearest town, especially with one shoe. The information boards along the path trace Samuel Marsden's journey to the Bay of Islands and while wine isn't mentioned, he is the man behind the first recorded plantings. Long before James Busby arrived with his cuttings at nearby Waitangi, Marsden recorded in his journal of 25 September 1819 that he could see the country's winemaking potential: 'New Zealand promises to be very favourable to the vine, as far as I can judge at present of the nature of the soils and climate. Should it succeed it will prove of vast importance in this part of the globe.'

Northland is the birthplace of wine in New Zealand and yet the rest of the country seems to have forgotten this: tell a winemaker in Marlborough that you've just been wine tasting in Northland and they'll likely scoff. 'People have written the area off because of the rainfall here,' says Rod MacIvor, the co-founder of Marsden Estate, which processes many of the region's grapes. 'But even when they started in Central Otago, they said they couldn't ripen grapes. The great thing about New Zealand is that we have no rules and we will give it a go.'

When MacIvor moved to Kerikeri in 1992 he had the intention of growing kiwi fruit, not grapes. The region had been producing fortified wine since thirsty Croatian immigrants started digging gum in the region but table wines were barely on the table. There were just two wineries – Okahu Estate and Longview Estate. Today, there are still only 67 hectares planted and twenty commercial producers but Northland has gained notoriety for being the home of the country's most expensive wine. Longview is now part-owned by Chinese investors and, since taking charge, the winery's sweet wine White Diamond – a wine that has been described by a local newspaper as 'the Northland go-to wine for a girls' night out' has spiralled in price from $30 a bottle to a retail price listed on the website of $1,206. Made from the hybrid Niagara, it has found new, wealthier, customers in the People's Republic.

GEOGRAPHY AND CLIMATE

Leaving Auckland behind, passing Matakana and heading further north, the landscape becomes ever-more rural: road signs provide a hotline number to report wandering cows. Inland is remote pine and ancient native forest so dense and seemingly untouched that you would not feel surprised if a brontosaurus casually sauntered out of the trees on to the road chewing on a native fern. In these rural areas, ramshackle weatherboard houses pepper the roadside, abandoned vehicles litter driveways. This is a poor region: more than one in five children live in poverty. But it is a poor region peppered with pockets of extreme wealth. The Bay of Islands, four hours' drive north of Auckland, is the land of the 'swallows' – the summer-following rich-listers who build their sea-view mansions on rolling hilltops and take their boats out to explore the Bay's 144 islands.

At a latitude of 35° S, this part of New Zealand is called the winterless north. Pruning can be done in T-shirts and bud burst arrives early, making for a long season. However, for Kiwi viticulturists used to fighting spring frosts further south, the temperate maritime climate of Northland means nights of wonderfully uninterrupted sleep. With an early start to the season, Pinot Gris can ripen as early as the end of January while most regions don't get started on their grapes for still wine until March or even April. The grapes are given plenty of warmth over the summer but the proximity of the sea means that maximum temperatures don't soar. Overnight temperatures can be as high as 15°C in summer, meaning that there isn't a wide diurnal temperature range. The lack of extremes and the steady warmth means that Northland has the country's highest number of growing degree days at 1,606 (median) compared with 1,034 in Marlborough's Wairau Valley and 1,334 in Hawke's Bay. However, that still only places it in Region II on Winkler's climate classification (I being the coolest, V the hottest) so it's far from being a hot climate.

The climate in Northland is not without its challenges. Its annual rainfall, at 1,680 mm, is double that of Marlborough, and humidity is high in this sub-tropical climate. Fungal-disease pressure is inevitable and growers use various methods to reduce it. Opening up the canopy allows better airflow, increases sunlight and enables sprays to penetrate. Vineyards with a sea view also benefit from the shore breezes.

The geography of Northland's wine producers means it is not easy to generalize its soil types. The southernmost point on the region's official wine trail is the town of Mangawhai. The trail runs up the east coast of New Zealand as far as Karikari Peninsula – a distance of 243 kilometres. Peter Jones, director of The Landing and chair of the Northland Winegrowers Association, says: 'When I was putting the GI (Geographical Indication) application together, I found out Northland has 220 different soil types whereas most GIs have 20!' Of course, they are not all suitable for growing grapes, and many of the vineyards in the region are a theme on clay, clay loam, sandy loam and silt loam. There are also some volcanic-inspired soils that have produced some promising Syrah. Many of the soils in this region hold moisture and, combined with the annual rainfall totals, this means that most vineyards in Northland are dry farmed.

THE EVOLUTION OF NORTHLAND

The town of Russell in the Bay of Islands was once described as the hell-hole of the South Pacific by the English naturalist and brains behind the evolutionary theory of natural selection, Charles Darwin. The former whaling port was resplendent with grogshops and brothels when he passed through aboard *HMS Beagle*. How times change: Russell is now a highly desirable place to live with Aucklanders and 'swallows' making this former hell-hole their little piece of paradise.

While Russell has evolved, so too have the region's wines in recent years. The wine list is strongly local at the Duke of Marlborough, the town's most famous pub – and the holder of New Zealand's first liquor licence (1827). But this is only a recent phenomenon, explains Anton Haagh, the pub's co-owner. 'In 2010, we started trying to buy wine off locals. I was really keen to support local wineries but the quality had to be there. It wasn't at that time and they lacked consistency. Since then, things have changed immeasurably – there's seven or eight labels I am now happy to list.'

Jones explains that one of the reasons for this improvement has been the input of Mark Nobilo, whose father Nikola founded Nobilo Wines in west Auckland in 1943. Mark was one of three Nobilo brothers and looked after the vineyard until the brand was sold to multinational drinks company Constellation in 2000. He has a bach (pronounced 'batch' and meaning a holiday home) in the area and has been helping local growers by running workshops and making vineyard visits, notes Jones. 'He has been instrumental in raising the quality of the viticulture – there's more awareness of preventative measures instead of trying to fix problems [when it's too late].'

The majority of vineyards in Northland are small-scale family-run operations; some are hobby vineyards. As a result, few have the money to build their own winemaking facility or the skills to make the wine. Many of the wines in the region have been made at Marsden Estate. In 2017, the facility made eighty-five different wines. However, the arrival of wealthy investors including Richard Margides, a Singapore-based Englishman, at Paroa Bay and California-based Kiwi Peter Cooper of The Landing will increase the number of independent winery facilities and raise the professionalism of the region further still.

WINE STYLES

Northland is best known for its Chardonnay and Syrah. The warm climate is conducive to making full-bodied, fully flavoured Chardonnay with fruit flavours in the riper spectrum such as peach and melon. The finest examples are hand picked, whole-bunch pressed and barrel fermented. Marsden Estate's Black Rocks Chardonnay is a benchmark style, having won many national awards. Unsurprisingly, many local producers would like to achieve similar acclaim and seek to emulate the Black Rocks style, which isn't too difficult as Marsden Estate is the main winemaking facility in the area. The downside of this is that there appears to be a lack of stylistic diversity when it comes to Chardonnay.

Syrah is the second most popular variety in the region, making a ripe yet elegant style with the best examples being seductively silken. If the fruit isn't picked at the right time, it can quickly lose its aromatic buoyancy and become flabby, so harvest dates are crucial. Ben Byrne, a promising young winemaker in Kerikeri, also uses a proportion of whole bunches in his fermentations to bring aromatic lift and spice.

Chambourcin is also planted in Northland. It is prized here for its resistance to humidity and fungal disease, and its naturally high acidity: in Northland, acidity levels can be low and acidification pre-fermentation is commonly practised. Less tolerant to humidity but more widely planted is Pinot Gris – its popularity is more a reflection of market demand than its suitability to Northland's climate. Its thin skins and tightly packed bunches are prone to swelling after rains (post-veraison) leading to skin splitting and botrytis. With more than 100 mm of monthly rainfall on average in January and February (compared with 40 to 50 mm in Marlborough), growing healthy Pinot Gris successfully in Northland isn't a simple undertaking. For those who do manage to get Pinot Gris safely to the winery (it is usually the first variety to be picked), the resulting wines are voluptuous, offering ripe red apple and pear fruit, a hint of spice and soft acidity. Sugar levels – and thus potential alcohol – can rise rapidly with Pinot Gris and picking decisions need to be made to ensure the wines don't become too alcoholic and unbalanced. Choosing when to pick can be tricky for many of the hobbyists who own vineyards and harvest their grapes when their jobs and lives permit.

Northland is never going to be a low-cost, high-volume producer. There is limited land that is suitable for viticulture and this lies along the coast, which is highly desirable and consequently expensive. Its remoteness and the scattered nature of its vineyards mean that the costs of sourcing goods and transportation are high. What's more, there is a lack of skilled labour and grapes must compete with kiwi fruit, which have a similar harvest period. Costs are high and nature always has the upper hand. Nevertheless, the Bay of Islands is a draw for wealthy visitors and many wineries have a cellar door, winery restaurant or luxury accommodation on site – or all three. The wine producers are defying the odds in this 'hell-hole of the South Pacific'. If I do go to hell, I hope it will be here.

PRODUCER PROFILES

Byrne Wines
Kerikeri
byrnewine.com

Northland boy Ben Byrne travelled to Australia and California to make wine before the lure of home was too hard to resist. Moving back to work at Marsden Estate, Byrne and his Czech wife Tereza set up their own label in 2013 leasing a windy block on volcanic soil at 200 metres elevation. This late-ripening vineyard is the source of his Waingaro Syrah and Viognier. Production is tiny and Byrne hasn't given up his day job quite yet but anyone who doubts that Northland can make fine wine should taste his Syrah.

Try this: Byrne Waingaro Syrah
A tantalizing combination of spicy black pepper, ripe black fruit and a floral note make this good enough to eat. Byrne uses a proportion of whole bunches in the fermentation providing lifted aromatics and giving this wine a real sense of purpose. Low yields are evident in the high level of fruit concentration and the oak is well handled. It's just a shame there isn't more of it to go around.

Visit
There is no cellar door but you can find Byrne pouring – and selling – his wines at Kerikeri market every Saturday morning.

Marsden Estate

Kerikeri

marsdenestate.co.nz

Rod MacIvor and his wife Cindy ended up growing grapes almost by accident. They moved to Northland in 1992 to grow kiwis, not grapes. However, a friend ended up with 1,500 surplus vines after the intended owner's marriage collapsed. MacIvor decided to plant them in 1993. Since then 4 hectares of vineyard have been planted while Marsden Estate has become the winemaking hub for Northland, producing wine for approximately twenty different growers. Its own vineyard is planted with Pinot Gris, Chardonnay, Muscat, Merlot, Pinotage, Chambourcin, Syrah and Tempranillo but Chardonnay is the winery's calling card.

Try this: Black Rocks Chardonnay

A mouthfilling, barrel-fermented Chardonnay that offers an attractive creamy texture. Expect ripe white stone fruit, peach kernel and a lees-derived savoury character.

Visit

Marsden Estate is just a few minutes outside of Kerikeri. Its charming and unpretentious restaurant and cellar door overlook the vines and a lake, complete with resident ducks for children to feed. Open seven days a week. Check website for opening times.

Okahu Estate

Kaitaia

okahuestate.co.nz

One of the founding fathers of the modern day Northland wine community, Monty Knight established Okahu Estate in 1984. It remained the most northerly vineyard in New Zealand until that claim to fame was snatched by Karikari Estate in the late 1990s. Okahu enjoyed its first big victory with its bold Kaz Shiraz, which upset the apple cart by winning a gold medal and a trophy at the Royal Easter Show in 1996. Northland could make wine? The Estate's warm, maritime climate and sandy black loam soils over clay produce rich, spicy reds, and in 2012 Okahu started growing Viognier.

Try this: Okahu Estate Syrah

A ripe warm-climate Syrah that is light, peppery and full of sweet red fruit. Its Chambourcin produced from relatively old vines is bold, aromatic and full of vigour.

Visit
The cellar door is open seven days a week during summer but closed in winter. Check the website for opening times.

Paroa Bay
Russell
paroabay.com
Paroa Bay is one of three Australasian wineries owned by Singapore-based Englishman Richard Margides (Yarra Yering and Urlar are the other two estates). A former golf course, the steep clay-based slopes of Paroa Bay's 5-hectare vineyard are now home to nine varieties from the cool climate Sauvignon Blanc to the late ripening Petit Verdot. The Bordeaux varieties are blended to make CMC, a wonderfully fragrant Cabernet Franc-dominant blend while the creamy, barrel-fermented Chardonnay offers opulence in spades. A small, modern winery and bottling line was installed on site in 2017.

Try this: Paroa Bay Syrah
An elegant, spicy and savoury Syrah with a generous lick of oak-derived vanilla. This Syrah offers an abundance of fine tannins.

Visit
Paroa Bay opened a cellar door and Italian-inspired restaurant – Sage – in 2017 overlooking the sparkling blue waters of the Bay of Islands. Sit on the terrace or gaze out of the floor-to-ceiling glass windows toward Roberton Island with its two natural lagoons; it is open for lunch and dinner Wednesday to Sunday. Paroa Bay also offers several accommodation options including Tarapunga, a luxury villa complete with a 17-metre infinity pool, gym, tennis courts, pétanque area, putting green, home theatre and a private deep-water boat to whisk you off to the best fishing spots and dolphin-watching areas.

The Landing

Pureurua peninsula
thelandingnz.com

Peter Cooper is a Northland boy done good. The lawyer turned property developer is now based in Newport Beach, California but in 2000 the call of home saw Cooper buy an enormous 400-hectare coastal property within spitting distance of Samuel Marsden's first settlement. In 2007, Chardonnay and Syrah were planted on some of its clay-based slopes and the first wines made in 2010. Success soon followed: the 2011, 2012 and 2014 Chardonnays won gold medals at the New Zealand International Wine Show. Since then, the vineyard (pictured below) has been extended to 9 hectares and includes small parcels of Italian reds – Sangiovese and Montepulciano – as well as Merlot, Malbec and Cabernet Franc. In addition to diversity of varieties, there is on-going experimentation with clones, and vines are planted on different aspects and slopes. Cooper's investment is on-going, with plans to build a winery on site by 2020.

Try this: The Landing Chardonnay
A barrel-fermented Chardonnay that is full and ripe with a savoury element and a creamy texture that caresses the palate. Low yields are reflected in the high level of peach-like fruit concentration.

Visit
The Landing is a gorgeous luxury retreat with four private villas available to rent. This hideaway caters to your every whim, complete with staff on hand to cook, clean, arrange massages and book helicopter rides to the exclusive Kauri Cliffs golf resort. There's also a boat on hand to help you discover some of the area's unspoiled 144 islands. But you might not want to leave this sanctuary with its natural beauty and, for those who like to actively relax, there's a tennis court, gym, and a natural swimming pool – the sea – on your doorstep. Did I mention that there's wine too?

5

AUCKLAND

The first trans-Tasman flight landed on a grassy paddock in south Auckland in 1928. On the shores of the Manukau Harbour, the paddock had a short landing airstrip, and more than fourteen hours after Charles Kingford Smith and Charles Ulm left Australian soil, they touched down in New Zealand. That paddock was home to a small flying club – and several resident cows. 'It was just a flying field when I was growing up,' says Villa Maria founder, George Fistonich. In 1961, Fistonich, now Sir George, founded his wine company and several years later Auckland airport was officially opened. Today, more than 19 million passengers wheel their suitcases through its sliding doors. The ascent of Villa Maria Wines has been no less spectacular but its home is still a couple of kilometres from what was once a humble airstrip. Should you find yourself in the airport with several hours to kill before catching your next flight, jump in a taxi and have lunch at the winery restaurant, surrounded by vines (see Chapter 15).

However, Villa Maria's origin as an Auckland winery and its evolution to become a New Zealand wine producer reflect the wine industry's shift away from New Zealand's largest city to the provinces. It was once the beating heart of New Zealand wine. The first half of the twentieth century is a tale of immigrants – predominantly of Dalmatian descent – toiling in a new country to buy land, plant vines and make wine. They settled in and around Auckland and supplied their friends, community and wider population with fortified wines and, later, table wine. It was not to last: urban development and the search for a climate better suited to the production of quality wines made from *Vitis vinifera* put paid to Auckland's dominance.

There remains a hardcore of producers in west Auckland but take a closer look and it soon becomes clear that Auckland is not the source of many of their wines. Don't despair for Auckland's wine scene just yet, however. While Auckland's original winemaking families were reaching their tentacles further afield, new wine regions were being explored in the wider Auckland region: Waiheke Island and Matakana. Attracted by the idyllic rural settings, a suitable climate and clay soils, small lifestyle wineries have been appearing since Kim and Jeanette Goldwater, who admitted they were 'a couple of innocent, middle-aged New Zealand do-it-your-selfers', first planted a hectare of Cabernet Sauvignon on Waiheke in 1978.

WEST AUCKLAND

There is still a core of quality-oriented producers resisting the encroachment of urbanization in west Auckland but the remaining vines outside the Babich cellar door and winery are a microcosm of Auckland's wine industry. These vines now represent just 0.5 per cent of their total crush and are surrounded by housing; the land will, says David Babich, be turned into housing at some point. Having made its first Marlborough Sauvignon Blanc in 1991 and purchased its first Marlborough vineyard in 1998, Babich now has around 500 hectares and a 5,500-tonne capacity winery in the region.

Similarly, Coopers Creek on the road out of Kumeu has been sourcing fruit beyond Auckland from the 1980s. Simon Nunns, the cycle-loving winemaker at Coopers Creek since 1997, is unequivocal about Auckland's grape-growing credentials: 'It has fertile clay-based soils and a warm, humid climate with high rainfall which gives every pathogen known to humankind an ability to flourish. You can grow good grapes in Auckland but it's a lot of hard work.' Indeed, with close to 1,400 mm of rainfall in Kumeu (mostly in the winter) compared with 700 mm in Marlborough, this is certainly more challenging when it comes to keeping fungal disease at bay – but at least the clay-rich soils of the area don't need irrigation. In terms of growing degree days, Kumeu is certainly warmer than most winegrowing regions of New Zealand, registering 1,401 days versus 1,068 in Marlborough's Wairau Valley (Anderson et al., 2012). However, that figure only places it in the lower reaches of Region II in Winkler's classification. It shares a growing-season temperature of 16.6°C with Rioja and the Yarra Valley. The reason that Kumeu's maximum daytime temperatures remain more modest than its latitude would suggest is that it sits on a narrow band of land: the Tasman Sea lies just 15 kilometres to the west and the Pacific Ocean 20 kilometres to the east, providing natural air conditioning.

The region's most famous producer, Kumeu River, consistently demonstrates that very good grapes – predominantly Chardonnay – can be grown here. It may come as a surprise that in this seemingly mild climate, frost can be an issue: despite their best efforts during the 2012–13 season, Kumeu River lost two-thirds of its crop. Frost also played its part in significantly reducing the size of the harvest in 2010 and 2015. 'People complain when we fly a helicopter at 3 a.m. to fight frost,' says Michael Brajkovich, Kumeu River winemaker and New Zealand's first Master of Wine. And there are more people to complain than ever. Urbanization is happening and Aucklanders are moving further and further out of the city in search of affordable homes or a semi-rural commute from the city. As a result, the highway that runs between Kumeu River's winery and its most prestigious vineyard, Maté's, is increasingly difficult to cross: a family of hedgehogs wouldn't stand a chance of crossing and remaining in 3D.

Without the Brajkovich family's constant pursuit of excellence in an area many fellow Dalmatians abandoned in favour of easier pickings, the wines of west Auckland would more often than not be overlooked. Its Chardonnays (see Chapter 3) have put Kumeu – and kept west Auckland – on the world wine map.

WAIHEKE ISLAND

Leave the hustle and bustle of Auckland's CBD behind, and forty minutes later you step off the ferry on to the shores of Waiheke Island. Long a hang out for artists, hippies, holiday makers and burned-out corporate types, Waiheke's laid-back attitude and climate has made this a haven for those wanting to escape the rat race. The arrival of a high-speed ferry ushered in a new era of residents – the commuter and second-home owner. It didn't take long for property prices to rise and, today, Waiheke Island is a curious blend of the alternative lifestylers, millionaires and everything in between. There are still no traffic lights or multinational fast-food outlets, but the rise and rise of tourism means double-decker buses whizz up and down and around the island's winding roads which has necessitated cutting back native trees, to the fury of local residents.

Waiheke now welcomes 900,000 visitors to the island who enjoy its sandy beaches, native bush – and wine. Vineyards and wine tasting are one of the key attractions for tourists who come to drink Chardonnay and Viognier, Syrah and Bordeaux blends on a lawn or terrace while looking out across the waters of the Hauraki Gulf. Waiheke now brands itself the 'Island of Wine', but that is a recent phenomenon. In his memoir *Vineyard Virgins* Waiheke pioneer Kim Goldwater recalls that the island was a place where 'the experts of the day declared that wine could not be satisfactorily grown. They prophesised that such an ill-considered endeavour would inevitably end in failure.' These naysayers were basing their negativity on experience: before the Goldwaters came along, the only wine that had been produced on Waiheke was a 'fairly ferocious fortified brew' from hybrid vines.

In the 1980s, the Goldwaters were followed by other pioneering producers including Stonyridge and Te Motu, all keen to grow and make Bordeaux varieties. Today, there are more than 200 hectares planted by some thirty growers on this 92-kilometre-square island. So, what has attracted Americans, Italians, the Swiss and French to Waiheke to make wine? The temperate maritime climate for starters. Sitting as it does in the sailing and fishing mecca of the Hauraki Gulf, the region is protected from the Pacific by the Coromandel Peninsula to the east and the Waitakere ranges to the west, meaning that it is actually drier than Auckland, very slightly sunnier and a little warmer. Unlike the South Island, Waiheke has a comparatively small diurnal temperature range with sea breezes acting as a natural conditioning unit on hot summer days while the water maintains higher minimum temperatures during the night. The long mild seasons with higher mean temperatures and higher sunshine hours than most New Zealand regions allow later-ripening varieties to have a fighting chance.

While the island is surrounded by water (it boasts 133.5 kilometres of coastline), the availability of water – too little or too much – can cause local growers headaches. While it is drier than Auckland, on average, Waiheke receives far more rainfall (730 mm) during the growing season than Hawke's Bay (421 mm), the country's most successful producer of Bordeaux blends and Syrah. It tends to be humid here so fungal-disease pressure is high and growers have to be vigilant with their spraying programmes. In 2016 and 2017, there was significant rainfall leading up to harvest: in 2017, Destiny Bay didn't pick a grape after rain fell in record quantities in March followed by the rainiest April since 1968.

In contrast, the lack of water has been an issue in other seasons: for example, in 2009–10, the island experienced its worst drought in fifty years. In such dry years, its producers are thankful for the water-retentive clay-based soils, which shrink and crack in summer, swell and become sticky in winter. It is simplistic to say that Waiheke's soils are clay; there is, of course, variation from site to site, hilltop to valley, but there is generally a high level of manganese found in the island's soils, a low level of organic matter, and a low pH. In tune with the country's sustainability message, irrigation is not commonplace here.

Wind is a bigger concern than on the mainland. 'Because we are an island, we get hammered by wind from all directions,' notes Martin Pickering, the winemaker at Stonyridge. The predominant winds come from the north east and south west, but sea breezes blow on to the shore from all sides. As a result, site selection is imperative. A sheltered, north-facing slope is a must for late-ripening varieties such as Cabernet Sauvignon, whereas earlier ripeners can be planted on higher, more exposed spots.

Waiheke's wines are not for the cheapskate. The high value of land on Waiheke and the limited number of suitable sites for viticulture keep costs of entry high, notes the island's submission for a Geographical Indication. Many sites are on slopes making them more time consuming to tend while yields are typically low. What's more, the industry's supplies need to be shipped in, adding to the cost of production. It is no surprise, therefore, that Waiheke producers are aiming for the top end of the market. While the premium can be justified on occasions, the price tag of many wines can be difficult to swallow. In these instances, they are best washed down with a romantic meal in a Waiheke winery restaurant overlooking the Hauraki Gulf.

When it comes to what's in the ground, Syrah has become the most planted variety on Waiheke – a major change from its Bordeaux-inspired beginnings in the 1980s. The warm, maritime climate and the small diurnal temperature shift allow Syrah to ripen fully, creating a medium- to full-bodied expression that has a distinctive savoury streak and a twist of spice alongside dark berry fruit. The grapes are ripe and round with low yields, giving a high level of mid-palate concentration while retaining a fresh finish.

Despite Syrah's growing popularity, it was the island's Cabernet–Merlot blends that first put it on the winegrowing map, and continue to be its standard bearer. The 1987 vintage of Stonyridge's flagship red Larose underlined the quality of the region's Bordeaux blends and, thirty years later, another Cabernet-based ultra-premium wine from the island, Destiny Bay's Magna Praemia, held its own at a prestigious international Cabernet tasting in Western Australia (see Chapter 3, Bordeaux reds for more information). The most successful blends are highly concentrated, textural and complex with a high percentage of new French oak playing a supporting role. The least successful are thin and weedy and still sport too much greenness.

White grapes are the minority on Waiheke but there are successful attempts at Pinot Gris, Chardonnay and Viognier. The warm climate gives fuller-bodied styles with ripe-fruit expression, generous alcohol and modest acidity. And, in keeping with the island's early Bordeaux theme, Man O'War also makes a textural, grassy, barrel-fermented Sauvignon/Semillon blend on the far eastern end of the island. Named Gravestone, it's not one to gift to elderly relatives.

MATAKANA

Heading north out of Auckland, it's about an hour's drive to the prosperous village of Matakana – traffic permitting: on a Friday night or the eve of a long weekend, the journey can be lengthy as half of Auckland seemingly heads for the long sandy beaches of the Matakana coast. This once-rural village has gone up in the world, with tourists flocking to enjoy its natural beauty and the bounty that nature provides, whether it's cheese, olives, wine or beer. Matakana has it all – there's even a former All Black running the local butcher's.

Tourism has become the most important economic activity in the region with the local population of 25,000 welcoming between 500,000 and 750,000 visitors annually, according to Matakana's application for a Geographical Indication. And many of them want to drink the region's wine: according to the New Zealand Tourism Research Institute, wine was second only to scenery on the list of most important things to do. As a result, Matakana wine tends to be consumed locally and the producers get a decent price for it, so there's not a great deal of incentive for them to export.

It's a young region – while the first vines were planted in the mid 1960s, the first *Vitis vinifera* vineyard dates from 1979 when Petar and James Vuletich founded the Antipodean brand. James went on to found Providence Vineyards, planting Merlot, Cabernet Franc and Malbec on a north-facing slope in 1990. There were plenty of new entrants in the 1990s: Ascension, Brick Bay, Gillman Vineyard, Hyperion, Matakana Estate and Ransom Wines. The trend was to plant Bordeaux varieties

– as it was in Waiheke – along with some Chardonnay and Pinot Gris. Since then, there has been growing diversity, with Syrah gaining in popularity, and Italian varieties. Heron's Flight, for example, started out with Chardonnay in 1987 and replaced it with Sangiovese and Dolcetto. The range of Matakana's offering is clear from the statistics: there are twenty-eight varieties planted on Matakana's 65 hectares of vineyard. This makes it very difficult to describe a distinctive Matakana-ness to wine lovers. 'There's not a style as such and everyone has their own thing going,' admits Richard Robson, chief winemaker at Matakana Estate.

However, the producers do have a common geography and climate. This is a warm, humid and maritime climate that can suffer from regular rainfall and the occasional sub-tropical storm. You can see the sea from many vineyards and sea breezes provide a cooling influence during the day; its insulating effect at night means that the diurnal temperature range is fairly unspectacular. This climate allows later-ripening varieties to grow but also means that low acidity levels may need pimping in the winery.

The moist, humid climate also requires careful attention in the vine-yard. Fungal disease is a major challenge and producers keep their cano-pies open and need to have a meticulous spray programme. It is hardly surprising that there was only one organic producer in the region at the last count, such is the disease pressure. In addition, the small family-run businesses here don't have the scale to risk losing an entire crop.

Rain at harvest is also a cause for concern, an extreme example being the 2017 vintage, when the remnants of two tropical cyclones dumped record rainfall across the North Island in April. Inevitably late-ripening reds took a hit and you're likely to see a lot of rosé from this harvest and remarkably few top Bordeaux blends. The average annual rainfall sits somewhere between 900 mm and 1,380 mm – depending on which weather station you choose – and, as the soil across the region is a variation on a theme of clay (i.e. sandy clay loam and clay loam), there's really no need to irrigate in Matakana, except for young vines.

It's unlikely that Matakana is going to become a large wine-producing region in the future, in part due to its challenging climate but also because of its proximity to Auckland. The distance between the city and this idyllic coastal setting is both a blessing and a curse, bringing prosperity to the area but also pushing land prices up. There are few suitable north-facing sites available for prospective growers – the flats are too fertile to make fine wine – and the rising cost of entry means that significant expansion is highly unlikely.

The wines are not cheap to make and that is reflected in the premium prices charged. However, quality is highly variable and value for money can be questionable. Many small wineries have been set up as lifestyle operations with cafes, visitor attractions and accommodation tacked on as an additional revenue stream. However, when you visit the region it will become immediately obvious why you would want to own a vineyard in this beautiful part of the world.

PRODUCER PROFILES

Coopers Creek
Huapai
cooperscreek.co.nz

In 1980, Penfold's NZ employees Andrew Hendry and Oregonian Randy Weaver bought an orchard in Huapai and founded Coopers Creek. While there was a small vineyard planted next to the winery, the pair sourced fruit from other parts of New Zealand, enjoying early success with its Hawke's Bay Chardonnay, the evocatively titled Swamp Road. In the late 1980s, Weaver's return to the United States saw Hendry become the major shareholder and, before the decade was out, it had made its first Marlborough Sauvignon Blanc. Today, the winemaker of more than twenty years, Simon Nunns, produces a wide array of varieties and styles. It still makes a few wines from its home of Huapai including a Pinot Gris, a Malbec/Merlot rosé and a Montepulciano, but wines from beyond Auckland's borders make up the majority of the portfolio. There are the usual suspects – Marlborough Sauvignon Blanc, Pinot Gris and Chardonnay (Swamp Road, now Swamp Reserve, is still in production despite its less than appetizing name) but the winery is gaining a reputation for its alternative whites including a wonderfully scented, round and fresh Albariño from Gisborne and a savoury, full-bodied, honeysuckle-esque Marsanne. When it comes to reds, Hawke's Bay dominates but there's also fun to be had with Lagrein and a varietal Montepulciano named Guido in Velvet Pants after Nunns' late dog. Luckily the wine doesn't smell of dog.

Try this: Coopers Creek The Bellringer Albariño
From the first vintage, the fruit sourced from Doug Bell's vineyard in Gisborne has made an Albariño that provides everything you could ever want from Rías Baixas. It is typically a dry, full-bodied and round style with a fresh fragrance reminiscent of apples and peaches followed up with an appetizing burst of fresh acidity on the finish.

Visit
The Coopers Creek cellar door is one of the most family friendly – there's a playground, giant chess set and you can bring your own picnic to enjoy with a glass of wine. The winery has become known for its free Sunday jazz sessions in summer and, best of all, it is just twenty-five minutes' drive from Auckland CBD.

Destiny Bay
Waiheke Island
destinybaywine.com

American couple Mike and Ann Spratt moved to Waiheke in 2000 with a plan to retire. They lived in a house on the top of a hill, which overlooked cows grazing in an almost amphitheatre-like setting. They bought the plot below, decided to buy vines – 'and then it got out of control,' jokes Mike, a former mergers and acquisitions specialist. Microbiology graduate Ann enrolled at the University of Auckland and took a masters in wine science while son Sean studied winemaking through the University of California, Davis. The family now produce super premium Bordeaux-inspired blends. Selection is meticulous in both the vineyard and winery and there's no chance of any nasty microbes ever making it to the bottle with DNA testing and an ozone machine on hand to ensure a fault-free wine without having to sterile filter. Its flagship wine, Magna Praemia, is a minimum of 70 per cent Cabernet Sauvignon with the other four Bordeaux varieties making up the remainder; Mystea is at least 60 per cent Cabernet while Destinae is an earlier-maturing red with Merlot making up 35 to 50 per cent of the blend. Oak is used to support the wine rather than overwhelm, spending between nine and fifteen months in barrel depending on taste.

Try this: Destiny Bay Magna Praemia
In the best years, this is gorgeous, seductive with incredible fruit

intensity and sumptuous tannins; this is a hugely complex wine that's all about texture.

Visit
Contact the winery to enquire about a private tasting through its website.

Gillman Vineyard
Matakana
gillmanvineyard.co.nz

The Gillman family became involved in the Matakana wine scene when James Vuletich founded Providence Vineyards in 1990. Toby Gillman and his father John volunteered to help plant the vineyard and would drive up in their Ford Escort at weekends before heading back to James's house to raid his wine cellar over dinner. After retiring from the world of surgery John and his wife moved up to Matakana and the family planted a close-spaced, low-trained 0.6-hectare vineyard – 0.4 hectares to Cabernet Franc and the rest to Merlot (with a dash of Malbec) on a slope of iron-rich volcanic clay. Gillman hasn't yet given up his day job as an accountant and he travels to the vineyard from Auckland on weekends to tend the vines. Nevertheless, he manages to produce something special on this small plot.

Try this: Gillman Vineyard
Gillman only makes one wine in his tiny cellar tacked on to his parents' house. The Right Bank-inspired blend is often released later than many more 'commercial' wineries to 'ensure the wine will show well' and provide restaurants with a red that has shed the rawness of youth. It is often a savoury, classically structured style with the high proportion of Cabernet Franc providing lovely floral and pencil-lead aromatics. It is an interesting wine to follow across the years, expressing vintage variation.

Visit
There is no cellar door but if you wish to arrange a private visit and tasting, contact Toby Gillman. His details can be found on the website.

Kumeu River
Kumeu
kumeuriver.co.nz

In 1944, Croatian immigrants Mick and Kate Brajkovich had finally saved enough working at local wineries to put a down payment on a 7.3-hectare property in Kumeu. Mick cleared the land with his son Maté and within four years they were producing wine. When Mick died in 1949 it was left to Maté to take over the reins from his father. His work in modernizing Kumeu River – known as San Marino Wines until 1989 – and his service to the New Zealand wine industry was recognized with an OBE. Maté passed away in 1992, three years after his son, Michael, the current winemaker, became New Zealand's first Master of Wine.

Chardonnay is now Kumeu River's jewel in its crown, representing two-thirds of planting, but it has taken some time to get where it is today. Maté planted Chardonnay back in 1965 but it was an old, virus-infected clone, and didn't ripen because it was on a vigorous rootstock. Despite initial setbacks, planting of Burgundy's white grape really began in earnest in 1981 and, in honour of his contribution, Kumeu River's top Chardonnay is named Maté's. The winery's main income, however, was derived from fortified wines until the 1980s. Maté's widow Melba remembers telling customers that they would no longer be making fortified wines: 'It was a real wrench to get rid of it because it was such a large part of our customer base. Some said: "What are we going to drink now?"'

However, the 1989 vintage marked the winery's entry to the big time – it won the International Wine Challenge's white wine of the show in 1991. Today, Kumeu River is the first winery you think of when asked to name New Zealand's best Chardonnay.

The Brajkovich family now makes five different Chardonnays. The entry point is the Village Chardonnay, which became a blend of Kumeu and Hawke's Bay fruit from 2016. It is often the best value Chardonnay in New Zealand with nice concentration and some textural interest from partial fermentation in old oak barrels and time spent on lees. The Estate Chardonnay is a blend of six different parcels in the area and offers lovely density on the supple mid-palate, integrated French oak and fine acidity. The single vineyard wines have their own personality from the powerful, clay-derived Coddington Vineyard to the more elegant, floral Hunting Hill, and the long-lived tribute to Michael's father Maté. A recent addition to the line-up has been a bottle-fermented sparkling wine. Fine and appetizing, it is a blend of 60 per cent Chardonnay and 40 per cent Pinot Noir. It spends thirty months on lees and the liqueur de dosage is a ten-year-old Chardonnay.

Try this: Kumeu River's Maté's Vineyard

In its youth, Maté's is tight and restrained needing time to show its true colours. But it is always intense and rich, detailed and citrus fresh on the long finish.

Visit

The cellar door is open Monday to Saturday year round.

Man O'War

Waiheke Island

manowarvineyards.co.nz

This is possibly my favourite place on Waiheke Island, and the bumpy, dusty road to Man O'War is worth every inch of the drive. At the far eastern end of the island, the Man O'War property is owned by one of New Zealand's richest families – the Spencers made their money in paper milling. They purchased four contiguous farms in the 1980s and joined them to form the Man O'War estate, which covers a massive 1,800 hectares. In 1993, they planted vines and there are now seventy-six separate blocks over 50 hectares with the whites sitting on top of volcanic hillsides and later-ripening reds on vertiginous clay-based slopes that seek shelter from the breeze. It also has a vineyard on the neighbouring Ponui Island, which is also home to forty Ponui donkeys – New Zealand's only feral donkey breed – about 1,500 Kiwis, a couple of sheep farmers and *Vitis vinifera*. The grapes are transported by barge to the shores of Man O'War Bay to be made into its Exiled Pinot Gris and its Warspite Cabernet Franc/Merlot/Malbec blend. Its cuvée names are inspired by battleships (Ironclad, Dreadnought) and mythology (Valhalla, Bellerophon). Man O'War is the largest single producer on the island, accounting for almost half the production.

Try this: Man O'War Dreadnought

This cuvée consistently encapsulates everything that is good in New Zealand Syrah – dark fruit, black pepper spice and smoked-meat flavours wrapped up in an elegant, medium-weight parcel with bags of freshness on the finish.

Visit
The cellar door sits on the edge of the beach and is the perfect place to while away an afternoon, eating, drinking, playing swingball or cricket, and taking a swim in the sheltered bay. It is open seven days a week during the summer, from 11 a.m. to 6 p.m.

Matakana Estate
Matakana
matakanaestate.co.nz
Founded in the early 1990s, the largest winery in Matakana went into liquidation in 2010 but Chinese-born New Zealand residents rescued the estate, and the winery was back in action for the 2014 harvest. Its home block sits on a north-facing, clay-based slope overlooking the main road into Matakana. It also sources fruit from vineyards across the country – Hawke's Bay, Marlborough and Wairarapa – so be careful to check the label if you're looking for Matakana-specific wines. The range produced on the estate includes the Reserve Pinot Gris – a full bodied, spicy example with textural interest; the barrel-fermented Reserve Chardonnay is rich, full bodied and offers savoury complexity.

Try this: Matakana Estate Reserve Syrah
The Reserve Syrah offers smoke, spice and savoury notes in a rather elegant, sartorial way.

Visit
The cellar door is open by appointment seven days a week. There is also accommodation on site: Matakana Lodge is a contemporary Tuscan villa sitting above the vineyard. Just a few minutes from Matakana village, the four-bed lodge boasts a heated indoor pool, spa room, home theatre, wine cellar and private chef service.

Obsidian
Waiheke Island
obsidian.co.nz
Sitting around 200 metres from the sands of Onetangi beach, Obsidian's 9 hectares of vineyard sit on four slopes. Planted in 1993, the non-irrigated, low-yielding sites were originally destined to make Bordeaux-style blends. While its two cuvées, The Obsidian and The Mayor, remain true to its early ambition, Waiheke's warm maritime

climate has led it down a Mediterranean-inspired path with plantings of Syrah, Tempranillo, Montepulciano and Viognier. It has a talented young team in both the vineyard and winery and is consistently one of the island's best producers.

Try this: Obsidian Reserve Syrah

A dense, rich and savoury Syrah sporting a complex array of flavours from ripe black fruit to spice, smoke and black pepper. In the best vintages, it is full and sumptuous yet maintains a wonderful freshness on the finish.

Visit

The unpretentious cellar door is open seven days a week in summer, 11 a.m. to 5 p.m. Check the website for winter opening times.

Passage Rock Wines

Waiheke Island

passagerock.co.nz

David Evans and his Swiss wife Veronika returned to New Zealand in 1993 and set up Passage Rock at the remote eastern end of the island. Initially they thought they were going to focus on Merlot – Bordeaux blends were the in-thing for Waiheke wine producers at that time – and they had just visited Pomerol's Petrus. Today, Passage Rock is better known for its Syrah, having won many awards, but does make a dense Merlot as well as several Bordeaux blends. It also makes a richly fruited Viognier.

Try this: Passage Rock Reserve Syrah

A lush, chocolatey Syrah with dark berry fruit, spice and well-judged oak, this is always a must-buy Waiheke Syrah.

Visit

The cellar door and informal bistro is open Wednesday to Sunday, 11 a.m. to 4 p.m. Be sure to try one of their wood-fired pizzas.

Puriri Hills Vineyard

Clevedon

puririhills.com

A native Virginian, Judy Fowler moved from the United States to New Zealand in 1996, founding Puriri Hills. A year later, having been advised that 6 of the 37.5 hectares on the property were suited to viticulture, she planted 1.6 hectares of Merlot and what she thought was Cabernet Franc (it turned out to be Carmenere), followed a little later by genuine Cabernet Franc, Malbec and Cabernet Sauvignon. The vines are dry farmed, and organic and biodynamic principles have been adopted. In a country dominated by drink-it-young Sauvignon Blanc, Puriri Hills has always bucked the trend, releasing its wines five to eight years after the vintage, when the team believes the wine has reached its drinking window. It offers three red Bordeaux blends: the earliest drinking wine, Estate, followed by the ageworthy Reserve range (renamed Harmonie du Noir from the 2012 vintage) and the flagship Pope. The barrels selected for the three tiers do not hail from specific parcels but are determined by tasting during élevage. All three wines are fermented in open-top fermenters before maturing in a high percentage of new French oak for eighteen to twenty-four months. The wines are not routinely fined or filtered before being bottled. They then rest in the cellars until Fowler deems them ready for release.

Try this: Puriri Hills Pope

The blend of Puriri Hills' top wine differs from year to year – sometimes Merlot dominates, in other years Cabernet Franc might take the lead role. Whatever the blend, it is usually intense and silky; in Cabernet Franc-rich years, it is particularly fragrant and precise. Drinks well for a decade or more.

Visit

The cellar is open weekends only, from 1 p.m. to 4 p.m. Telephone ahead on +64 9 292 9264 or email through the website in advance to confirm that it will be open.

6

GISBORNE

Captain James Cook was born in the village of Marton, Middlesbrough, about ten minutes' drive from my birthplace. While a Middlesbrough company was responsible for building the Sydney Harbour Bridge before shipping it half way around the world, it doesn't have many famous sons – the music of Chris Rea and the magic tricks of the late Paul Daniels are unlikely to be discussed in more than two centuries' time – so it was inevitable that my childhood would be speckled with school trips and wet-weekend outings to the town's Captain Cook museum.

To my eight-year-old self whose summer holidays involved nauseating journeys across the North Sea to Norway, Cook's long sea voyages held little romance. However, the tales of exotic places he visited on the other side of the globe made the British winter in north-east England seem even more dreary and dark. In addition to a large collection of Pacific artefacts, and a glass case filled with stuffed animals including a koala and exotic birds, the museum regales visitors with his journey on *HMS Endeavour*. His first encounter with Gisborne locals when he dropped anchor was far from successful, leading to several violent encounters and the deaths of nine Māori. Cook soon weighed anchor and left the waters of Poverty Bay, so named by Cook '... as it afforded no one thing we wanted'. Thankfully, the locals are much more hospitable today.

Not only was Gisborne Captain Cook's first glimpse of New Zealand, this easternmost region of the country is also the first place to see the sunrise. Its vineyards are the first in the world to enjoy the warming rays of the sun at the break of dawn. The Māori name for the area is Tairawhiti, the coast upon which the sun shines. Its abundant sunshine (2,475 hours per year) and moderately warm conditions make the flats of Poverty Bay a bountiful land for agriculture. However, this is a region of farmers nurturing apples and kiwi fruit, sweetcorn and avocados – or whatever the most profitable crop is at the time. Grapes are not currently in favour: between 2008 and 2018, the vineyard area fell by more than 40 per cent. The sun has set on Gisborne's day as the country's largest wine-producing region and it needs to find a new way.

HISTORY

Born in Nottingham, England in 1800, William Williams was the youngest of nine children and travelled to New Zealand as a missionary, where he planted grapevines on the mission station around 1840 with the aim of making altar wine. Another European missionary, the Frenchman Father Lampila, planted vines and built a church in 1850 in Gisborne – thinking he was in Hawke's Bay: a stiff southerly had blown him off course. Finding he was more than 200 kilometres north of his intended destination he packed up and trekked south, but returned two years later to find the vines in good health and made a barrel of wine. Sadly he didn't get to enjoy the bounty. Joseph Mackay's *Historic Poverty Bay and the East Coast* explains that Lampila asked the captain of a whaling ship to transport the wine back to Hawke's Bay but the sailors opened the barrel on the return journey, supped the wine and replaced it with sea water.

Despite the strength of the temperance movement in New Zealand, there were several producers in Gisborne swimming against the tide. Friedrich Wohnsiedler, a German immigrant who had run a butcher's shop in Gisborne, was forced from meat to wine. The entry in the encyclopaedia of New Zealand explains that in 1914 anti-German sentiment led to a mass attack on his shop in the town's main street. He and his wife fled with their three young children out of a top-storey window and across planks to an adjacent building. Pork lovers' loss was to be wine lovers' gain, for the Wohnsiedlers retreated to Waihirere and there established Poverty Bay's first significant winery. He was assisted by an Austrian blacksmith, Peter Gurschka, who also made his own wine. The Waihirere wine label grew, producing fortified wines for the local market. After his death in 1958, Wohnsiedler's sons took over the business and with an injection of capital, production rapidly increased. The family company was acquired by Montana Wines in 1973 but the butcher-turned-winemaker's name lived on through Montana's Wohnsiedler Müller-Thurgau, which became one of the country's biggest sellers.

It was in the mid 1960s that many larger enterprises realized that Gisborne was a source of cheap and plentiful grapes with its fertile soils and clement weather. The region's application for a Geographical Indication notes that in the four years from 1965 to 1969, Gisborne's vineyard area increased from 27 to 263 hectares, although most of the varieties planted were better suited to quantity rather than quality. The mushrooming vineyards pumped out large volumes of innocuous Müller-Thurgau, Chasselas and Palomino: a yield of 20 tonnes per hectare was not unusual. Despite the vine pull of 1986, there were still close to 200 hectares of Müller-Thurgau in Gisborne at the turn of the millennium. Today, the image of Gisborne as a bulk wine producer persists despite Marlborough overtaking Gisborne as the country's largest wine producer in the early 1990s. One grape grower explains: 'Growers often had sheep farms and grew grapes because they wanted to make a lot of money. We got a name as a bulk region because growers could crop [vines] heavily. Grapes were a low-priced commodity.' While hybrid varieties like Müller-Thurgau and Albany Surprise were underwhelming, a group of quality-oriented producers were developing their own interpretation of Gisborne. Bill Irwin was planting the first Mendoza clones of Chardonnay, which he had imported, as well as Sauvignon Blanc, Chenin Blanc and Gewürztraminer on the Matawhero vineyard in 1968, 'while the rest of the district was being bastardized by Müller-Thurgau,' says his son Denis. Having sold grapes in the early years, the first vintage of Matawhero Wines was produced in 200-litre plastic barrels in 1975. The Gewürztraminer and Chardonnay were a huge success and Irwin is incredibly proud that in 1977, Queen Elizabeth II was served one of his wines on a visit to New Zealand. James and Annie Millton were equally dynamic and had a long-term vision for making quality wine. Their vineyards, farmed biodynamically today, and the wines they produce offer all the evidence needed to convince any sceptics that Gisborne can produce fine wines.

GEOGRAPHY AND CLIMATE

The Gisborne region boasts New Zealand's most easterly point. In this remote rural setting, it enjoys a temperate, maritime climate with high sunshine hours (2,475 annually). It is surrounded by hills which form a protective horseshoe, opening to the sea only on its eastern side. The area suitable for growing crops and vines forms a triangle with the shores of Poverty Bay lapping at its base. The triangle narrows to a peak in Ormond, 16 kilometres inland. In this mild climate, frost rarely troubles growers, particularly those closest to the coast. It isn't unheard of but Geordie Witters, co-founder of TW Wines, points out 'We've only been frosted badly three times since 1983.' The proximity of the ocean is a major factor in the Gisborne climate as cooling sea breezes flow through the vineyards during the late morning. It also means that summer evenings are mild, reducing the diurnal temperature range.

Despite its protected location, Gisborne is a little wetter than many other east coast wine regions in New Zealand with annual rainfall around 1,000 mm compared with 700 mm in Marlborough. Although the region's wettest month is July – winter in the southern hemisphere – rain is common at harvest time, which is a challenge for growers: March and April receive close to 100 mm of rain on average during each of these critical months. The worst scenario is the arrival of former tropical cyclones, which can bring wet weather, humidity and high winds just as the grapes are ready to be picked. However, its moderately warm days (there are 1,725 growing degree days according to the region's GI application) are made warmer by dry north-westerly winds, and its mild nights mean that Gisborne is often one of the first regions in New Zealand to start harvesting. This is an advantage for growers hoping to avoid autumn rains. Ripening grapes in Gisborne is no problem; the issue lies with getting the ripe fruit to the winery before adverse weather arrives. Canopy and crop management is essential to ensure this happens.

WHAT LIES BENEATH

The majority of Gisborne's vineyard holdings lie on a former flood plain. In the 1950s a flood control scheme was established but historic flooding has left behind alluvial clay, loam and silt soils, which are rich and fertile. Unlike the soils of the Gimblett Gravels or Central Otago, which are unsuitable for growing other crops economically, Gisborne's soils are attractive to farmers growing such crops as maize, lettuces, avocados, kiwi fruit and apples. It is a region that can produce abundant yields but grape growers with quality ambitions need to control the vigour of their sites, and cover crops including chicory are increasingly common to increase competition. Higher planting density is also an option if vine heights and canopies are correctly managed: Steve Voysey, owner of Spade Oak Vineyard, has increased the density of his Viognier vineyard, reducing row spacing from 3 metres to 1.5 metres. Devigorating rootstocks including Riparia Gloire and 101-14 are also part of the mix in Gisborne's vineyard. One of the major advantages of Gisborne's moisture-retaining soil and climate combination is that dry farming is possible here. The lines of black irrigation hose running the length of rows at shin height are conspicuous by their absence in many Gisborne vineyards. This means the local wine industry is putting little pressure on local water supplies, and with concerns in some parts of the country about future water availability, Gisborne's future as a wine producer seems far more sustainable.

Gisborne is not just a single entity. The wine community has identified nine districts within Gisborne that have distinctive characters including vines that lie on slopes inland. These include the narrow Ormond Valley, which inspired Nick Nobilo's ultra-premium Gewürztraminer project, Vinoptima, and what's known as the 'Golden Slope', a slim 10-kilometre strip on a base of clay overlaid with light black topsoil, speckled with vineyards. Proving that it's not all flatland viticulture, the region's hillside vineyards have made some of the finest wines. Biodynamic producer Millton Vineyards grows vines on both flat sites and precipitous slopes: Naboth's Vineyard was inspired by a trip to Germany's steep vineyard sites. After purchasing adjoining slopes in 2000, Clos de Ste. Anne was established bringing the total planted area on these slopes to 9 hectares. The Chardonnay, Chenin Blanc and Viognier hailing from these vineyards show the heady heights that Gisborne can reach when made with tender loving care. Similarly, McDiarmid Hill is an elevated site on the western edge of the Gisborne wine region, sitting next door to a lime quarry. Villa Maria makes a silken barrel-fermented Chardonnay off this gently sloping site. Standing above the vineyard high above the valley floor, Tony Green, the company's Gisborne viticulturist, explains how the region has changed its approach to viticulture with a focus on lower yields and less emphasis on chemicals: 'In the early days of SWINZ, we used to do a count of our species in the vineyard and we would get to one. Now we can count into double figures. Between the rows, we pick flowers, clover, thistles, barley grass, rye …'

WINE STYLES

Gisborne is the self-proclaimed 'Chardonnay capital of New Zealand' and there were once signs erected celebrating its dedication to this non-aromatic white variety. There are efforts to keep it on the map: a group of local producers has created a Classic Chardonnay group dedicated to marketing their rich barrel-fermented Chardonnays, which should 'melt even the coldest heart'. However, it is no longer the country's most important Chardonnay producer by volume: that title now lies with Marlborough. The reason for this is that a large number of Chardonnay vineyards have been uprooted since 2009 when the New Zealand arm of Pernod Ricard pulled the plug on many grape-growing contracts due to a decline in Chardonnay sales; fellow drinks giant Constellation also reduced its intake of Gisborne fruit the same year. From 1,084 hectares out of a total of 2,083 in 2010, Chardonnay represented just 620 hectares of Gisborne's 1,246 in 2017. It is still the most-planted variety making full-bodied, round Chardonnays with ripe stone fruit that are enjoyable in youth. The wines are softer and richer than offerings from the cooler climes of the South Island. Styles vary dependent on price point from simple, fruity and unoaked to savoury, barrel-fermented styles with wild yeast and lees work adding complexity. The region is also known for producing Chardonnay destined for large-volume sparkling wine brands including Lindauer, which was sold by Pernod Ricard to Australasian drinks company Lion.

Aromatic whites are collectively the most important wines after Chardonnay. Pinot Gris, which is also used by Lindauer to make a carbonated sparkling wine, is now the second most important variety in Gisborne. It is an early ripener so it can get to the winery before heavy rains arrive but, with its naturally compact bunches and thin skins, the variety needs to be carefully managed in the vineyard to avoid any splitting and subsequent fungal disease. Generally fermented in stainless steel at cool temperatures to preserve freshness and aromas, the wines are full bodied with soft acidity. From dry to sweet and everything in between, they offer ripe red apple fruit, pear and spice aromas. Its Alsatian bedfellow Gewürztraminer has a long and successful history in Gisborne's warmer climes, achieving heady floral voluptuousness. It has been in the Gisborne palette of varieties since the pioneering Bill Irwin of Matawhero imported and planted virus-free Gewürztraminer in the early 1970s, and was soon winning recognition around the world. It is a rather difficult variety to sell with its distinctive personality and naturally low acidity but in the Ormond area it has found a home, making premium and super-premium wines, which are popular in China.

This being New Zealand, it is inevitable that Sauvignon Blanc will make an appearance. It covers 120 hectares (2017) of Gisborne's fertile land making full, rich, tropical styles that are less piquant and racy than the cooler South Island examples. This is not what you should come to Gisborne to drink, however. What makes Gisborne really interesting right now is its seemingly ever-growing band of alternative whites. The country's biggest vine importer and nursery, Riversun, is based in Gisborne so they have a lot of options for experimenting with new varieties and clones close to home, and a white Spanish variety seems to be settling in nicely. Since its first vintage in 2011, Coopers Creek's Bellringer Albariño has been a hit. Grown by former design engineer Doug Bell and his co-founding partner Delwyn, the variety is well suited to a damp maritime climate. Its home in Spain, Rías Baixas, receives 1,800 mm of rainfall annually – making Gisborne look positively arid. The resulting wines are scented, full-bodied yet fresh whites that are a dead ringer for Spain's best. It's not just Albariño that should renew interest in Gisborne. Millton Vineyards has been a long-time supporter of Chenin Blanc and has taken it to new heights on hillsides in Gisborne, making complex, ageworthy examples. It also excels at sumptuous Viognier. Meanwhile, Spade Oak produces a rare Petit Manseng and TW Wines produces taut, long-lived Verdelho. The Bells have been growing a range of alternative varieties including Fiano, Lagrein, Marsanne and Vermentino as part of a trial with the

Gisborne winegrowers' association and the local polytechnic. While the results shone in the glass, the trial has now come to an end and many of the varieties have been pulled out, replaced with economically viable alternatives. While it's a shame to see them go it has prompted others to plant some of the varieties; James and Annie Millton have planted Vermentino as a result of the trials, for example.

When it comes to reds, Gisborne doesn't have a signature variety or style. Merlot and Pinot Noir are the two most planted varieties but collectively they only account for 100 hectares of vineyards. The majority of Pinot Noir planted in Gisborne is destined for blending and carbonating as part of a sparkling wine. There are a few ambitious examples from low-yielding hillside sites that are sensitively oaked and offer soft, ripe expressions.

PRODUCER PROFILES

Historically Gisborne has been a region of grape growers selling their fruit to large enterprises. The large companies, dictated by drinking trends, have been the final arbiter in planting decisions in the region. There are relatively few smaller wineries based in Gisborne dedicated to making high-quality wine for the export market. However, there are quality-conscious wineries outside of Gisborne, which make highly successful wines from Gisborne fruit including Coopers Creek (particularly the fruit from Doug Bell) and Villa Maria (barrel fermented Gisborne Reserve Chardonnay).

Longbush Wines
Gisborne
longbushwines.com
The Thorpe family are a big deal in Gisborne. Not only do they own Longbush Wines, the family's tree also has branches in other agricultural products from cheese and kiwi fruit to game. There are four Thorpe brothers. Richard went into the family horticulture business before co-founding Waimata Cheese, now the country's third-largest speciality cheese producer, but the others are involved with wine. Geoff established New Zealand's leading vine nursery, Riversun, in 1982. Bill established Longbush Wines and their sibling John became winemaker

in 1990, eventually taking over the winery business. Starting his career in hospitality before moving into the world of wine production, John explains that China represents 85 per cent of its sales; the People's Republic loves the friendly sun-drenched wines of Gisborne, particularly the lychee-like Gewürztraminer. Its modern Family Label range has high ambitions and is only produced in the best vintages from hand-picked fruit. The varietals include Chardonnay, Gewürztraminer and Viognier. There are also two *blanc de blancs* and a sparkling Muscat for a bit of fun and, in a particularly clement year, you might find a red wine in the line-up. The label's fruit is sourced from six long-serving grape growers and the vines are dry farmed.

Try this: The Family Company Gewürztraminer
A full-bodied, perfumed wine with lots of juicy, fleshy fruit and excellent balance. It spends twelve to eighteen hours on skins before undergoing a cool fermentation.

Visit
There is a cellar door, which is open by appointment only. Contact details can be found on the website.

Matawhero Wines
Gisborne
matawhero.co.nz

Sitting at the end of the cul-de-sac on Riverpoint Road, Matawhero Wines has entered a new phase in its history. Australian Kirsten Searle and her Gisborne-born husband Richard purchased the estate in 2008, forty years after Bill Irwin and his flamboyant son Denis established the vineyard. In the 1970s and early 1980s its Gewürztraminer and Chardonnay were highly acclaimed both domestically and internationally but its glory days were far behind and the brand was in need of regeneration. The 15-hectare vineyard on silty clay has been replanted under the Searle family's ownership, with Kim Crawford as consultant winemaker. In addition to the Matawhero range, which stays true to its roots, they have created the Church House range, which offers a taste of alternative Gisborne. Having dabbled with varieties including Arneis, Albariño, Chenin Blanc, Grüner Veltliner and Malbec, in the long term Albariño and Chenin Blanc look set to make the cut. The new owners are keen to honour the winery's past and, in September 2017, launched a flagship Chardonnay: Irwin. Produced from vines planted in 2013 on silt loam on the Golden Slope in Gisborne, the wine is fermented in American and Hungarian oak and the first vintage, 2016, produced a full bodied, creamy and sweetly fruited Chardonnay.

Try this: Matawhero Wines Gewürztraminer
If you're going to drink Gewürztraminer in Gisborne this has to be your first port of call: it was the first vineyard in New Zealand to plant the variety. Unfortunately the original vines have been ripped out and have been replanted under the new ownership. The wine is bright and incredibly floral with all the roses and lychees you could ever desire in a Gewürztraminer nose.

Visit
The new owners have reopened the cellar door, which is open five days a week in summer. There is also a four-bedroom vineyard cottage with swimming pool available to hire. For more details, visit the Matawhero website.

Millton Vineyards and Winery
Gisborne
millton.co.nz
Annie Millton grew up in Gisborne surrounded by vines that her father had planted in the late 1960s. She met James, a South Islander, during his cadetship at Montana Wines in the mid 1970s. Love blossomed between the teenagers and several years later the young couple looked at buying land in Central Otago. During their reconnaissance mission they decided that the hot summers and cold winters weren't much fun for them – or for fledgling grapevines. Moreover, there were grapes in the ground, and a supportive family, back in Gisborne. Partners in life and wine, the Milltons established their winery on the banks of the Te Arai river in 1984. One of their first wines, a high solids Chenin Blanc, was not well received, however: 'We were so proud of it and it was rejected as faulty at the Air New Zealand Awards. Positive sulphides wasn't an understandable thing in those days, once again we were ahead of our time.' The Milltons had the last laugh: in 2008, the Te Arai Chenin Blanc was named as one of the '1001 wines to drink before you die'.

The vineyards were farmed organically and biodynamically long before it became fashionable. In 1986 they received organic certification and, after James read a Rudolf Steiner book on biodynamics on a four-day walk around Lake Waikaremoana, they became the first producer in the southern hemisphere to adopt biodynamic practices. At this time, Gisborne was a land of conventional viticulture, pursuing quantity over quality. Did people think they were crazy? Yes, says James: 'Everyone thought we were absolute lunatics then they started asking us about it because they could see they were using so many chemicals but the vines were becoming resistant to them and they were having problems.'

In addition to farming the vineyard biodynamically since the 1980s, there is no irrigation used across the five sites, making their vines dry farmed. The original Opou Vineyard planted by Annie's parents in 1969 continues to bear fruit: both Chardonnay and Riesling (and Navel oranges) are grown here. The Te Arai Vineyard, sitting on the banks of the Te Arai river, is also home to Annie and James, the winery, barrel hall and native tuis who take full advantage of the bird bath at the cellar door. Here, the fruit is grown for several wines including Muskats @ Dawn, a fabulous low-alcohol sparkling wine perfect for breakfast. Its most iconic sites are the steep slopes of Naboth's Vineyard (planted in 1980) and the adjacent Clos de Ste. Anne (2000–1). The upper slopes (pictured above) are planted to Chardonnay, Pinot Noir, Syrah and Viognier while the lower, clay-based slopes of the Clos produce a range of wines including La Bas (see Try This). The Milltons have also gained a deserved reputation for their Chenin Blancs from the Te Arai Vineyard, partially fermented in demi-muids giving a round, off-dry Vouvray-esque style. The Chardonnay in Naboth's Vineyard, is planted on an east-facing hillside – making it one of the first vineyards, if not the first, in the world to see the light of the new day. The resulting wine is good enough to eat: full and rich without heaviness, it caresses the palate. With bottle age, it takes on mealy, lanolin and savoury characters.

Viognier is also one of Millton Vineyards' specialisms, making three separate cuvées off three sites: Clos de Ste. Anne, Riverpoint Vineyard and Clos Samuel – a block close to the Te Arai river, which can become infected with noble rot in some vintages. The dry Viogniers both offer everything you could ever want from a Viognier: full in body with curves in all the right places, it is always balanced. The flavours are varietally classic: orange, florals and peaches abound. It also produces red wines – a rich, savoury Syrah and a soft, richly fruited Pinot Noir. Its well-priced Crazy by Nature label, so named because people thought these biodynamic Gisborne growers had a screw loose, also includes Cosmo, a Malbec, Syrah and Viognier blend.

The future of Millton looks assured with son Samuel joining the family business. There's also continued experimentation with the addition of Vermentino and Roussanne in 2014 and the arrival of two clay amphoras that are used to ferment Chenin Blanc and Syrah.

Try this: Millton Vineyards Clos de Ste. Anne La Bas Chenin Blanc
A dry, rich, savoury and powerful Chenin Blanc with lanolin, nutty and quince flavours. It can age gracefully for a decade, becoming increasingly gourmand.

Visit
Enjoy an informal tasting at the cellar door, open seven days a week during summer, before taking a seat under the shade of an umbrella, enjoying a glass of Chenin Blanc and watching the native tui dance around the garden that has been lovingly nurtured by Annie Millton.

Spade Oak Vineyard
Gisborne
spadeoak.co.nz
Steve Voysey started as a winemaker for Montana in 1987 and moved to Gisborne with the company after being promoted in the early

1990s. He purchased a vineyard there with his wife Eileen in 1993 to supplement his winemaking income, and the grapes were sold for the next two decades. His long-term employer Pernod Ricard pulled out of many Gisborne growing contracts in 2009 and sold the contract winery facility to New Zealand company Indevin. Voysey continued his work as a consultant at Indevin but decided it was now or never to create his own label from the vineyard he knew so well. Spade Oak was born – the name inspired by a property his grandfather farmed on the banks of the River Thames in England. Rich, creamy Chardonnay and voluptuous Viognier are at the heart of the Spade Oak brand but there is also a more experimental side. Voysey is having a bit of fun planting alternative varieties under the Heart of Gold range including Albariño, St Laurent, Tempranillo and even an intriguing Petit Manseng that is available in 375 ml bottles only. The varietal wine varies in style and sweetness levels from vintage to vintage.

Try this: Spade Oak Vineyard Heart of Gold Albariño
Planted in 2009, Voysey's young Albariño vines are making a wine that is gaining more fruit intensity year on year. Fermented in stainless steel to retain the fruit's aromatic purity, it offers red apple and peach aromas. Dry, full bodied and zesty, this is proving to be a variety well suited to the Gisborne climate.

Visit
Visits are by appointment only. Contact details are on the website.

TW Wines
Gisborne
twwines.co.nz
TW Wines was founded by the irrepressible Geordie Witters and Paul Tietjen, who started as contract grape growers for large companies. Witters hails from a sheep- and beef-farming family and, in 1972, decided to give grapes a go. At that time, the priority was high yields rather than high quality and the fruit destined to be picked early for sparkling wines might be cropped as high as 18 to 20 tonnes to the hectare. Tietjen, a fourth-generation New Zealander, produced grapes for wineries like Nobilo, Coopers Creek and Kim Crawford. On a fishing trip in 1997, the pair decided that they would team up to launch their own label – with significantly lower yields. Sitting on the well-

regarded Golden Slope district, they make three creamy Chardonnays, a rich Viognier and a juicy rosé; they also produce an inky Malbec and a herbal Carmenere. Ask them to show you their oldest original Chardonnay vines and you will be whisked off to see forty-year-old Charlene and Charmaine.

Try this: TW Wines Verdelho
If you can get hold of an older example from a warm, dry vintage, you will be pleasantly surprised with the graceful evolution of this Verdelho. One of the very few examples of this varietal in New Zealand (Hawke's Bay's Esk Valley also produces an excellent one), which is perhaps best known for producing Madeira, it becomes nutty and creamy with attractive lanolin-like characters. Its naturally huge acidity makes for a brisk and lively finish.

Visit
For a vineyard tour and tasting, email or call TW Wines to make arrangements. Details can be found on the website.

Vinoptima
Gisborne
vinoptima.co.nz

Nick Nobilo has been a leading light in the New Zealand wine industry since the 1960s, introducing winemaking techniques and developing varieties including Pinot Noir in the early 1970s. His father, Nikola, who emigrated from the Dalmatian island of Korcula in 1937, founded Nobilo Wines and shared his passion with his sons. In the early 1970s, Nick persuaded a grape grower in Gisborne to plant Gewürztraminer as well as Müller-Thurgau. Nobilo admits to a lifelong love affair with the aromatic grape and, following the sale of the family company to BRL Hardy (now Constellation Brands) in 2000, Nobilo decided to pursue his passion for this singular variety. He went to Gisborne and selected the best vines from the vineyard, planted in the early 1970s, and planted out the Vinoptima vineyard with the cuttings, as well as five clones sourced from Alsace. He built a winery in 2003 and the first vintage followed in 2004. The aim was – and remains – to make Gewürztraminer to rival the Grands Crus of Alsace. The top wine, Reserve, is fermented in 1,200-litre German oak oval vessels and 2,000-litre stainless steel tanks, which are then blended and aged for twelve months before being bottled. It spends five years in bottle before release. In 2004, Nobilo produced a botrytized wine from just a few rows that was subsequently awarded 97 points by *The Wine Advocate*, the highest score given to a New Zealand wine at that time. Its more affordable cuvée, Bond Road, is made from fruit sourced from a nearby vineyard. There is also a botrytized Gewürztraminer, when nature permits. Setting up a business based on one rather under-appreciated variety was never going to be an easy sell but the company has found success in China. Now in his 70s, Nobilo was looking for new blood to take the business forward at the time of publication.

Try this: Vinoptima Ormond Reserve Gewürztraminer
Always exotic, spicy and classically varietal, the intense palate fills the mouth with scents of lychees, ginger and roses. Off-dry or medium-dry in style, depending on the vintage, it is succulent and decadent.

Visit
There is no cellar but appointments can be made in advance. Contact details are available on the website.

7

HAWKE'S BAY

A giant banner dominated the New Zealand wine trade's annual tasting in London. It was a familiar sight: the view from Rippon Vineyard over Lake Wanaka, Central Otago. Its beauty is undisputed: vines sit on the shores of a lake carved by a glacier more than 10,000 years ago; snow-capped mountains rise up in the distance. A tiny island sits like a green dumpling in the vast depths of its cold, dark waters, sometimes braved by mad triathletes in thick wetsuits. This image has become synonymous with the country's wine industry, just as Central Otago Pinot Noir has become New Zealand's most famous red wine. It has earned its reputation and worked tirelessly to put itself on the map but it is far from being New Zealand's longest-serving red-winemaking area. That honour goes to Hawke's Bay and it is high time that the region and its reds won the recognition it deserves. The next giant banner should sport the distinctive ridge of Te Mata Peak.

As early as 1851 there was wine in Hawke's Bay. Mission Estate Winery, formerly known as Mission Vineyards, was established by missionaries a decade before gold was discovered in Central Otago. Te Mata Estate, Vidal and the estate now known as Esk Valley were up and running by the 1920s – half a century before the first Sauvignon Blanc was planted in Marlborough and sixty years before Central Otago released its first Pinot Noir. Standing beneath the banner of Rippon Estate, Trinity Hill's winemaker Warren Gibson considered why more people aren't talking and writing about Hawke's Bay. 'We are not the new kids on the block,' he says.

The region's wine history starts in the unlikely location of Le Havre, France. On Christmas Eve 1836, nine Marist priests and the newly appointed Bishop of the South Pacific, Jean Baptiste Françoise Pompallier, set sail from the shores of the English Channel on what was a fairly convoluted route to New Zealand. They went via Chile and refuelled, then dropped two Fathers off in what is now part of French Polynesia; one came to a sticky end, losing his head for repeatedly attempting to convert the son of a chief to the Catholic faith. What was left of the party then headed to Sydney before eventually landing in the far north of New Zealand in 1838.

More than a decade later, the French missionaries headed south, bound for Napier in Hawke's Bay. This was no straightforward trip either: they mistakenly ended up in Gisborne after their ship was blown off course. When they finally made it to Hawke's Bay they established a mission but trouble was brewing. In 1857 fighting between two rival Māori over land ownership forced the missionaries to abandon their station and vines for another part of the Bay, explains Mark Sweet in his comprehensive history of the region, *Wine Stories from Hawke's Bay*. The Fathers and Brothers grew grapes for sacramental wine but, being French, it was also considered part of their daily diet. The locals also enjoyed the Society of Mary's wines: records show that in 1895, 703 gallons of mainly dry red wine were sold, according to the *History of Mission Vineyards, 1838–1979*.

Wine production in Hawke's Bay had expanded beyond the grounds of the Mission by 1895, the year that Romeo Bragato toured New Zealand to report on the prospects for viticulture and wine at the end of the earth. Here he visited the producers and tasted the wines of Greenmeadows Vineyards, Te Mata Station and Frimley Orchards. The men behind the vineyards at Greenmeadows and Te Mata were two of the largest landowners in the area. Greenmeadows' Henry Tiffen was a successful businessman who ventured into vine growing late in life: he was 71 when he took some vines from his friend William Beetham's property in the Wairarapa to his Hawke's Bay station. He only lived for another six years but in that time he created the largest vineyard in the country with Pinot Noir, Pinot Blanc, Pinot Meunier and Hermitage (Syrah). Bragato visited and reported: 'The soil and climate and quality of the grape, clearly prove the capabilities of this district for producing champagne and other wines.' Following Tiffen's death, his devout Baptist niece took over the vineyards, gradually reducing the vineyard in an era of temperance and, by 1923, explains Sweet, Tiffen's vines were no more.

Bragato also spent time with Bernard Chambers at Te Mata Station during his whistlestop tour. Chambers had inherited nearly 2,000 hectares of land from his father and, having been inspired by trips to vineyards in Europe and California, planted his first cuttings in 1892. Encouraged by Bragato's praise for his 'beautiful wine', he became Hawke's Bay wines' biggest champion for the next twenty years, planting vines, building a cellar and employing a full-time winemaker from Australia. In the face of growing support for temperance, Chambers expanded the operation to 14 hectares and tripled production to 45,500 litres in the decade to 1913, according to Department of Agriculture figures. He now took on the mantle as New Zealand's biggest producer. Despite increased quantities, Chambers focused on making quality table wine, and he was rewarded at several international wine competitions. In 1908, Te Mata won golds at the Franco-British exhibition in London; two years later at the London Japan-British Exhibition there were multiple golds for Te Mata's wines, a gold for Frimley and silver medals for both Greenmeadows and Mission. The legendary French-born English wine merchant and author André Simon (1877–1970) tasted Te Mata's 1912 red blend in 1964 with New Zealand's leading wine writer of the period, Frank Thorpy, and Thorpy recorded Simon's comments: 'Remarkable, quite remarkable. One would not have thought it would have kept this long. This really is quite good, there is not the slightest trace of acidity or vinegar. No sign of decay at all. A very mellow wine.' Describing a wine as fault free is hardly high praise, but fifty-two years after the Pinot Meunier and Cabernet Sauvignon grapes were plucked from their vines in the Havelock Hills, this comment suggests that the wine was imbued with the ageworthy qualities that elevate a good wine to a fine wine.

Unfortunately, for Te Mata and Hawke's Bay, fortified wine was the order of the day for the first half of the twentieth century and, like King Canute, a handful of table wine producers could not stop the tide of sherry and port lookalikes. It was almost inevitable that after selling Te Mata in 1917, it became 'a factory of sorts' writes Keith Stewart in *Te Mata: the First 100 Years*, making cheap fortified wine. The 1912 'claret' that Simon and Thorpy had tasted was 'a glimpse of what could have been' for the winery and Hawke's Bay.

It was a similar story at Mission Vineyards. Originally a producer of dry white and red wines, it bowed to public demand in the mid 1900s, buying a pot still in order to make fortifying spirit. In the first half of the twentieth century, the Brothers were on the receiving end of several unkind acts of God – losing almost all of their wine in a fire that gutted their cellars in 1929 and, just two years later, on 3 February 1931, a huge earthquake shook the entire region leading to a huge wine spillage at Mission and the devastation of the city of Napier. Nevertheless they persevered. Today, Mission no longer makes fortified wines but when current winemaker Paul Mooney, a science graduate who took over the reins from Brother John in 1979, started work at the estate many of the grapes picked from their 44.5 hectares of vines were still destined for port and sherry production.

It was up to pioneering individuals to fulfil Hawke's Bay's potential as a quality wine-producing region, as Bragato had envisioned before the turn of the century: 'The Hawke's Bay Province is, in my opinion, the most suitable for vine-growing I have visited in New Zealand. It possesses thousands of acres which, by reason of the nature of the soil, natural drainage, and sufficiency of heat, will produce grapes of both table and wine-making varieties in rich abundance.'

Dennis Kaska (1921–1974)

Born in Hungary in 1921, Kaska emigrated to New Zealand in 1950 and took up a position at the national viticultural research station Te Kauwhata for seven years, making some very fine experimental wines, before moving to Hawke's Bay to oversee production at McWilliam's Wines. Kaska, explains *Wine Stories from Hawke's Bay*, was the man behind the country's most popular table wines in the 1960s: the medium-dry Müller-Thurgau-based white Cresta Doré and the hybrid-dominant Bakano red. He was also hugely influential in making small parcels of high-quality Cabernet Sauvignon and Chardonnay, which were praised as being some of the finest ever made in New Zealand. Having studied in Hungary, Montpellier and Paris, he had a trained eye and was the first to spot phylloxera's presence in Hawke's Bay in late 1964. He died in 1974, aged fifty-three.

Tom McDonald (1907–1987)

French multinational drinks company Pernod Ricard owns the Church Road winery, which dedicates its 'McDonald Series' and its flagship red range 'TOM' to the man who left school at fourteen and went on to manage the country's largest wine producer. The story goes that Tom 'the Grizzly Bear' McDonald took a job with one of the former Marist brothers. Bartholomew Steinmetz had left the Order and bought 2 hectares of land, planting a vineyard which McDonald leased from him aged just nineteen. Despite a strong temperance movement and the Depression, McDonald survived by growing table grapes, fruit and vegetables. He also planted Cabernet Sauvignon. It was his trial block of Cabernet Sauvignon that proved to be the variety's trailblazer. McDonald famously presented French-born wine writer André Simon with a bottle of Bordeaux first-growth Château Margaux 1949 and a bottle of his Cabernet Sauvignon from the same year during his 1964 visit to the Bay. Simon reported in *Wine and Food* that McDonald's Cabernet was 'rare and convincing proof that New Zealand can bring forth table wines of a very high standard of quality'. He continued: 'The Margaux had a sweeter finish and a more welcoming bouquet, greater breed, but it did not shame the New Zealand cousin of the same vintage.' In 1962 McDonald's Wines merged with McWilliam's where he remained until he retired in 1976. In addition to his winery duties, the story of Church Road, *A Love Affair with Wine*, explains that he liked tending roses, collecting stamps and playing golf, as well as being active in industry matters as president of the Hawke's Bay Winegrowers Association, and later, chair of the Wine Institute of New Zealand. He died just short of his eightieth birthday in 1987 but he had overseen a seismic shift in the Hawke's Bay's wine trade, and his legacy lives on.

It would take fifty years before the quality-oriented cogs of Hawke's Bay's wine industry would begin to turn with any real momentum. There were individual pioneers during that time, like Tom McDonald and Dennis Kaska, but they were lone voices in a sea of sweet fortified production. But with legislative changes and cultural attitudes shifting, the 1970s and 1980s marked the beginning of a brighter future for Hawke's Bay – and for the rest of the New Zealand wine industry. The vine pull in the mid 1980s bid farewell to 500 hectares of inferior hybrid vines as well as sherry-producing Palomino, and said hello to Chardonnay, Merlot and Cabernet Sauvignon. The first Syrah vines were planted in what would become the Gimblett Gravels. Subsequently, curious wine investors and winemakers were turning up, and buying up: the last thirty years have witnessed the arrival of international investment from France (Church Road), Germany (Elephant Hill), the United States (Craggy Range) and more recently China (Paritua Vineyards). The Marist Order moved to Auckland in 1990 but Mission is still 100 per cent owned by its founders, the Society of Mary. More than 150 years after the first Brothers arrived in the region, Hawke's Bay remains a blessed place to produce wine.

GEOGRAPHY AND CLIMATE

On the east coast of New Zealand's North Island, Hawke's Bay has a temperate maritime climate. At its most easterly point, vines sit on the shores of the Pacific Ocean (and when the tide is particularly high, have been known to be *in* the ocean) and flow westwards across former river beds, heading inland and upwards to altitudes of 250 metres in central Hawke's Bay.

In the red section, New Zealand's cool climate makes it conducive to planting Pinot Noir but, less than 300 kilometres north of Martinborough, Hawke's Bay is much warmer. Tony Bish, founding winemaker at Sacred Hill, says: 'We have to break the paradigm that all of New Zealand is cool climate.' In terms of other wine regions, it is a little warmer than Bordeaux albeit significantly cooler than Napa Valley, and that is reflected in the grape varieties planted and the wine styles produced.

The majority of Hawke's Bay's 5000-plus hectares of grapevines lie on the Heretaunga Plains, which includes the increasingly respected Gimblett Gravels and Bridge Pa Triangle. The history of this vinous landscape stretches back 250,000 years, which seems like a very long time ago for most of us but for geologists is very recent. Three rivers with names that trip up most visitors to the region – the Ngaruroro (the g is not pronounced so Na-roo-row-row), the Tukituki and the Tutaekuri – have flowed, flooded and changed course as they have snaked their way to the Pacific over their lifetime. The result is that most of Hawke's Bay's vineyards now lie on former river beds. The composition of the soils varies from place to place – there are twenty-five different soil types in Hawke's Bay – but the Heretaunga Plains area is essentially the remains of rivers depositing their load en route to the coast. Both the Bridge Pa Triangle and Gimblett Gravels, for example, are terraces left behind by the Ngaruroro river. In 1867, the river changed course and left 'pure gravel beds with lenses of sand, silt and clay at various depths,' explains the Gimblett Gravels Wine Growing Association. Although the Gimblett Gravels and Bridge Pa both have the same gravel foundation, the older Bridge Pa has a deeper layer of topsoil, consisting of sandy loam or clay loam, which is said to imbue its red wines with more perfume and softer tannins.

Further inland, there are similar soil types left behind by the Ngaruroro river but on elevated terraces. According to Hawke's Bay's 2017 dossier supporting the application for a Geographical Indication for Hawke's Bay: 'These regions – Crownthorpe on the northern bank and Mangatahi on the southern – are extensive, and vineyard plantings can be a little cooler and damper than the Heretaunga Plains. Similar terraces straddle the Tutaekuri River as it approaches the plains.' Meanwhile, in the Havelock Hills and the coastal plantings of Te Awanga, there is a silica pan that runs through its gravel-based soils. For many local producers who have tasted the wines of Burgundy and Saint-Émilion, however, limestone would be the ultimate soil. Te Mata Peak is a ridge of limestone, and limestone quarries are situated just a few miles south of Hastings, so it certainly exists in the region although not all limestone is born equal – nor is their date of birth the same. Nevertheless, it wouldn't be surprising if some enterprising winemakers (with plenty of money to burn, which discounts most of them) went on a treasure hunt. Rod McDonald says: 'There are some beautiful north-facing slopes that are on limestone that we haven't planted but you would need to charge $50 a bottle or more to make it worthwhile.' In 2001, husband and wife team Rodger Tynan and Rosie Butler took that leap of faith far from the heart of Hawke's Bay's wine scene. Drive thirty minutes south of Hastings and you'll discover Pinot Noir planted on loess-covered limestone. Rather appropriately, they named the brand

Lime Rock but, after seventeen years of work, retirement beckoned and they put the vineyard, winery and brand up for sale in early 2018.

What is greywacke?

Is it:

1. A hard, grey sandstone that makes up the 'basement rock' of large swathes of New Zealand;

2. The name of Kevin Judd's very fine Marlborough wine brand, or

3. The first name of a cat – Greywacke Jones – in the Hairy MacLary series of children's books? (Parents of children under five will be well acquainted with author Lynley Dodd's canine and feline characters.)

The answer? All of the above. However, in Hawke's Bay the basement rock of greywacke (pronounced 'grey-wacky') is of most significance. This is how it is formed: sand and mud accumulated as sediments deep under the sea were compressed and then uplifted to form mountains millions of year ago. Nature has taken its course; these mountains eroded and fragments were transported by rivers and broken down over time.

When it comes to climate, Hawke's Bay can ripen Syrah, Merlot and, in warmer years, Cabernet Sauvignon. This is a feat few regions in New Zealand can manage. Nevertheless, the region also produces Sauvignon Blanc and Pinot Noir. The easiest way to understand this seeming anomaly is to slice the region into three sections: the coast, the plains and the hills.

From the start of the season, the differences in climate between the coast, river plains and hills is keenly felt. The moderating temperature of the Pacific Ocean means that frost machines aren't needed in the coastal village of Te Awanga, yet less than 20 kilometres from the shore, spring frost is a risk. The Heretaunga Plains and the vineyards at altitude are speckled with frost fans. Alwyn Corban, who co-founded Ngatarawa Wines in 1981 and was a pioneer of the Bridge Pa district, remembers frost-free days: 'Until 2001, frost was not an issue but then we had a bad frost and then another horrible frost in 2003. That's why we all put in the wind machines.'

Moving into summer, coastal vineyards benefit from the cooling sea breezes that ripple through the vineyards on a daily basis. The proximity of the ocean makes for lower maximum temperatures during the day but higher minimum temperatures during the night compared with sites further inland. Producers here note that this leads to wines with lower acidity and higher pH as well as lower fragrance. The cooler daytime temperatures mean that this is one of the places to successfully grow Sauvignon Blanc in Hawke's Bay, but Cabernet Sauvignon struggles. While the Crownthorpe and Mangatahi Terraces, and the higher sites above the Tutaekuri River in the Dartmoor Valley to the north (home to Sacred Hill's Riflemans Chardonnay and Te Mata's Woodthorpe Terraces), are a little too far inland to benefit from the sea breezes experienced at Te Awanga, the effect of altitude allows Chardonnay, Gamay and Syrah to thrive in this area.

In the vine-dense Heretaunga Plains, there is clearly a difference in the everyday summer climate compared with the coast and the high inland terraces. Elephant Hill has its home block, winery and sleek cellar door on the coast in the village of Te Awanga as well as owning vineyards in the Bridge Pa Triangle and the Gimblett Gravels. Its viticulturist Jon Peet explains: 'I can go from Te Awanga to Gimblett Gravels and it can be 7°C warmer. It's like stepping into an oven when you go into the Gravels vineyard. The stones heat up so much if there's no wind.' Those stones retain heat after the sun goes down. Over the course of the night, temperatures eventually drop lower inland than at the coast, but it is a slow process.

The warmer temperatures experienced on the Plains mean that grapes tend to ripen more rapidly. Peet notes, for example, that Syrah might be picked on their Gravels site in the last week of March whereas at its Te Awanga site it will be the third week of April. Similarly, Matt Stafford, chief winemaker at Craggy Range, explains how Chardonnay ripens later on the cooler, more vigorous Kidnappers Vineyard at Te Awanga than at the bony Gravels. 'We pick two to three weeks later at Kidnappers. We would probably be picking at 23 to 24 Brix [equivalent to 13.6 to 14.4 per cent potential alcohol] in the Gimblett Gravels but we will be happy if we can pick at 21 to 22 Brix [12.2 to 12.9 per cent potential alcohol] three weeks later.'

Going 'rogue'

Leafroll is an issue for New Zealand wine producers and in the late noughties Gimblett Gravels was feeling the strain. The viral disease is spread by grafting or via the mealybug. The effects include reduced yields and slower ripening, leading to less sugar accumulation, unripe tannins and lower colour. That's a major issue for cool climate viticulture and for late-ripening varieties such as Cabernet Sauvignon, which is popular in Hawke's Bay. A six-year study led by PhD student Vaughn Bell starting in 2009 across Gimblett Gravels attempted to reduce the viral incidence below 1 per cent. The study found that by removing or roguing the infected vines (and removing the roots, which can be a source of further infection) and careful monitoring, the disease can be significantly reduced. The malady is fairly easy to spot: the leaves of infected vines turn dark red and droop while the leaf's veins remain green. It might look pretty and make you burst with autumnal feelings but it's bad news for the vine. Vineyard owners were advised to remove entire blocks if the incidence of leafroll was higher than 20 per cent.

There have been some major casualties: Craggy Range's block of Chardonnay responsible for its exquisite Les Beaux Cailloux had to be ripped out, as it was starting to infect their neighbouring red blocks, while Delegat, the company behind Oyster Bay, replanted its Gimblett vineyards.

There is a parasitic wasp that preys on the mealybug but the bony soils of Gimblett Gravels aren't a natural habitat. 'The virus is spread by mealybugs. We're trying to control that population and the difficult thing is the parasitic wasp is only attracted by flowering species and the land here is so poor,' says Matt Stafford, winemaker at Craggy Range. 'We are looking at how we can naturally find some hardy plants to create positive competition [with the vines] and attract the parasitic wasp.' There's an additional issue in that the mealybugs leave a secretion that ants love, and the ants scare away the wasps.

Despite the issues facing the local producers, by working together and implementing Bell's strategies, the number of vines infected dropped from 13 per cent in 2010 to 2.5 per cent in 2014, showing that its spread can be controlled.

One of the major challenges for Hawke's Bay grape growers is harvest rain – and the occasional tail end of a tropical cyclone, whether it was Cyclone Pam in March 2015, or Cyclones Debbie and Cook in mid-April 2017 or, for the small band of producers making wine in Hawke's Bay in 1988, Cyclone Bola. Even the tail end of a cyclone can cause huge damage, and the damage is most severe for those producers sitting on the shore of the east coast. Greg Collinge, the 1970 Citroën DS-driving owner of Supernatural Wine Co., whose organic vineyard looks out to sea laments: 'We are the first dumping point when the wind blows from the east.' Having vineyards across the region can spread the risk, and the free-draining soils of the Heretaunga Plains mitigate the effect of rain particularly if drying winds follow the downpour.

An unwelcome downpour close to harvest means that slip skin – whereby the skin slips off the berry when pressure is applied – is not unusual here. If you see a local winemaker giving his vines a damn good kick in the run-up to harvest, they might be lamenting a Black Caps defeat [the New Zealand cricket team] or checking for slip skin, a botrytis infection of the grapes. Slip skin can affect seemingly healthy, ripe grapes in the days before harvest. It normally develops if there is a sudden burst of heavy rain just before picking. While it is difficult to spot with the naked eye, you need to harvest quickly to prevent botrytis spreading so any suspect vines need to be given a good old jiggle (or a kick), and the affected grapes will drop off. It can be an issue in Hawke's Bay and, in 2011, there was plenty of kicking of vines and sadly slip skin did play a part, particularly with Merlot. Stafford explains the team saw 'our last parcel of Merlot destined for Sophia [its flagship Bordeaux blend] slip before our eyes within eight hours of walking through the blocks – the difference between a $70 bottle and not even making the grade for a $27 wine.'

Despite the threat of rainfall, the availability of water and water rights have been a hot topic in the Bay, particularly for those growers on the free-draining Heretaunga Plains. Without irrigation here, growing vines would be nigh on impossible. Hawke's Bay receives around 750 mm of rain throughout the year with July (winter in New Zealand) being the wettest month. While European vineyards with similar rainfall are forced by law to survive without irrigation, the gravel-dominant soils of Hawke's Bay regularly demand irrigation to prevent the vines keeling over. Steve Smith MW, the founding winemaker at Craggy Range and now co-director of Aotearoa New Zealand Fine Wine Estates says: 'The Gimblett Gravels definitely needs the opportunity to irrigate – you can't dry farm but it is all about water management. To keep vines going on a really hot day on a site with 5,500 vines per hectares – which is quite close spacing – you'd need about 70 cubic metres [70,000 litres] per hectare. At Craggy [Range], we could have gone for a couple of weeks without irrigation but in some places, it might be three or four days.' There are cynical – or jealous – wine producers in other parts of the country that call Gimblett Gravels viticulture hydroponics. Scathing compatriots aside, most of the wine industry's water needs are provided by underground aquifers, which are topped up by rainfall in the winter months. For those sites not endowed with acquifers, water has to be drawn from rivers, bores or dams.

CHAMPIONING HAWKE'S BAY

Hawke's Bay does a lot of things well, as geographer Warren Moran points out in his book *New Zealand Wine*: 'Although it grows only about one quarter of Marlborough's total area in vines, it has nine varieties each with over 100 hectares planted. Marlborough has 5.' This diversity is not simple to convey to someone who lives thousands of miles away; it is much easier when a region has a signature varietal like Marlborough and Sauvignon Blanc, Central Otago and Pinot Noir. 'The challenge for Hawke's Bay is to become as well known as Marlborough and Central Otago,' says Fongyee Walker MW whose company, Dragon Phoenix Wine Consulting, has organized a series of educational roadshows across the People's Republic of China for the Hawke's Bay Winegrowers association. Yet the lack of a star variety is not a big concern in the opinion of the country's first Master of Wine. 'In China, one of the key buying cues is region rather than grape, perhaps a knock-on from the Bordeaux effect, so it's important for Hawke's Bay to establish itself as a high-quality production area regardless of the varieties.'

What Hawke's Bay does have is a storied history, unlike many other New Zealand wine regions. Vines have been growing in Hawke's Bay for more than 150 years despite the best efforts of the temperance movement and pious licensing laws. Mission Estate Winery is the oldest producer in the country and Te Mata boasts the oldest winery building (1896). Mission can also lay claim to being the only winery in New Zealand where Tom Jones, Rod Stewart (twice), Barry Gibb and Engelbert Humperdinck have performed.

With a host of the country's finest wines on its books including Te Mata Coleraine, Trinity Hill Homage Syrah and Sacred Hill's Riflemans Chardonnay, there's little doubt that Hawke's Bay can produce outstanding quality reds and whites. From the coast to former river beds like the Gimblett Gravels and climbing up to the Crownthorpe Terraces, the general standard of wine production across its seventy-six wineries is good to excellent. But it's not the first region that comes to mind when buying New Zealand. Gaetan Turner, president of South World Wines, is based in Paris and sells Elephant Hill's wines across France, which sounds like a task akin to selling ice to Eskimos yet you'll now find Hawke's Bay wines in Michelin-starred restaurants from Paris to Monaco. His customers – if they know anything about New Zealand wine – have heard of Marlborough but not Hawke's Bay. 'But there's a different story to tell and then we show them the photos of Elephant Hill and it blows them away.'

As it should. Elephant Hill is a wine-photographer's dream location: the untamed Pacific waters ebb and flow within metres of its vineyards. The rugged peninsula of Cape Kidnappers, which juts out into the ocean, provides a dramatic backdrop. Drive fifteen minutes inland to the arty town of Havelock North and there is more natural beauty: follow Craggy Range's winemaker Matt Stafford on Instagram and his images of morning runs up Te Mata Peak or along the local beaches (sometimes meeting a seal along the way) attest to the spectacular landscape of this region. What's more, its main city, Napier, was destroyed by an earthquake in 1931 and was rebuilt in Art Deco style, making it a mecca for architecture lovers. Admittedly, the region doesn't have the drama of Central Otago's mountain ranges but it has plenty of vistas worthy of appearing on a banner at the country's annual trade tastings.

And it also has its own event that is ripe for attracting international wine lovers. For the past twenty-five years, it has organized New Zealand's equivalent of the Hospices de Beaune. While bidders from the four corners of the globe attend the Burgundy auction, attempting to secure a parcel from the latest vintage, the make-up of the Hawke's Bay event is rather more local and the region could seek to raise its profile beyond New Zealand shores. There has been a string of excellent vintages (2013, 2014, 2015) and the prices that the wines have attained, while impressive in New Zealand terms, look like absolute bargains compared to the prices paid at the Burgundy charity auction. The event also provides an opportunity for outsiders to understand the region's laid-back attitude: no shirt and tie needed here, there's beer to drink at the auction, and winemakers present their lots in their idiosyncratic way. At the 2015 auction, Clearview Estate donated a personalized blending session to make a quarter-barrique of wine (56 litres), followed by a meal that was clearly going to involve a lot of wine: 'This will be a lunch that you won't remember,' announced the winery's kooky owner Tim Turvey at the auctioneer's podium before the bidding climbed to $7,000. There's a lot to like about Hawke's Bay, its wines and people.

WINE STYLES

When it comes to Hawke's Bay reds, Pinot Noir is but a scratch in a body of Merlot and Cabernet. Across the Bay, producers offer everything from a straight Merlot or Cabernet Sauvignon to a full melting-vat of Bordeaux varieties in one bottle, but the region is slowly hoping its blended wines can cut the leash from its association with 'Bordeaux' blends because the wines are grown and made in Hawke's Bay – but that might take centuries. The red 'Bordeaux' varieties make up a quarter of all the vines planted in Hawke's Bay, making it the home of New Zealand red blends. Merlot typically dominates blends as the late-ripening Cabernet Sauvignon can struggle to reach full maturity in cool or wet vintages such as 2011 and 2012. The resulting wine style could be compared to Right Bank Bordeaux in warm years: offering ripe fruit, structured tannins and fresh acidity. When it comes to nuance, the wines of Bridge Pa exhibit a softer tannin structure and more perfume than the Gimblett Gravels, which needs the generosity of Merlot to flesh out its frame. There are also producers who use a proportion of Cabernet Franc and Malbec to bring extra complexity to the blend, and there are some producers making very attractive varietal bottlings. But making great Bordeaux-inspired reds is hardly novel. Gordon Russell, senior winemaker at Esk Valley is realistic: 'No matter how good our Bordeaux blends are, there is a sea of wines like them across the world.'

However, the region has another red variety that makes an idiosyncratic style. Syrah offers the elegance, spice and savoury nuances of the northern Rhône with sweet New World blackberry fruit. It is a unique and characterful combination. John Hancock, Trinity Hill's founding winemaker agrees: 'It's a little bit like Pinot Noir. It's transparent and shows where it is grown very well. Our Chardonnay, which we make exceptionally well, and the Bordeaux-style blends could, on tasting, be from anywhere but the Syrah is distinctly Hawke's Bay – it's that spicy, savoury, medium-bodied style. It manifests itself slightly differently across the region but it's still distinctly Hawke's Bay. You can't reproduce it anywhere else: it's like Sauvignon Blanc in Marlborough or Pinot Noir in Central Otago.'

Despite the adoration of its producers and the admiration of wine critics around the world, who have claimed Syrah should be the next big thing, it has not yet translated into sales. The bigger, bolder style of Australian Shiraz continues to dominate the category – even domestically, where the Shiraz/Syrah shelves are dominated by South Australian Shiraz while the local Syrahs often occupy an embarrassingly small and dusty corner.

While Hawke's Bay is responsible for almost 9 out of 10 hectares of Cabernet, Merlot and three-quarters of the Syrah grown in New Zealand, the region isn't just a red-wine producer. More than 50 per cent of plantings are white, and Chardonnay is the most popular variety. The styles range from unoaked, citrus-driven, precise styles to barrel-fermented, richly texured Chardonnay. Site plays an important part in the style of Chardonnay with fruit grown on the coast and at altitude picked around three weeks later than on the Plains. The resulting wines are fresh, fine and sport lower alcohol levels.

In the white department, Chardonnay might be Hawke's Bay's calling card but Sauvignon Blanc plantings come a close second. The region's temperate maritime climate and lower diurnal temperature range create a different aromatic profile and structure compared with cooler Marlborough Sauvignons. Expect a more weighty expression on the mid palate and a grassy, citrus-infused nose. Winemaking varies hugely across the region from the conventional stainless steel, inoculated yeast route, which produces a crisp, linear style, to full-bodied, barrel-fermented styles, including Te Mata's Cape Crest, which is also one of the precious few that add a splash of Semillon and Sauvignon Gris. There's even an organic producer making unfined, unfiltered, unsulphured *pétillant naturel* Sauvignon Blanc: Supernatural Wine Co.

Of course there's Pinot Gris in the mix. From just 5 hectares in 1990 to 12 hectares at the turn of the century, plantings have since mushroomed to 422 hectares. It is not Hawke's Bay's calling card by any means, with many examples offering little interest and high alcohol, but there is a handful of producers making some interesting styles and creating textural interest with techniques including sensitive skin contact, wild yeast and fermentation in used barrels.

There are also small but important plantings of other varieties from Gamay and Tempranillo to Albariño and Viognier. The region's diversity and willingness to experiment with new blends will increase, believes Michael Henley, chair of Hawke's Bay Winegrowers: 'We have only had one generation of wine drinkers in New Zealand – my parents' generation. Our generation is more inclined to experiment. When I worked at Trinity Hill, we would always show our Marsanne/Viognier blend, Tempranillo and Syrah [to cellar door visitors]. If wineries are smart they will show we are more than supermarket wine. A wine style or brand starts at home and a rise in tourism [and winery visitors] is going to push this. It's coming but it's just going to take time: we are still a young region.'

PRODUCER PROFILES

Church Road
Taradale
church-road.co.nz

Now owned by French drinks company Pernod Ricard, Church Road can trace its winemaking history back to the late nineteenth century: in 1897, Bartholomew Steinmetz, a former member of the Mission, founded Taradale Vineyards with 2 hectares of land purchased from the Tiffen estate. This is the site we know today as Church Road. Aged fourteen, a young Tom McDonald started working on the vineyard and within five years was left in charge of the estate when Steinmetz returned to Europe. In 1936, after Steinmetz's death, McDonald bought the winery and continued his work. In 1944, McDonald sold the winery but stayed on as winery manager; the winery was now known as McDonald's Wines and, under new ownership, a winery was built on the Church Road site. It was during this time that he pioneered some of New Zealand's earliest commercial Chardonnay and introduced French oak barrel-matured Cabernet Sauvignon, which New Zealand's leading wine writer of the era named 'the finest commercial wine made in my lifetime'. In 1962, Australian wine company McWilliam's acquired McDonald's Wines, injecting capital and know-how. McDonald remained as production manager until retiring in 1975; a year later his contribution to the New Zealand wine industry was recognized, receiving the Order of the British Empire (OBE). His name is also honoured by Church Road's flagship TOM range, which was first produced in 1995. In the late 1980s, Montana (now Brancott Estate, which is owned by Pernod Ricard) entered Hawke's Bay, buying vineyards and the McDonald winery, which would later become known as the Church Road winery. Not only did they acquire property, they also bought into the history of a New Zealand pioneer.

The winery's focus has not shifted from the varieties McDonald championed – Chardonnay, Merlot and Cabernet Sauvignon – but time has brought diversity. The winery offers the drinker a number of tiers. The Church Road range is hugely popular in the domestic market, offering exceptional value for money, the characterful McDonald range includes several interesting varietals such as Verdelho, Sauvignon Gris and Marzemino. Church Road gets really serious when stepping up to the Grand Reserve tier. Both the Grand Reserve and flagship TOM ranges are only made in very good vintages.

Try this: Church Road Grand Reserve Syrah
A rich, fleshy and polished Syrah sourced from Gimblett Gravels. High level of fruit concentration reflects the low yields. It is highly fragrant with blackberry fruit, floral notes and subtle black-pepper notes. In youth, there is a liberal lick of vanilla derived from one-third new French oak barrels. A small proportion of Hungarian oak barrels are also used.

Visit
Church Road's cellar door is open seven days a week with tours running

twice daily. Join the 11 o'clock tour and finish your visit with lunch at the winery restaurant. Visit the website for more details.

Craggy Range
Havelock North
craggyrange.com

Established in the early 1990s by Australian-based American-born entrepreneur Terry Peabody and Master of Wine Steve Smith, the brand's upmarket HQ sits underneath Te Mata Peak in Hawke's Bay (pictured below). While it also owns vineyards in Martinborough and Marlborough, its 'prestige' wines Le Sol Syrah and Sophia (a Bordeaux blend) are the essence of Gimblett Gravels. Its flagship Chardonnay Les Beaux Cailloux ceased production after the 2011 vintage due to leafroll virus, which is a major challenge for this stony subregion of Hawke's Bay. Having been replanted about 100 metres from the original site, its comeback 2016 vintage was released in mid 2018. For a taste of Chardonnay grown by the Hawke's Bay coastline, you can't go wrong with the suave, concentrated yet fresh Kidnappers Vineyard. The winery also has vineyards on Martinborough's Te Muna Road, producing tangy Sauvignon Blanc and suave Pinot Noir (see Chapter 8).

Try this: Craggy Range Sophia

New World wines have been stereotyped as offering sweet fruit but this is broody and complex. Hailing from Gimblett Gravels, this Bordeaux blend offers a richly aromatic nose, full of spice, dark cocoa and fruit cake. Smooth and supple in the mouth, with a taut and dry finish, this is a wine with poise. High levels of fruit concentration indicate low yields and you're left with stone-licking texture from the Gravels.

Visit

The service at Craggy Range's cellar door is as slick and professional as you'll get in Hawke's Bay. Visitors can enjoy four different tasting experiences from $7.50 for four tastings (refunded if wine is purchased) to $60 for the 'Ultimate Prestige Collection' which includes two vintages of its flagship wines: Aroha, Le Sol and Sophia. Booking is required for the fine wine tastings. The winery also has an on-site restaurant, Terroir, which was refurbished in 2018, as well as vineyard cottage accommodation and a four-bedroom luxury lodge overlooking the Tukituki River.

Elephant Hill

Te Awanga
elephanthill.co.nz

This is a relative newcomer to the Bay's winemaking scene, founded in 2003 by a German couple, Reydan and Roger Weiss, who fell in love with the coastal village of Te Awanga and could see the potential for producing wine here. The vineyards are so close to the sea that at high tide anyone with a decent throwing arm could get a stone in the water. The winery is now run by their son, former banker Andreas Weiss. Sitting on the shore of the Pacific, plantings of later-ripening varieties have been pulled up and the site now excels at restrained and almost salty Sauvignon Blanc and citrus-fresh, barrel-fermented Chardonnay. The estate includes vineyards in Gimblett Gravels and the Bridge Pa Triangle, which are crucial to the complexity of its spicy, savoury Syrahs.

Try this: Elephant Hill Salomé Chardonnay

The year 2016 marked the inaugural vintage of this Chardonnay in its 'Icon' range. Cropped at only one kilo to the vine, there are very few cases made but it produces a wine with a high level of fruit concentration while remaining delicate. Taut and fresh with mouthwatering acidity, the classy nutty new French oak is well handled.

Visit

The modern, sleek cellar door is open seven days a week from 11 a.m. with a $5 charge redeemable against any purchase. It's worth putting a few hours aside to have lunch in the stylish modern restaurant, which serves up some of the best views and finest food in the region. In 2018, the winery also opened up a luxury lodge above the winery which enjoys uninterrupted views over the vines across the Pacific Ocean and out to Cape Kidnappers. It can accommodate up to eight people and boasts an impressive array of artwork collected by co-founder Reydan Weiss, Philippe Starck-designed furniture, a 20-metre private pool, use of a Range Rover, and a private tour and tasting, among other things.

Esk Valley

Esk Valley
eskvalley.co.nz

Founded by Englishman Robert Bird in 1933, the site of Glenvale Winery & Cellars sits in a sheltered spot, 10 kilometres north of Napier. It's impossible to miss – the historic whitewashed buildings stand bright against the green vines and deep blue New Zealand sky. Having catered to the demand for popular fortified styles until the 1970s, Glenvale moved to table wines labelling its wines Esk Valley, a valley to the north where it nurtured most of its grapes. However, financial difficulties led to receivership in 1980 and, in 1986, George Fistonich of Villa Maria purchased the winery and vineyards. While the winemaking has since become more high-tech, there's a focus on traditional methods and original concrete fermentation vats are still used for its reds. The brand's most interesting vineyard site is its home block The Terraces, which was originally planted in 1940 and given a new lease of life in 1989. The configuration of this 1-hectare block is Douro Valley-like although the varieties planted – Malbec, Merlot and Cabernet Franc – are not. This red spends up to two years in barrel before being sold *en primeur*. Esk Valley also sources grapes from its vineyards in Gimblett Gravels, which are used for its Winemakers Reserve range of red wines – also fermented in the open-top concrete tanks. The winery also produces an entry-level Esk Valley range which sources fruit from both Hawke's Bay and Marlborough.

Try this: Esk Valley Verdelho

The first Verdelho vines to be planted in New Zealand since the 1890s produce a dry, weighty style with lots of tangy citrus fruit flavours and a streak of minerally acidity. While the rest of the country hasn't followed suit (there are just 7 hectares nationwide), it is a delightful wine to enjoy for its vibrancy – and its rarity value.

Visit

The cellar shop is open seven days a week from 10 a.m. to 4.30 p.m. Tours can be arranged by appointment.

Sacred Hill

Dartmoor Valley
sacredhill.com

Sheep-farming brothers David and Mark Mason with friend and winemaker Tony Bish founded Sacred Hill in 1986, with the simple philosophy of 'making more wine than they could drink and sharing the rest'. The sheep were shipped out and a fruit salad of vines planted on their farm high up in the Dartmoor Valley. By the mid-1990s, it was clear that Chardonnay was the star of the show: the Rifleman's Vineyard is considered one of New Zealand's finest Chardonnay sites. The secret ingredients are Mendoza-clone Chardonnay vines planted on their own roots in 1988 on soils made up of 10,000-year-old volcanic ash and deep red metals overlaying limestone, at around 100 metres altitude. The winemaking is hands off: the must is settled for a short period before wild yeasts are allowed to do their own thing on the cloudy juice in French oak barrels. At the turn of the century, Sacred Hill ventured into the Gimblett Gravels and it is here, on the former riverbed of the Ngaruroro River, that its flagship reds are produced including the rich yet elegant Deerstalkers Syrah, and two Bordeaux blends: Helmsman is a Pauillac-like Cabernet-dominant blend while Brokenstone is a more supple Merlot-led style for earlier drinking. The winery has also acquired significant holdings in Marlborough.

Try this: Sacred Hill Deerstalkers Syrah

In order to buy this piece of land in Gimblett Gravels, Sacred Hill had to relocate and rebuild the clubhouse of the then owners: the local deerstalkers' association. They now have an all-singing, all-dancing

HQ and the land's bony soil has produced a rich and polished Syrah with a high level of concentration and poise, mellow and balanced with a peppery character over the pure blackberry fruit. It has fine chalky tannins with a burst of acid freshness on the clean, long finish.

Visit
The cellar door is open for a series of summer events only. Visit the website for more details.

Supernatural Wine Co.
Te Awanga
millarroad.co.nz

Former City banker Greg Collinge and winemaker Hayden Penny have shunned convention in Hawke's Bay to focus on Sauvignon Blanc and Pinot Gris that are grown organically, and in the winery there's a low-intervention, low-sulphur approach. First planted in 2004 on a hillside overlooking the Pacific Ocean, there are now 7 or 8 hectares of Sauvignon Blanc (depending on whether you ask Collinge or Penny) and 0.8 hectare of Pinot Gris which produce an array of unorthodox wines sporting craft-beer-esque labels, topped with a crown seal. Expect the unexpected when you open the bottles – they have probably been fermented wild and on their skins, undergone full malolactic fermentation and been bottled unfined, unfiltered and unsulphured. There's also a *pétillant naturel*. Good on them for daring to be different.

Try this: Supernatural Wine Co. Green Glow Sauvignon Blanc
Destemmed without crushing, leaving whole berries in the ferment. This mid-gold wine spends two weeks on skins, goes through full malolactic conversion and spends six months on lees before being bottled unfined and unfiltered. The result is a rich, full-bodied and phenolic off-the-wall Sauvignon Blanc that's more about texture than aromatics. Bone dry with intense nutty and grassy flavours. And the label glows in the dark.

Visit
Tasting is by appointment only.

Te Awanga Estate
Te Awanga
teawangaestate.co.nz

From the 2018 vintage, the Rod McDonald Wines label became known as Te Awanga Estate. The man behind the Syrah which won the title of best red in show at the 2017 edition of the International Wine Challenge (IWC), and who drives a temperamental 45-year-old white Mercedes to work, has steadily built up his holdings across Hawke's Bay after leaving Vidal in 2006. The 20-hectare Te Awanga home block sits less than 500 metres from the Pacific Ocean, making elegant Syrah and creamy Chardonnay. The fruit for his Quarter Acre range (the label behind the IWC-winning Syrah) is sourced from small parcels dotted around Hawke's Bay and the fermentations are all indigenous, which McDonald uses across all of his wines. There's also a shift to organic practices with half of the vineyards already certified organic and the balance in transition. His most serious wines are bottled under the Trademark label while the One Off range is self-explanatory.

Try this: Rod McDonald Trademark Syrah
A youthful wine with time on its side, it offers pure blackberry essence and fine stone-licking tannins. While it is super chewy, there is plenty of concentration in the mid palate and the fresh acidity pulls the wine like a needle with a thread, providing a fine, lingering finish.

Visit
The unpretentious cellar door, within spitting distance of the Pacific Ocean, is open Wednesday to Sunday from 11 a.m. to 5 p.m., increasing to seven days a week during the summer months (January to March). In addition to tasting the full range of wines, there are pizzas, platters and other bowls of goodness to be devoured. Once a month, you're encouraged to down tools and spend a lazy Sunday afternoon on the lawn listening to live music. Dog lovers should watch out for McDonald's Border terrier, Cricket, chasing rabbits through the vines.

Te Mata Estate
Havelock North
temata.co.nz

New Zealand's oldest winery buildings belong to Te Mata and sit in the Havelock Hills. This is home to Coleraine, New Zealand's closest thing to a Bordeaux classed growth. First planted by Bernard Chambers in 1892, Te Mata has been operating continuously since then although it took the efforts of John Buck, a New Zealander who cut his teeth in the London and Bordeaux wine trade, to revive the winery's fortunes. Having sold his wine shops in Wellington, Buck was able to buy the winery in 1974. The vineyards were in disarray and needed to be replanted, while winery buildings were renovated and re-equipped. It was clear from the early 1980s that the estate was going to excel at Bordeaux blends – Coleraine and its more affordable sibling Awatea are considered two of New Zealand's finest examples. Since then, it has expanded its Hawke's Bay holdings to the Bridge Pa Triangle, the home of its fine Syrah, Bullnose. In 1994, it ventured further north to the Dartmoor Valley and planted Woodthorpe Terraces, which is home to its joyous single vineyard Gamay and citrussy Viognier, as well as its largest plantings of Merlot, Syrah, Chardonnay and Sauvignon Blanc. Buck has now retired and passed the Te Mata reins to his sons Nick (CEO), Jonathan (vineyard manager, Woodthorpe) and Toby, sales and marketing manager.

Try this: Te Mata Estate Coleraine

At the risk of this being a cliché, this Coleraine would give Bordeaux's best a run for their money. It is a powerful and intense wine yet remains elegant and precise. Richly aromatic, giving ripe, black fruit and an attractive herbal note. Densely fruited on the mid palate followed up with abundant sinewy tannins. There's lots of new French oak used in the making of this wine, but it's integrated, adding Christmas spices to the mix.

Visit

The cellar door is open every day in summer from 10 a.m. to 5 p.m. (Sunday, 11 a.m. to 4 p.m.) and Monday to Saturday in winter (10 a.m. to 5 p.m.). Bookings for private tours and tastings must be made at least twenty-four hours in advance. Visit the website for more details.

Trinity Hill

Roys Hill
trinityhill.com

Founded in 1993 by cricket-mad Australian John Hancock and the London-based Kiwi owners of Bleeding Heart restaurant, Trinity Hill has become even more international since Charles Banks's management company took a stake in the business. Despite going through a period of upheaval in 2017 – which saw the imprisonment of Banks for fraud, and the departure of both Hancock and its CEO Michael Henley – Trinity Hill's vines and wines are oblivious to the turbulence. Based in Gimblett Gravels from day one, its flagship Syrah, Homage, was first made in 2002 and is only made when the quality is deemed sufficiently high; it is consistently one of New Zealand's finest Syrahs. Its premium Gimblett Gravels range offers plenty to keep wine lovers interested, from Hawke's Bay's signature Syrah style to The Gimblett, a classically fashioned Bordeaux blend. There's also a bit of alternative fun to be had with a voluptuous Marsanne/Viognier blend, a fleshy Tempranillo and an Italian-inspired Montepulciano.

Try this: Trinity Hill Homage Syrah
The flagship Syrah from Trinity Hill keeps on getting better and better. It is very fine and elegant, offering incredible intensity with an almost weightless appeal. An increasing proportion of whole-bunch fermentation has introduced lifted blue and black fruit aromatics, and spice. With abundant tannins and plentiful freshness this wine offers appeal in youth and over the medium- to long-term.

Visit
The cellar door is open seven days a week, from 10 a.m. to 5 p.m.

Vidal Estate
Hastings
vidal.co.nz

In 1888, Spaniard Anthony Joseph Vidal joined his winemaking uncle in Wanganui before moving to Hastings in Hawke's Bay. He bought a racing stable with just over an acre of land in 1905, turning the stables into a cellar to make wine. Vidal Estate was born. Focusing on fortified wines to meet market demand, his sons took over the business upon his death in 1933. After spending a short time in the hands of Australian-based Seppelt in the early 1970s, Villa Maria purchased the winery in 1976 and reinvigorated the brand. Just three years later, to much fanfare, it became the first New Zealand winery to have a restaurant on site. Vidal's strongest suit is barrel-fermented Chardonnay, inky Syrah and richly fruited Merlot/Cabernet blends. Its Legacy Chardonnay is a Marmite wine: some say it is one of the finest Chardonnays in the world, others feel it is too reductive. Having tasted older examples, the struck-match character wanes with bottle age, leaving a powerful, citrussy wine. In warm, dry seasons, the Legacy reds are perfumed, polished and sumptuous. If you don't have a racehorse owner's budget, however, the Reserve tier offers a more affordable snapshot of Gimblett Gravels reds. Vidal has also introduced Marlborough whites and Pinot Noir to its portfolio.

Try this: Vidal Legacy Syrah
In a dry, warm year, this Syrah is ripe and voluptuous in its youth with plenty of rich red and black fruit on the mid palate. Extraction is always judicious and low yields are reflected in the superb concentration. One for the cellar.

Visit
New Zealand's first winery restaurant is still in operation for lunch and dinner. The on-site cellar door is open Monday to Saturday, 10 a.m. to 5 p.m.

8

WAIRARAPA

'Pinot Noir was my favourite variety but La Tâche was not for sale and no one from Musigny called me. It was pretty clear that to get started in wine we would have to go to the New World. We went to all of the wine regions in New Zealand but we always came back to Martinborough – we fell in love with the place.'

Kai Schubert, Schubert Wines

In the late 1990s, the lure of Martinborough's savoury, textural Pinot Noirs and the sprouting of a wine community in this town were too hard to resist for German oenologist Kai Schubert and his partner Marion Deimling. If he had toured New Zealand two decades earlier, there would have been little to attract an ambitious winemaker from the other side of the world to this area. Martinborough was a small sheep-farming town that was in decline in the 1970s and its future looked bleak. It was established in 1879 by an immigrant from Northern Ireland, John Martin, who made his fortune in the Central Otago gold rush – but a hundred years later the town needed a new lease of life. In a bid to reinvigorate its fortunes, the Martinborough Borough Council called a seminar to explore the prospects for horticulture in the area.

Grapes weren't front of mind at that meeting although a book publisher, Alister Taylor, had already planted wine grapes, including Chardonnay and Gewürztraminer, as well as citrus and fruit trees on his Martinborough property. However, one of the attendees, Derek Milne, a soil scientist working for the now-defunct government-run Department of Scientific and Industrial Research (DSIR), wondered why grapes weren't getting much airtime. He was a wine lover and having compiled a comprehensive analysis of New Zealand's climate and soils, he concluded that Martinborough, as well as Marlborough and Waipara, were perfectly suited to viticulture. Fellow DSIR scientist Dr Neil McCallum took the plunge in 1979, planting grapes on Puruatanga Road, an avenue that is now lined with some of New Zealand's finest Pinot Noir vineyards (as well as being home to the local cemetery). Following McCallum's lead, Milne put his money where his report was and planted what would become Martinborough Vineyard; Ata Rangi and Chiffney (now Margrain) soon followed. When Martinborough Vineyard hired the first professional winemaker, Australian Larry McKenna, in 1986, it was a very different town to modern-day Martinborough. 'It was a country town in decline,' recalls McKenna. 'There were no cafes, no hipsters; there were two fish and chip shops and a pub. Today, it is quite the tourist destination for Wellingtonians.'

Martinborough now thrives off winegrowing 'and its spinoffs', according to a short history of the town, *The Look of Martinborough*. The book recounts a story of an American wine writer who was due to visit Ata Rangi in 1991 but there was nowhere decent for him to stay. A local couple opened their home to save the visitor from a low-grade motel or a basic hotel. How times change: there are now more than a dozen bed and breakfast options, two hotels and as many as a hundred cottages for rent; good luck trying to find a bed during Toast Martinborough, though. Since 1991, the town of 1,300 residents has steeled itself for an annual 8,000-strong crowd descending on its wineries every November to taste Riesling, Pinot Noir and Syrah followed by some wine-fuelled dancing. It is not uncommon for tickets to sell out in fifteen minutes and the event generates around $1.6 million.

Since the release of McCallum's first wine in 1984, Martinborough has swelled to more than forty wineries covering almost 700 hectares. However, the vinous history of the Wairarapa began long before its soil scientist pioneers were born. In 1883, wealthy landowner William Beetham and his French wife Marie Zelie Hermance Frere planted vines on their land – including Pinot Noir, a wine that was exhibited in Paris in 1897. During his tour of New Zealand in 1895, Romeo Bragato visited Beetham's 1.6 hectares of vineyard at Lansdowne Station and tasted a six-year-old Hermitage (Syrah) of 'prime quality'. In his

Report on the Prospects of Viticulture in New Zealand, Bragato predicted that both Wairarapa and Hawke's Bay would one day be 'studded with vineyards'. The rise of temperance put paid to Bragato and Beetham's ambitions for New Zealand wine and the vineyards of the Wairarapa. The Masterton district voted to go 'dry' in 1909 and this marked the end of Wairarapa's vineyards – and its fifteen pubs – until liquor licences were restored in 1946. William Beetham and his wife did not live to see the revival of the region's vineyards but their influence in the restoration of viticulture lived on: Derek Milne, the author of the report sparking the first planting in Martinborough – in 1979 – married William and Marie Zelie's great-great-niece. In New Zealand there is no such thing as six degrees of separation – two will do. It is fitting that the winery Milne founded, Martinborough Vineyard, has named its top Pinot Noir in honour of the Frenchwoman.

GEOGRAPHY AND CLIMATE

'This is an extreme environment,' says Lance Redgwell, the founder of Cambridge Road Vineyard. It's difficult to imagine the havoc the elements inflict on Martinborough on a balmy summer's day, as we hop across an unimposing fence that separates his vineyard from Ata Rangi, but 'the wind is tumultuous'. And, if you look carefully at the trees in the area, they do sport a comb-over appearance from the constant onslaught of the wind. 'The weather wants to push [the vines] down like a set of dominoes. When the wind hits extreme velocity – say 120 kilometres an hour – it can snap the shoots off,' explains Redgwell. In such a gusty climate, it's not uncommon to see shoots clipped to the fruiting wires like a pair of underpants pegged to a washing line.

Sitting at the bottom of New Zealand's North Island, there's no getting away from the wind. The Aorangi Mountains provide some natural protection from the cold southerly winds whistling their way up off the sea. Rows of trees, known as shelter belts, are a common sight between vineyards in Martinborough in a bid to reduce the ferocity of gusts. However, as the dossier containing Martinborough's application for a Geographical Indication (GI) evidences, the mountains to the east and west act 'as a wind funnel from the notoriously windy Cook Strait'. The Martinborough GI is the closest in Wairarapa to the coast, and among the windiest in the country. The spring winds are often cold and this affects flowering, reducing yields and creating fewer berries in a bunch. As a result, bunch weights in Martinborough are significantly lower than, say, across the Cook Strait in the more sheltered Marlborough region. Producers across Wairarapa talk of small berries and unusually thick grape skins, which give greater colour and tannic structure to their savoury Pinots.

It's not only the southerly winds that have growers on edge during the spring. Frost likes to pay regular visits to the region. In November 2006, Hiroyuki Kusuda, a rugby-loving Japanese wine producer making tiny quantities of painstakingly selected fruit, lost 80 per cent of his Syrah crop to the frost and he wasn't alone. Frost wiped out chunks of the region's fledgling crop. Dutchman Wilco Lam, the winemaker at Dry River in 2010, was working at Alana Estate in 2006: 'Everyone was screwed by the frost and they said we are not going to take this any longer. Everyone started putting wind machines in. That has kept yields economical although 6 to 8 tonnes is a lot around here. Prior to that it was unbelievable how people survived.' Frosts still visit the vineyards of the Wairarapa but the damage inflicted has been minimized by the frost-fighting measures adopted.

As spring turns to summer, the Wairarapa generally enjoys high sunshine hours (2,035 hours annually) and warm days (the mean maximum temperature during the growing season is 16.4°C and it has 1,280 growing degree days). It remains the coolest and driest wine region in the North Island but does have an advantage over its more northerly compatriots: the Aorangis to the east offer shelter from harvest rainfall while the Rimutaka and Tararua Ranges to the west act as a rain shadow. The Wairarapa has a moderate annual rainfall (755 mm annually compared with 690 mm in Dijon, Burgundy and 850 mm in Bordeaux). However, long dry spells and low humidity combined with warm norwesterlies mean that irrigation is common in the region, particularly on free-draining alluvial sites.

Despite the warmth of summer, you'll need to pack a jumper at night, as the area experiences a generous diurnal temperature range. It is not uncommon to have a daytime temperature approaching 25 to 30°C, falling to 10°C at night. These differences are not as marked as, say, in Central Otago but it is still chilly, explains Schubert: 'Martinborough is not the ideal barbecue climate: once the sun drops, that's it. It's bloody cold but that keeps the acidity and the fruitiness.' The cooler night-time temperatures also help to extend the growing season and imbue its Pinot Noirs with greater aromatic expression and deeper colour. When harvest finally arrives, the weather tends to be more settled – that's why the Wairarapa hot air balloon festival takes place as autumn descends and the gusts of spring have lost their puff.

BEYOND MARTINBOROUGH

Gladstone is a twenty-five minute drive north-east of Martinborough and en route you can visit one of the local tourist attractions: Stonehenge Aotearoa, a full-scale adaptation of the real stone circle in southern England. Keep your eyes peeled for Gladstone; you might miss it if you blink. There are no hotels, coffee shops or antiques dealers here, unlike Martinborough. Instead there's an isolated pub affectionately known as The Gladdy and a meat-processing works called Cabernet Meats. You couldn't make this stuff up. Paddy Borthwick, the raconteur behind the eponymous label, explains that this is sheep and beef farming territory. He'd know: not only does he make wine in Gladstone, the family's 1,600-hectare property Te Whanga Station is home to 7,000 Angus stud cattle and 10,000 sheep, and he comes from a long line of ambitious butchers. Borthwick expanded the family's interests to wine in the 1990s and you'll find his vineyard and winery on Dakins Road, which is the focal point for wine producers in Gladstone. Here you'll find other brands like Johner and Urlar, as well as Martinborough-based Schubert's main vineyard holdings: Block B was the source of fruit for Schubert's wine, which won the International Pinot Noir trophy at the Decanter World Wine Awards in 2010, beating Pinots from nineteen other countries.

Climatically, there is little difference between Martinborough and Gladstone (and Masterton). Heading north from Martinborough, the vineyards are similarly affected by the southerlies in spring, lowering yields, and the drying norwesters in summer. There are minor differences: further inland, the maximum daytime temperatures might be marginally higher and the night-time low marginally lower, giving a greater diurnal temperature range. There is also a slightly higher frost risk during the growing season – frost fans line Dakins Road – and there's a little more rainfall in Gladstone and Masterton than Martinborough. Jon McNab of Gladstone-based Fairmount Estate admits: 'There's not a lot of difference climatically between the sub-regions. We normally have a cool spring, hot and dry summer, and long dry autumn.'

When it comes to soil types across the region, McNab adds: 'The soils are very similar: free draining, alluvial on the old river bed, low-lying generally.' The river responsible for leaving these deep alluvial river terraces eminently suited to wine production across the Wairarapa is the Ruamahanga. It has etched a course towards Palliser Bay, leaving behind striking cliffs, escarpments – and river gravels. Vines across the region are planted on free-draining river terraces covered by silt loam and, depending on site, wind-blown loess. A tributary of the Ruamahanga, the Huangarua River runs almost parallel to the vine-laden Puruatanga Road in Martinborough – originally known as the Martinborough Terrace – and is also responsible for the Te Muna alluvial terraces upon which Craggy Range and Escarpment Vineyard produce deeply coloured, nuanced Pinot Noir. Larry McKenna, co-founder of Escarpment, explains: 'We are all here for the alluvial gravel terraces. We prize the free-draining warm soils.'

In short, Wairarapa is a theme on river gravels. There are variations on a theme, of course. Upstream in Gladstone, the river gravels are larger than those found in Martinborough, which is said to affect the texture of the wines. The boniest, stoniest soils across the region are the most free draining and warm up quickly whereas those sites sporting deeper levels of wind-blown loess have a greater water-holding capacity and take longer to warm up during the day, slowing ripening. Clay can be found, if you go looking, and there's even a lime quarry on Dry River Road (but you won't find Dry River Wines here, which has confused many a tourist), suggesting there are myriad possibilities in the future.

CHAMPIONING THE WAIRARAPA

Gaining recognition for Wairarapa wines is difficult. Wairarapa isn't easy to get your head – or tongue – around. To make it even more complicated for non-New Zealanders, they throw in another wine producing region with almost the same letters – Waipara. And then there's Waiheke and Waitaki ('wai' means water in Māori). Even Kiwis are confused. Paul Mason, the winemaker at Martinborough Vineyards since 2007, admits: 'When I grew up in Auckland, I didn't know where Wairarapa was!'

The size of the Wairarapa winegrowing region doesn't help in its bid for global recognition. Its vineyards account for 3 per cent of the country's plantings but it produces just 1 per cent of the country's wine. The region's low yields – an average of 5 tonnes per hectare – mean this is not a place to make entry-level Sauvignon Blanc. As a result, multinational wine companies and their demanding shareholders have stayed away. You won't find Constellation or Pernod Ricard executives swanning around town; this is a place of small-volume, quality-oriented producers. Ata Rangi's winemaker, Helen Masters, explains: 'The same person who makes the wine sells the wine. It's not as flash as other regions because it doesn't have the scale.' But that small scale also means you're likely to meet the owner when you drop in to taste their wines.

WINE STYLES

Despite its small size and negligible marketing budget Martinborough, in particular, has become synonymous with fine Pinot Noir within the global wine community. The region had been on the radar of diplomat turned Martinborough winemaker Hiroyuki Kusuda from his initial taste of its wines while working for the Japanese consulate in Sydney: 'It was the first wine from outside Burgundy that made me think "I smell Pinot", so the name Martinborough was firmly in my head ... but it's still little known apart from among Pinotphiles.' The area's unique conditions contribute to its quality and style: the windy environment and consequent low yields and small berries are conducive to high levels of colour, structure and concentration. Its cool and long growing season, and the marked shift in day and night-time temperatures, develops fruit intensity while retaining vibrant acidity. While there are some fruity examples for drinking in their youth, most wineries in Martinborough aim to produce a Pinot Noir that benefits from maturation in bottle.

Producers aim to reflect their place – Escarpment, for example, releases four single vineyard Pinot Noirs from Martinborough. Nevertheless, there are winemaking choices that differ from producer to producer, creating a stylistic interpretation of place. Kusuda, for example, selects the fruit for his wines berry by berry. There are no stems in the ferment, whereas less than five minutes down the road at Escarpment, McKenna isn't afraid of stems – in a good year, the ferment might contain 50 to 60 per cent of whole bunches. Dry River doesn't practise post-fermentation maceration, pressing its Pinot Noir as soon as the wine to avoid any harsh extraction. Nor does it rack once in barrel in a bid to exclude oxygen during maturation and imbue the wine with extra longevity. Meanwhile, at Cambridge Road, Redgwell is a proponent of making wine as naturally as possible – and breaking the rules. Don't expect his wines to be fined, filtered nor any sulphur added, and if the mood takes him, he might blend his Pinot Noir with Syrah or even Riesling.

While Pinot Noir is the region's signature variety and represents around 50 per cent of plantings, it isn't all red: around a third of the vines in Wairarapa are Sauvignon Blanc. While it's 130 kilometres between Martinborough and Blenheim in Marlborough, as the crow flies, and the vines have their feet in former riverbeds on both sides of the Cook Strait, Wairarapa's expression of Sauvignon Blanc differs in its aromatic profile. Say goodbye to the exuberant tropical fruit of Marlborough and say hello to its purity of grassy, gooseberry and citrus-fruit aromas. The style is comparatively restrained and generally offers a high level of concentration with firm but balanced acidity. Winemakers experiment with a number of techniques to add aromatic and textural interest such as wild yeast, skin contact, barrel fermentation and lees stirring.

Sauvignon Blanc doesn't have a monopoly on Wairarapa whites, however. Some of the country's finest Chardonnay is made here, typically from the Mendoza clone. The wines reflect their place – the Wairarapa winds contribute to low yielding, richly concentrated grapes while the long, cool growing seasons and significant diurnal temperature swings deliver Chardonnays that offer cooler climate aromas of nectarine, apple and citrus fruit. The Mendoza clone typically displays hen and chicken – a condition leading to variable berry size on the same bunch. This gives an inimitable diversity of ripe and less ripe characters in a wine, as well as a streak of scintillating acidity. Ambitious Wairarapa winemakers commonly employ techniques including whole-bunch pressing, barrel fermentation in French oak, malolactic fermentation and lees contact to bring texture, structure and complexity.

Pinot Gris plantings now outweigh Chardonnay and Riesling. The wine style varies from producer to producer but Wairarapa's long and cool season imbues this typically low-acid style with a welcome burst of freshness. The region's best producers do a very respectable job in delivering a pure, varietally classic expression, adding interest with indigenous yeast fermentation and different fermentation vessels. Nevertheless, it pains me that Pinot Gris covers twice as much land as Riesling in Wairarapa. The best Rieslings are dry, steely and taut with piercing aromas that slice through the air. The variety's naturally high levels of acidity and purity of fragrance are retained in this cool, dry climate. There are also very successful off-dry and sweet styles but the region's naturally low humidity means botrytis is uncommon. Winemakers keep it simple in the winery to maintain its purity.

Syrah is a minority sport in the Wairarapa – it accounts for just 1 per cent of the region's vines but it cannot be ignored: this red variety produces an idiosyncratic style at the bottom of the North Island and it has won over many fans at home and abroad with its highly spiced nose, savoury complexity and softly textured yet elegant mouthfeel. However, those who give Syrah a go here should be prepared to have their nerves shot. A month after the Pinot Noir has been harvested, the Syrah finally ripens – or not. This means stable autumn weather is a crucial factor in the success of Syrah and, as the grape skins start to soften on the vine in late April, there is a fine line between greatness and garbage. Somewhat ironically, Syrah is vigorous and needs to have some serious crop thinning to get over the finish line even in this windy, typically low-yielding region.

PRODUCER PROFILES

Ata Rangi
Martinborough
atarangi.co.nz

Following the publication of Derek Milne's report identifying Martinborough's suitability for wine, single dad Clive Paton sold his milking cows and in 1980 bought a piece of gravelly land. He started planting vines as one of the pioneers of the area, and won his first gold medal for Pinot Noir in 1986. Clive's sister Alison bought an adjoining piece of land in 1982 and his wife Phyll joined the business in 1987. Since then, Ata Rangi has established its name as one of New Zealand's finest Pinot Noir producers. The Ata Rangi Pinot Noir is always elegant with finely textured tannins and cool acidity. It shows a high level of damson-like fruit concentration and a savoury twist. Always complex and long, it is a pleasure to drink and worthy of cellaring for eight to ten years, and more. It is interesting to compare the Ata Rangi Pinot Noir with the McCrone single vineyard expression. The McCrone site nearby has a higher proportion of clay, making for a richer, rounder expression with an abundance of mouth-coating tannin. In the white department, the Craighall vineyard, which is literally across the road from the Ata Rangi home block, produces a richly fruited, nutty Mendoza-clone Chardonnay that's never short on mouth-watering acidity. It's also worth seeking out the Riesling, Pinot Gris and Sauvignon Blanc.

Try this: Ata Rangi Pinot Noir
Scented and lifted, this shows both intensity with delicacy. The texture is smooth and supple. The flavours are complex and nuanced with spice and florals, making for a beautiful wine that you want to sink into. Tight and finely pixellated tannins lead to a long, drawn-out finish.

Visit
Information on booking for the twice-daily tastings at Ata Rangi's cellar door can be found on its website.

Above: First planted in 2007, The Landing in Northland's Bay of Islands lies adjacent to the site where Samuel Marsden, the missionary who planted New Zealand's first grapevines, in 1819, held the country's first Christian service.

Below: In an amphitheatre on Waiheke Island, a short ferry ride from Auckland CBD, Destiny Bay specializes in premium Bordeaux blends.

Above: Home to 40 donkeys, 1,500 kiwis and several vineyards, ripe grapes from Ponui Island have to be transported by barge to Man O'War's winery on Waiheke Island.

Below: On the east coast of the North Island, Gisborne enjoys a warm, sunny and sometimes humid climate. Gewürztraminer has long been at home in its fertile soils and Vinoptima's vineyards have been the source of some of its finest cuvées.

Above: Sacred Hill's Rifleman's Vineyard sits on white cliffs overlooking the Tutaekuri River. The Chardonnay vines that make its flagship Chardonnay were planted on their own roots in 1988.

Below: Te Mata Peak's imposing form and distinctive ridge tower above the Hawke's Bay landscape, affording panoramic views across the region, including the Tukituki River.

Above: Following veraison, nets are a common sight across New Zealand, as grape growers attempt to thwart hungry birds keen to eat their ripening crop. Palliser in Martinborough (pictured) specializes in Sauvignon Blanc, Chardonnay and Pinot Noir.

Below: Escarpment Vineyard sits on Te Muna Road, which is slightly higher, more exposed and cooler than sites in Martinborough township. The risks are high but the rewards can be great.

Above: In the vineyards of Cloudy Bay, one of Marlborough's most famous wine producers, the Pinot Noir harvest is in full swing. Founded in 1985 by David Hohnen, the winery now belongs to the wine arm of luxury goods empire LVMH.

Below: The Croation founders of Brancott Estate, formerly known as Montana Wines, planted the first vines in Marlborough in 1973. Sauvignon Blanc took root in 1975.

Above: Aromatic white wines thrive on Nelson's Waimea Plains, close to the waters of Tasman Bay. The sea acts as a moderating force in Nelson, reducing temperature extremes during both day and night.

Below: Neudorf Vineyards is nestled in the rolling Moutere Hills, where clay-gravel soils enable viticulturists to dry farm. Taken from Rosie's Block, this photograph shows the original vineyard in full autumn glory, the bucolic cellar door and the winery.

Above: Planted on its own roots, Black Estate's Home Vineyard is now overlooked by one of New Zealand's most acclaimed vineyard restaurants. The winery's star has risen since moving to new ownership in 2007.

Below: In the Omihi area of Waipara Valley, North Canterbury, Greystone makes acclaimed aromatic whites, Chardonnay and Pinot Noir on hillside sites.

Above: One of Waitaki's pioneering wine producers, Ostler, has vineyards across the valley. This vineyard overlooking Lake Waitaki is 30 kilometres further inland than its original site 'Clos Ostler', which means it is warmer and ripens more reliably.

Below: The vines hugging the slopes of Rocky Point Vineyard look across Lake Dunstan toward the snow-capped Pisa range. This is winemaking on the edge: Central Otago is the most southerly wine region in the world, sitting at a latitude of 45°S.

Cambridge Road Vineyard

Martinborough
cambridgeroad.co.nz

The ability to buy a mature vineyard next door to Ata Rangi lured winemaker Lance Redgwell to Martinborough in late 2006. Buying a vineyard that was first planted in 1986 and was farmed organically, Redgwell has since adopted biodynamic practices. While he specializes in Pinot Noir and Syrah, he also makes more edgy wines including whites that don't shy from skin contact, left of centre blends, and two no-added-sulphite *pétillant naturel* cuvées under crown cap. He has a no fining, no filtration policy for all wines.

Try this: Cambridge Road Estate Pinot Noir

An unadulterated, unfined, unfiltered Pinot Noir with incredible fruit concentration, layer upon layer of spicy complexity and structure. Requires a patient owner who is prepared to let it shake off its youthful audacity.

Visit

The cellar door is open weekdays from 11 a.m. in summer; during the winter, it is open at weekends from 11 a.m., and weekdays by appointment only.

Craggy Range

Martinborough/Hawke's Bay
craggyrange.com

While Craggy's headquarters is in Hawke's Bay, it has become a major producer of fine Martinborough wine. At the end of 2017, it purchased an additional 100 hectares in Te Muna, which will make it the biggest vineyard owner in Wairarapa. While the Te Muna vineyard (pictured overleaf) is predominantly Pinot Noir and Sauvignon Blanc, it also makes an Alsatian field blend, Te Muna Four, which is made in tiny quantities and is vintage dependent but worth seeking out for its intrigue.

Try this: Craggy Range Aroha Te Muna Vineyard Pinot Noir

Sumptuous and svelte, this is always a gorgeously textured Pinot Noir. Broody and concentrated, there is a high proportion of whole-bunch fermentation bringing florals, spice and a fine line that zips this wine into a focused finish.

Visit
There is no Craggy Range cellar door in Martinborough. Tastings are held at its Giants Winery, on the outskirts of Havelock North, Hawke's Bay.

Dry River Wines
Martinborough
dryriver.co.nz

The first vineyard to be planted in Martinborough in 1979. Inspired by fellow soil scientist Derek Milne's report, which extolled the virtues of Martinborough as a wine-producing area, Dr Neil McCallum took the plunge and planted what would become Dry River Wines. Since 2003, the vineyard has been owned by New York financier and philanthropist Julian Robertson, the man behind New Zealand's most exclusive golf resorts Cape Kidnappers and Kauri Cliffs. It aims to be certified organic by 2019. In the vineyard, there is an extreme leaf-plucking regime: you won't find a leaf shading the swelling fruit. The aim is for both higher and riper phenolics, while in the winery there is no post-fermentation maceration. 'We'd rather not have long fermentation on reds for the extraction of tannins from seeds and stems because those are not the phenolics that we are after. We are trying to extract real gentle phenolics that have developed in the vineyard,' explains Wilco Lam, Dry River's Dutch winemaker. There is also no racking to avoid oxidation during its maturation in French oak barrels with the aim of creating a long-lived wine. In addition to Pinot Noir, Dry River is one of the handful of Martinborough locals making Syrah in a spicy, personality-filled yet light-bodied style. The dry Craighall Riesling (it often has 5 to 6 grams per litre of residual sugar but combined with high acidity, gives the impression of dryness) offers a delicate, citrus and floral expression with a linear finish. It can be enjoyed in its youth but having tasted a 20-year-old example, age brings beauty.

Try this: Dry River Pinot Noir
Dry River's Pinot is a blend of three blocks, which each bring their own personality. For example, the Craighall vineyard tends to give a more structured and dense expression than other parcels. It offers up generous fruit (for Martinborough) and the whole bunch component brings spicy, smoked charcuterie, with firm acidity and a taut tannic structure on the tea-leaf-like finish. This is a wine that is enjoyable young but deserves a place in the cellar for ten years and more.

Visit
There's no cellar door at Dry River and visits are by appointment only.

Escarpment Vineyard
Martinborough
escarpment.co.nz

Founded by the Kirby family and the McKennas in 1998, Escarpment was purchased in early 2018 by Australian winery Torbreck Wines, whose owner is American tech billionaire Peter Kight. It has always been a champion of the Te Muna Road area of Martinborough with 19 hectares under vine. Pinot Noir represents around 70 per cent of the vineyard with Pinot Gris, Chardonnay, Pinot Blanc and Riesling making up the remainder. Te Muna is higher, more exposed and marginally cooler than vineyards 'in town'. This means frosts can be harder, winds can be stronger and ripening can be later – but there are always seasons that are exceptions to the rule. Escarpment produces Pinot Noir with a high proportion of whole bunches in its Pinot Noir fermentations. In good years, you can expect 50 to 60 per cent whole bunch in Escarpment wines whereas in cooler years, like 2012, when the fruit and stems aren't so ripe, that ratio falls to around 25 per cent. The four wines in its single vineyard 'Insight Series' are a reflection of place and are must-buys for Pinotphiles. The floral-scented Kiwa and the more muscular Te Rehua Pinot Noirs hail from leased blocks in

Martinborough town and are often the first to be picked. The Kupe block is my personal favourite but, having been planted on its own roots due to a lack of grafted vine material in 1999, the vines behind Kupe are slowly being pulled out and replanted due to phylloxera. Escarpment also produces some fine whites: a dry and taut Riesling, a food-friendly savoury Pinot Blanc and a flinty Chardonnay.

Try this: Escarpment Vineyard Kupe Pinot Noir
Always classy, fragrant and unadulterated, Kupe fills the mouth with fragrance: pure damson, cinnamon, spice and herbal elements. An abundance of resolved tannin coats the palate, melting harmoniously on the long, drawn-out tea-leaf finish. A complex, concentrated and memorable wine.

Visit
There is no cellar door but barrel-room tastings can be made by appointment, Monday to Friday.

Gladstone Vineyard
Gladstone
gladstonevineyard.co.nz
Founded by an Australian vet in 1986 on the former riverbed of the Ruamahanga, Gladstone Vineyard has been owned and run by two Glaswegians since 1996. They have since added to the original vineyard, purchasing 10 hectares on nearby Dakins Road. Its Sauvignon Blanc is everything you'd hope for from Wairarapa: crisp, fresh and citrus-driven. It has an extra layer of texture, thanks to a proportion of barrel-fermented wine. In the relatively cool climes of Gladstone, its Pinot Gris retains freshness and has more interest than the average Gris with some parcels undergoing skin contact or fermentation in old oak barrels. The winery's 12,000 Miles range is a more affordable expression of Gladstone Vineyard.

Try this: Gladstone Vineyard Pinot Noir
Soft, ripe and round Pinot Noir style with a hint of savoury complexity on the fresh finish.

Visit
The cellar door is open daily from 11 a.m. to 4.30 p.m. Tastings are

free or you can sit in the wine garden with a picnic while sampling a tasting tray of its current release reds and whites (four 50 ml samples) for a small fee.

Kusuda Wines
Martinborough
kusudawines.co/english

Tokyo-born Hiroyuki 'Hiro' Kusuda produces tiny amounts of soulful Pinot Noir, Syrah and Riesling. Martinborough had been on his radar since his initial taste of its Pinot Noir while working for the Japanese consulate in Sydney. Wine was a lifelong passion and its lure proved too hard to resist: he quit his job to study winemaking at Geisenheim in Germany in 1997 (he didn't yet speak German) and his thesis took him to Martinborough, where he was hosted by fellow Geisenheim graduate Kai Schubert. Over a glass of wine with Schubert, Kusuda decided his young family's future was in Martinborough. He leased a vineyard block in 2001 and made his first wine in 2002. Kusuda's attention to detail is unparalleled, and his rigorous fruit selection would leave an accountant aghast. The owner-winemaker selects the fruit for his wines berry by berry with his picking team of 'housewives, professionals and students' – volunteers who have flown from Japan at their own expense to help at the winery. 'It's boring and painful work,' admits Kusuda, but there are perks: he holds back 300 to 400 bottles of wine after each harvest to replenish the cellar for next year's thirsty volunteers. The painstaking methods appear to be worth the effort: his Pinot Noir and Syrah show incredible velvety texture and are almost meditative while his dry Riesling is pure and intensely concentrated, with acidity that cuts through the wine with laser-like precision.

Try this: Kusuda Wines Pinot Noir
Kusuda's Pinots are all about sumptuous texture and a wonderful sensation of relaxation in the glass. Offering savoury notes, a hint of spice and subtle plum; mellifluous, it is always harmonious and round. Tiny yields and small berries which are individually selected mean a high level of fruit concentration and subtle savoury fine-grained tannins.

Visit
Kusuda Wines is not open to the public.

Martinborough Vineyard

Martinborough
martinborough-vineyard.co.nz

Derek Milne, the scientist and author of the paper concluding Martinborough was perfectly suited to viticulture, was one of the founders of Martinborough Vineyard in 1980. With around 6 hectares of vineyard planted in 1985, Australian winemaker Larry McKenna took a job with the fledgling company in this fledgling region and remains in Martinborough to this day. It quickly became the darling of the town, taking the best Pinot Noir title for three years running (1988–90) with its elegant, savoury expression. When McKenna left to set up Escarpment Vineyard in 1999, the mantle was handed to Claire Mulholland and, in 2007, to Paul Mason.

After a slight stumble, wealthy American Bill Foley's wine business Foley Family Wines purchased the now 60-hectare estate in 2014, having bought fellow Martinborough vineyard Te Kairanga in 2011, as well as Vavasour and Grove Mill in Marlborough. He also owns the luxury lodge Wharekauhau in Wairarapa. The new owner appointed Master of Wine Alastair Maling as chief group winemaker, giving Mason an extra set of brains to draw on. Its greatest asset, however, is its original own-rooted Pinot Noir vines, which have been farmed organically since the late noughties. Its flagship wine, Marie Zelie Reserve Pinot Noir, pays homage to the Frenchwoman who pioneered the region's vineyards in the late nineteenth century with her husband William Beetham. She was also the great-great-aunt of Derek Milne's wife. The wine is only produced in excellent vintages and is a barrel selection sourced from the oldest parcels. The result is a delicate and fragrant wine with a dense core of fruit and finely woven tannins. Its Home Block Chardonnay has won international acclaim: the 2012 vintage was named top wine in *Decanter* magazine's eighty-strong blind tasting of Chardonnays from around the world (outside Burgundy). Other wines of interest include a Sauvignon Blanc, Pinot Gris, Riesling and a rare Syrah/Viognier blend while there is also a well-priced second label, Te Tera, which offers juicy Sauvignon Blanc, Pinot Gris and Pinot Noir.

Try this: Martinborough Vineyard Pinot Noir
A truly classic expression of Martinborough, offering elegance, texture

and structure in a refined package. It displays floral aromas, savoury tones and fine fruit.

Visit
The cellar door is open seven days a week, but an appointment must be made on Wednesdays and Thursdays.

Palliser Estate
Martinborough
palliser.co.nz

Wyatt Creech was born in the US but grew up in Wairarapa, becoming a Member of Parliament for the region and spending a brief period as Deputy Prime Minister. He planted vines in Martinborough in 1984 and four years later formed a public company with a large number of shareholders (there were more than 200 in 2017). Larry McKenna made Palliser Estate's first wine in 1988 before Alan Johnson took over the reins and he remains at the helm three decades on. The company's dynamo was the winery's second largest shareholder, the late Richard Riddiford. He ran the company for twenty-five years until stepping down in 2015 and worked tirelessly to put Palliser and Martinborough on the world's wine map. Since his death, a new team is guiding the brand forward which includes the introduction of organic farming in 2016. The label has always maintained a focus on Pinot Noir – nearly half of all plantings are dedicated to the red variety while Sauvignon Blanc (23 per cent of plantings) and Chardonnay are its most important whites. There is also a little Riesling and Pinot Gris. The wines are consistently good to very good, particularly the fresh and bright Sauvignon Blanc (see Try This). Its top cuvée, The Great Ted Pinot Noir, is a serious, dense blend of its best wines that spends up to eighteen months in oak with a high proportion of new barrels. The second-tier Pencarrow label offers more affordable drinking to be enjoyed in youth.

Try this: Palliser Estate Sauvignon Blanc
A pure expression of Wairarapa Sauvignon Blanc that is produced without any funny business: fermented in stainless steel to preserve the fine grassy, citrus and tropical fruit, it is light in body with some time on lees to build mid-palate weight. Fine and fresh.

Visit

The cellar door is open seven days a week from 10.30 a.m. to 4 p.m. There is a service charge of $5.

Schubert Wines

Martinborough
schubert.co.nz

In 1998, Geisenheim graduates Kai Schubert and Marion Deimling said goodbye to Germany and hello to New Zealand, buying a piece of land in Gladstone. While Schubert Wines' cellar door is in the heart of Martinborough, it only has 2 hectares under vine here while the majority of its plantings (12.5 hectares) are situated on Dakins Road, Gladstone. This organic producer specializes in succulent yet fresh Pinot Noir, producing three cuvées including Marion's Vineyard and Block B, whose 2008 vintage won the International Pinot Noir trophy at the Decanter World Wine Awards in 2010. Having purchased the Martinborough home block off an Italian 'who planted everything but Pinot Noir', you can still find an array of varieties here: Syrah, Merlot, Chardonnay, Pinot Gris and even some Müller-Thurgau (these three whites are used to produce Tribianco: a round, full-bodied and gentle barrel-fermented blend).

Try this: Schubert Wines Block B Pinot Noir

This block brings together five different Dijon clones and offers ripe plums, a herbal element and dried fruit character. Soft yet focused on the mid palate, it sports a savoury finish. A fine line of acidity and resolved yet abundant tannins leave a taut structure.

Visit

The cute cellar door in Martinborough is open most days from 11 a.m. to 3 p.m. for tastings. There is a small charge of $5 per person.

PART 3
SOUTH ISLAND

9

MARLBOROUGH

It's not the Smithsonian, but Marlborough Museum should be on every wine visitor's list of places to visit. It took me six years of living in New Zealand to step inside its doors and when I mentioned I'd finally visited its wine exhibition, most local winemakers responded with 'Oh, I've still not been there'. They should: a community that does not know its past is like a vine without roots. The history of Marlborough's wine industry is a wonderful reminder of how young it is and how quickly success has graced its vineyards. It celebrates the pioneers of the modern era, which started in 1973, and commemorates those who first planted vines a century earlier.

One of the region's earliest pioneers was David Herd. Look left as you leave Blenheim airport and there is a bronze statue of the Scotsman who first planted vines circa 1873, a hundred years before Montana made the first plantings of the modern era. Leaving the mills of Dundee behind in 1852, Herd set sail with his wife and daughter for Australia before making the journey to New Zealand in 1854. He managed a 20,000 acre station in Marlborough for two decades and was finally able to purchase a piece of land in what is known as the Southern Valleys today. He named the property Auntsfield and planted Muscat vines supported by manuka posts, and made wine until his death in 1905. His son-in-law Bill Paynter continued his winemaking legacy in the face of the growing temperance movement but the vines were removed in 1931. This part of Marlborough's history might have been forgotten if it wasn't for cinematographer Graeme Cowley. Having been involved in Kiwi classics like *Goodbye Pork Pie* and *Smash Palace*, he was in the market for a piece of land. In 1998, after a 'nightmarish' two-year process, he purchased a piece of land in the hills: 'We weren't allowed to check on the soils but there was a comment that "they used to grow grapes up here in the old days" and it was something that stayed with me. I started doing some research.' And so the history of David Herd and Auntsfield was revived. The Muscat vineyard with manuka posts has been recreated; the original winery, which had collapsed and was buried under a pile of rubbish, has been restored. And there's a bronze statue of the pioneering Scotsman at the airport.

Herd wasn't the only man making wine in the late nineteenth and early twentieth centuries. Born to English parents, George Freeth established a vineyard near Picton just a few years after Herd founded Auntsfield. His company, Mount Pleasant Wine Vaults, made fruit wine for the local community and operated until 1958. Another important figure in the early history of Marlborough wine was Mansoor Peters. He left his native Lebanon for New Zealand in the 1890s and ran the general store in Blenheim. He also had a licence to make wine but it wouldn't have been particularly fine – vines were grown on fences and on a shed behind the store, according to the Museum, and was fermented in barrels with honey and water added for good measure.

The cultural, social and legal climate did not support the growth of a wine industry in Marlborough – or in New Zealand – in the first half of the twentieth century, and it was long considered too cold to grow grapes successfully. That was until Frank Yukich, director of Montana Wines, turned up in 1973 and bought close to 1,200 hectares of land for $1.3 million, paying the deposit out of his own pocket. The Montana board were kept in the dark and when they were told, they weren't happy. It took reports from a handful of scientists as far away as California to convince them that growing grapes in Marlborough wasn't a folly. The first vine was planted at a commemorative ceremony in August 1973 and it was a publicity coup. The *Marlborough Express* reported that Yukich had brought in a coach-load of journalists and he confidently declared that 'wines from here will become world famous' – but others weren't convinced and the problems in the vineyard early on suggested they had made a big mistake.

However, land was cheap, Marlborough had a dry climate with plentiful sunshine, and the stainless steel tanks from the dairy industry were perfectly suited to fermenting wine. Gradually the sheep were moved on and the vines moved in. In 1986, there were 1.6 million sheep in the region and 1,000 hectares of vines. In 2007 Marlborough's sheep population had been reduced to 597,000 and vines had spread their roots over more than 13,000 hectares, despite land prices rising from $8,000 to $255,600 per hectare in that time. Yukich had taken a gamble and it had paid off handsomely.

By the mid 1980s, the wines of Marlborough were making as bold a statement as Yukich had uttered in 1973. The founder of Margaret River's Cape Mentelle, David Hohnen, had tasted the potential of Marlborough Sauvignon Blanc in 1984 and the next year was making the first vintage of Cloudy Bay. Acclaim quickly followed. The region's place on the wine map was further cemented when Hunter's Fumé Blanc won the public vote at the Sunday Times Wine Club Vintage Festival in London in 1986 (see Chapter 1 for more details). The region's inimitable Sauvignon Blanc style was waking up tired palates and started collecting international silverware. It was inevitable that others wanted a piece of the action. Even Queen Elizabeth II turned up to see what all the fuss was about in 1990. She was taken up to enjoy the view on 'Rob's Nob', a rocky outcrop named by former Prime Minister Robert Muldoon during a visit in 1984, which is now home to Brancott Estate Cellar Door. Gerry Gregg, then winery manager of Montana Wines, took Her Royal Highness to a viewing platform they had erected for her visit before sampling a glass of Montana 'Rhine Riesling' and a lunch of spit-roasted lamb. During the lunch, John Stichbury, the fun-loving founder of Jackson Estate, spied an opportunity when the Queen supped her Rhine Riesling. He threw a napkin over his arm in a bid to disguise himself as a waiter and bagged himself Her Royal Highness's wine glass, bottle and menu. The glass is on display at the Marlborough Museum.

Having dined like a Kiwi, the Queen planted a Sauvignon Blanc vine and Villa Maria's George Fistonich planted a second on behalf of the absent Prince Philip. These two vines marked the start of a rapid expansion in the region. From 1,423 hectares in 1990, plantings almost trebled to 4,050 hectares at the turn of the century. By 2005, it had swelled to 16,608 hectares. Five years later, the figure stood at 22,500. There are now more than 26,000 hectares of vines planted across Marlborough. In the period between 2010 and 2017, 1.2 billion litres of wine left Marlborough for the world, according to data from the Ministry of Primary Industries.

GEOGRAPHY AND CLIMATE

Marlborough sits at the north-eastern end of the South Island. On a clear day, you can look across the water and see the North Island, where a dark cloud is usually depositing rain and high winds on the country's politicians in Wellington, the capital. The cold southerly winds that race up the east coast from Antarctica are buffeted by the Kaikoura Ranges, which protect Marlborough, sending the southerlies whistling into Wellington and Martinborough. While Wellingtonians are suffering the chilling effects of these winds, it can be sunny and settled in Marlborough thanks to the natural protection it is afforded by the Kaikouras and surrounding mountain ranges. In fact, Marlborough can often lay claim to the most sunshine hours in New Zealand (annual average 2,475 hours, 1981–2010), hence the Māori name for the Wairau Valley, Kei puta te Wairau: 'Place with the hole in the cloud'.

Marlborough is also relatively dry and vines on its free-draining stony soils typically require irrigation. The lush tree-covered Richmond Range (tree covered if the commercial loggers haven't harvested them, that is) to the north receives around 2,000 mm of rain annually and bears the brunt of the precipitation, leaving the Wairau Valley, the heart of Marlborough's wine industry, with around 700 mm of rain each year. The further you head south across the Wairau Valley, the progressively drier the conditions become. By the time you reach the Wither Hills south of Blenheim, a popular walking spot, the brittle, brown grass in summer testifies to the increasing aridity. Rising up in the south, the Blairich Range boasts a peak more than 1,500 metres high, providing yet more protection. It separates the Wairau Valley from the Awatere, making this increasingly important subregion even drier. In short, the further south you are in Marlborough, the drier the climate.

However, the east–west axis also plays a significant role in the vineyard. Grapes now stretch all the way to the windswept beach of Rarangi. From sea level, the region very gently rises to around 50 metres in the town of Renwick (around 20 kilometres west of the coast). Head further west – and inland – for another 9 kilometres to the vast

Waihopai vineyard created by Ara Wines, now owned by Bankhouse Estate, and the elevation is around 100 metres. The increase in elevation and the diminishing maritime influence means that diurnal temperature ranges can be larger inland. There is no cooling sea breeze to enjoy 30 kilometres inland and no warming influence at night, so take a sweater if you want to sit out on an evening in Marlborough. It is also more frosty the further inland you go and the frost-fighting machine companies are doing good business here.

WHAT LIES BENEATH

The soils of Marlborough are based on former riverbeds and glacial outwash. At the last count, there were a whopping eighty-seven different soil types identified in Marlborough but they are all variations on a theme of river gravels, sand, silt, loam and clay. The Wairau River – and its tributaries – have deposited their loads during times of flood throughout the valley. Today, the river winds its way down from the ski fields in the west to the vine-filled Wairau Valley, before flowing into the salty waters of Cloudy Bay in the east. This being a flood plain, the soils on the valley floor are inherently variable and can change within a small distance. Clive Dougall, the winemaker at Seresin Estate for more than a decade, turned organic consultant, shares his experience: 'We dug hundreds of soil pits. In the Noa vineyard [a block adjacent to the winery] we found the thickest clay I've ever seen in my life – it was like potter's clay. The rest of the block is a liquorice allsorts: silt, gravels.'

Variation within single rows is even visible to the naked eye. Pull up at the side of the road between Blenheim and Renwick and look down a row. You're likely to see ridges and dips within a 20-metre spacing; there are patches of deep silts generating verdant canopies adjacent to bony, stony soils that stress the vine. Damian Martin, science group leader, viticulture and winemaking, for Plant and Food Research in Marlborough, explains: 'It's one of the features of the Marlborough style, that combination of vines growing on bony soils that are under stress next to vines that are grown on deep soils that grow like triffids.'

The free-draining alluvial soils on the river flats become heavier and less free draining to the east of the railway line in Blenheim. Within spitting distance of the sea, these loamy alluviums are a result of rivers slowing and depositing finer material. In combination with a higher water table close to the coast, these fertile sites ripen a heavier crop load than the well-drained stony soils further inland.

CARVING UP MARLBOROUGH

Marlborough is often referred to as one entity but the region's development in the hills of the Southern Valleys and the expansion of the Awatere Valley are an essential chapter in the modern story of Marlborough.

The Southern Valleys spread like fingers from the Wairau Valley into the foothills of the Blairich Range. The north-facing slopes first attracted viticulturist Mike Eaton to plant the now-renowned Clayvin vineyard in 1991. At that time, water was an issue. In an attempt to prevent the soils drying out Eaton covered the vineyard in a layer of polythene, remembers Hätsch Kalberer, the winemaker at Fromm, who has been making wine from Clayvin since it first bore fruit. It was not until 2004 that the valleys became truly viable as a winegrowing area with the creation of an irrigation scheme supplying an area of 4,400 hectares. 'It made it viable for people to establish vineyards in the Southern Valleys,' says James Healy, co-founder of Dog Point. It certainly has: the local winegrowers' association estimates that a quarter of all Marlborough's vineyards are now situated in one of the five Southern Valleys: Ben Morvan, Brancott, Fairhall, Omaka and Waihopai. Sheltered from the sea breeze in their own private amphitheatres, it can get warmer here during the summer days and cooler at night.

Pinot Noir is finding its home on the slopes of the Southern Valleys thanks to their northern exposure, warmer daytime temperatures and the loess and clay soils. The resulting wines have greater depth and more sumptuous palate texture than Pinot Noir produced on the free-draining alluvial soils in the Wairau Valley. The red wines from this part of Marlborough are turning the region from a fruity, friendly Pinot Noir producer into a serious player. Anna Flowerday, an Australian winemaker who bought Te Whare Ra in 2003 with her Marlborough-born winemaking husband, says, 'When I moved here, there would have been four or five Marlborough Pinot Noirs that I would have defended; now there are more than fifteen or twenty and they have all come from the Southern Valleys.'

THE AWATERE VALLEY

Little has been written about the Awatere Valley: it came late to the Marlborough Sauvignon Blanc party and it is hardly a tourist destination. Situated about 20 kilometres south-east of Blenheim, there are few cellar doors and no fancy winery restaurants although in the small town of Seddon you can get a good pie for lunch. There are few wineries based in the Awatere, and yet this valley now represents close to a third of all vineyards in Marlborough and it would be New Zealand's second largest wine-producing region in its own right, if it wasn't lumped in with the Wairau and Southern Valleys.

The first vineyard was planted in 1986 by the Vavasour family and Awatere local Stu Marfell, the chief winemaker since 2002, remembers going along to its first harvest with his mum and brother to help pick (and eat) the grapes: 'In 1989, there weren't a lot of people around to pick grapes and a lot of farmers' wives came along to help out.' It wasn't long before producers in the Wairau jumped in their cars and journeyed over the winding Weld and Dashwood Pass in search of land which was significantly cheaper, but there was a big question mark over whether or not it was warm enough. 'When they were developing the Seaview and Dashwood areas on the coast [in the lower Awatere], the people working on it would say they were off to Siberia,' laughs Damian Martin. Data collated by the Marlborough Research Centre shows that the average annual air temperature in Blenheim is slightly warmer than Dashwood in the Awatere (13.24°C versus 12.9°C for the period 2002–11).

Ripening remains one of the biggest challenges facing growers. Jeff Fyfe is chief winemaker at Yealands Estate, which has more than 1,000 hectares under vine in the Seaview area of the Awatere, making it the largest privately owned vineyard in the valley. He explains: 'We have budburst at the same time as the Wairau but we harvest two to three weeks later. It's much cooler and the growing season is much longer, which means we have our fingers firmly crossed while everyone else [in the Wairau] is harvesting.' Ripening occurs even later at elevation in the area known as the Upper Awatere: the vineyards of the Awatere begin in the low-lying coastal areas and snake their way upstream perched atop dramatic terraces carved by the river. The Awatere Valley Road follows the course of the river, sandwiched between two imposing mountain ranges. At elevations of 250 to 300 metres, ripening can be a week later than at vineyards at sea level, and harvest has been known to take place as late as May. The threat of autumn rains and frost at this late stage in the season and at these altitudes makes growing grapes here a risky business.

The wind is also a major challenge for grape growers in the Awatere. While the warm, dry norwester affects all parts of Marlborough, the Awatere Valley is more exposed to coastal winds. Weather stations in the Awatere Valley attest to the fact that it is far windier here than in the Wairau Valley and, from 2000 to 2012, the mean daily wind run for the Awatere was 373.2 kilometres versus 277.9 kilometres in Blenheim (the wind run is an indication of the average wind speed over twenty-four hours so a daily wind run of 240 kilometres per hour gives a mean wind speed of 10 kilometres per hour). With maximum winds sometimes creeping above 100 kilometres per hour, it is not uncommon for young shoots to snap such is the wind's force. The wind is often responsible for smaller crops, smaller berries and thicker skins but with so much natural ventilation, disease pressure is relatively low.

The cooler climes of the Awatere mean this is not the place to plant late-ripening varieties, as Vavasour discovered to its detriment. 'In the late 1980s, they didn't know what was going to grow well so they planted a bit of everything – even a reasonable amount of Bordeaux varieties,' says Marfell. 'I think they thought it was a bit warmer than it actually is and when I started in 2002, we were still making a straight Cabernet Sauvignon. It was pretty herbaceous – definitely on the green side – but when we stopped making it, we actually got a bit of hate mail. I guess there were people who must have enjoyed those flavours!'

Unsurprisingly, Sauvignon Blanc is the most planted variety in the Awatere Valley and it produces a crisp style that is aromatically less overt than the Wairau Valley. It often sports a herbaceous character reminiscent of green capsicum or peas, which several studies have shown is linked to higher concentrations of isobutyl methoxypyrazine. Awatere Sauvignons tend to be more subtle in the tropical fruit department; in the Upper Awatere, elderflower or blackcurrant bud is an oft-used descriptor and some say the region's 'minerality' or oyster-shell characters are hallmarks of the area's whites. Its wines always have a low pH and striking acidity, giving the wines a powerful – and if not carefully managed, eyewatering

– finish. Fyfe says: 'For me the single biggest character of Awatere is its minerality. It produces a different type of acidity – it is naturally higher and we will adjust the acidity, if required, which brings the pH up and gives a broader palate weight and more texture.'

Following the lead of the Wairau, Pinot Noir is the Awatere's most planted red. The Valley's cooler climate can imbue the wines with herbal and floral aromas – even without any whole cluster influence – and a brightness of acidity. The windy conditions, leading to small berry sizes and thicker skins, can create more darkly coloured Pinots than you might expect. In the more sheltered Upper Awatere, loess and clay also bring depth and texture.

WINE STYLES

Marlborough is the home of New Zealand Sauvignon Blanc (see Chapter 3). The region counted 20,600 hectares of this aromatic white variety in 2018, according to the country's Vineyard Register Report, which represented 80 per cent of all Marlborough's vines. There were a little more than 23,100 hectares of Sauvignon Blanc in New Zealand, which means that 89 per cent of the country's Sauvignon Blanc is in Marlborough.

Marlborough became famous for turning up the volume on Sauvignon Blanc, making an exuberant style that blended herbaceous characters with a bowl of tropical fruit. It was piercing, easy to understand and totally different from anything anyone had ever tasted. The classic Marlborough Sauvignon Blanc continues to provide an inimitable green yet tropical style with mouthwatering acidity. This is the region's bread and butter and it knows what side its bread is buttered.

While sticking to their knitting, winemakers and highly involved wine consumers are looking for what's next. It's already here and the answer is more refined, texturally interesting Sauvignon Blanc. Techniques including hand picking, whole-bunch pressing, wild yeast, barrel fermentation and lees ageing have brought a new wave of Marlborough Sauvignon Blanc.

Pinot Noir represents just 11 per cent of Marlborough's vineyard but in the context of New Zealand that's almost half of the country's Pinot (2,657 hectares out of 5,653 hectares nationally). Marlborough has a little bit of catching up to do with Martinborough and Central Otago when it comes to its Pinot Noir credentials. Dog Point's Ivan Sutherland admits the region was a 'late starter' to the Pinot game: until the Southern Valleys' Irrigation Scheme was established in 2004, the variety was planted on the free-draining alluvial river flats that produced pretty Pinot without much substance. They still do, particularly when yields are high. Since the Southern Valleys have opened up, the best Pinot Noir, offering depth and weight, has come from the north-facing clay and loess slopes. Ambitious producers have discarded the Pinot Noir clones that were planted for sparkling wine in favour of vine material better suited to making fine Pinot, and these vines are starting to reach some level of maturity. The winemakers are also becoming more mature, understanding the personality of their fruit and making decisions accordingly. For example, Clive Dougall, the former winemaker at Seresin Estate, decided that cold soak and whole-bunch fermentation was not conducive to making a complex Pinot Noir. 'We have a lot of fruit power so if we cold soak and leave it on skins for a short time you end up with a very fruity wine and I want to lose that fruitiness,' he says. Instead, he leaves the wine on skins for five or even six weeks. Meanwhile, oak use has become more sensitive. Admittedly there are still plenty of entry-level, fruity Pinot Noirs in Marlborough that have been given some oak treatment and don't have the *cojones* to cope, but at the other end of the price spectrum oak is increasingly playing the support role rather than a star part. Ben Cowley of Auntsfield explains: 'We are finding with older vines that we are pulling back on new oak for Pinot Noir because we are getting naturally ripe tannins from the fruit.'

Marlborough Pinot Noir has come a long way in a short time. It will never usurp Sauvignon Blanc and there will remain plenty of simple, fruity examples but the finest are increasing in complexity year on year. This is one to watch.

Similarly, there are some fine Chardonnays hailing from Marlborough. Its potential was recognized in 1997 when Montana (now Brancott Estate) won the best white wine of the year at the International Wine Challenge with its 1996 Marlborough Chardonnay. Now home to a third of all New Zealand's Chardonnay vineyards, Marlborough's cool climate is conducive to making pure citrus and stone-fruited Chardonnay with a fine line of acidity. There is a wide variety of

Chardonnays ranging from fun, fruity and unoaked styles to serious, barrel-fermented, savoury examples. Ambitious producers use a variety of techniques to build texture and complexity including wild yeast, solids, French oak and lees work.

Chardonnay currently vies with Pinot Gris as the region's third most-planted variety. A little more than 1,000 hectares are planted, reflecting the market's love for the variety rather than a burning desire to grow this grape in Marlborough. Wineries produce everything from crisp, dry Pinot Grigio styles to lush, sweet Pinot Gris although the majority are generally off-dry. There is a handful of producers making more interesting styles allowing wild yeast to ferment the juice in old oak, but the volumes are small. More interesting still are the Riesling and Gewürztraminer wines that offer incredible fruit purity and a sensation of brightness on the palate whether dry or sweet.

The region is also home to some of the finest sparkling wine producers in New Zealand: vintage Pelorus (made by LVMH-owned Cloudy Bay), No. 1 Family Estate and older vintages of both Deutz and Daniel Le Brun show that when it's good, it's very, very good. Its cool climate, abundant sunshine, modest rainfall and vineyards full of Chardonnay and Pinot Noir suggest this is an odds-on favourite. Yet there are very few producers focused on the pursuit of beautiful bubbles and its potential has not been fully realized. Compared with Sauvignon Blanc, it takes a long time to produce and costs significantly more. Nevertheless, a small group of producers in Marlborough has set up an association in a bid to take this category more seriously. Established in August 2013, members of Methode Marlborough must make sparkling wine from the three Champagne varieties – Chardonnay, Pinot Noir and Pinot Meunier – and the wines must spend eighteen months on lees before disgorgement.

PRODUCER PROFILES

Auntsfield Estate

Southern Valleys

auntsfield.co.nz

Wellington filmmaker Graeme Cowley and wife Linda bought Auntsfield in 1998. Sitting at the end of Paynters Road in the Southern Valleys, there was not a vineyard to be seen and the pair had to travel to Waiheke Island 'to work out where to plant the vines on the hills'. Having heard that vines once grew on the property, Graeme set about researching its past and discovered that he had purchased the land where Marlborough pioneer David Herd had established the region's first vineyard around 125 years earlier. In addition to planting Sauvignon Blanc, Pinot Noir and a little bit of Chardonnay on the property with his sons, viticulturist Ben and winemaker Luc, the family reconstructed Herd's 382-vine Muscat vineyard and restored the original cellar, which had collapsed and was buried under a pile of rubbish. There is as much care for the modern vineyard as there is for the past at Auntsfield and its hillside Sauvignon Blanc is clean, pure and vibrant with lees work bringing additional palate weight. Its single block Chardonnay Cob Cottage is a savoury barrel-fermented style with a firm line of acidity providing a taut finish. In 2005, a hundred years after Herd's death, Auntsfield introduced Heritage, a Pinot Noir from the steepest part of the vineyard. It is a bunch selection from its highest vines on the highest block in the Southern Valleys and includes a teaspoon of wine from the 1905 vintage.

Auntsfield's original cellar

Try this: Auntsfield Estate Pinot Noir Hawk Hill
From a low-yielding clay–loess slope, Hawk Hill makes a broody, suave Pinot Noir with ripe dark fruit, spice and abundant, finely textured tannins.

Visit
Cellar door tastings are by appointment only, Monday to Friday. The historic vineyard and cellar tour is highly recommended, costing $20 per person (minimum two guests). Booking details can be found on the Auntsfield website.

Brancott Estate
Wairau Valley
brancottestate.com

Formerly known as Montana Wines, Brancott Estate was born in 2010 to avoid confusion in the US market. Many North Americans associated Montana Wines with the state of Montana, rather than Marlborough, New Zealand. While it is now focused on Marlborough, the company was founded in west Auckland by Croation immigrant Ivan Yukich. Its first wine was released in 1944 and, under Yukich's sons, Maté and Frank, grew rapidly in the 1960s and 1970s, expanding to Gisborne and, in 1973, buying up virgin land in Marlborough. Frank proclaimed that, 'wines from here will become world famous', and his crystal ball reading proved to be accurate. At this time, multinational drinks company Seagram had taken a 40 per cent share in Montana. It has since been under several different owners and it currently sits in the portfolio of French drinks company Pernod Ricard. Brancott Estate is one of New Zealand's biggest producers today, making entry level Sauvignon Blanc and Pinot Noir among other things, but it is also at the forefront of industry innovation and research, assisting generously in industry – and student – projects on Sauvignon Blanc, lower-alcohol wines and Pinot Noir. It has a mind-boggling seven ranges within the portfolio: the Terroir Series, for example, explores Marlborough's subregions, Flight comprises its lighter-in-alcohol wines and Living Land is the winery's organic range.

Try this: Brancott Estate Chosen Rows Sauvignon Blanc
This is Brancott's flagship white and is the culmination of a project which began in 2008, aiming to make ultra-premium Sauvignon Blanc.

By lowering cropping loads in the vineyard and playing around in the winery with pressing regimes, wild yeast, oak and lees, Chosen Rows came to fruition in 2010. The resulting style offers richness on the palate, complexity and balance. It captures aromatics in both the savoury spectrum, as well as offering Sauvignon's signature green capsicum and grassy notes. The finish is both powerful and textural. This is top-end stuff with a top-end price point to boot.

Visit

Offering fabulous views over the Fairhall area – and if it's a clear day, you might glimpse the North Island – Brancott Estate's Cellar Door and Restaurant sits on the rocky knoll once known as Rob's Nob. The sleek, light-filled building is open daily from 10 a.m. to 4.30 p.m., offering a range of tastings and tours of the vineyard by bicycle and helicopter. You can even get up close and personal with a falcon. There's a restaurant on site with local produce inspiring the menu. The website has full details and booking information.

Cloudy Bay Vineyards
Wairau Valley
cloudybay.co.nz

After tasting an electric Marlborough Sauvignon Blanc in 1984, Cape Mentelle founder David Hohnen jumped on a plane to New Zealand and a year later was making the first Cloudy Bay Sauvignon Blanc. Hohnen bought some grapes from Corbans and hired Kevin Judd, who was working at Selaks in Auckland during the 1985 vintage. Judd telephoned instructions to Hohnen who transported the grapes from Marlborough across the Cook Strait to be processed at the Corbans winery in Gisborne. Needless to say there was plenty of skin contact. Hohnen moved fast: by the end of 1985 he had built a winery, and Judd became the full-time winemaker until 2009. The 1986 vintage received critical acclaim and the brand soon built up a loyal following. It was a huge marketing success, building an aura of scarcity and exclusivity that had customers signing up to waiting lists.

It was not only thirsty consumers who wanted a piece of the Cloudy Bay action: in 1990 Veuve Clicquot Ponsardin invested in Cloudy Bay vineyards and the winery is now part of the Moët Hennessy wine division. It's not all Sauvignon Blanc at Cloudy Bay, although it does represent 70 per cent of production. It produces a classy, savoury 100 per cent barrel-fermented Chardonnay with a citrussy backbone, a gentle Marlborough Pinot Noir and, since the 2010 vintage, a more ballsy example from Central Otago – Te Wahi. As part of a luxury group embracing some of Champagne's finest names: Dom Pérignon, Krug, Moët & Chandon, Ruinart and Veuve Clicquot, it is to be expected that it does sparkling wine well. The vintage expression of Pelorus is made only in the best years, and is a blend of around 60 per cent Pinot Noir and 40 per cent Chardonnay, picked from select low-yielding sites within the Wairau Valley. The wine spends between four and seven years on lees, depending on the vintage. Its barrel-fermented Sauvignon Blanc Te Koko was first produced in 1996. Striking the balance between Marlborough's exuberant fruit and wood can be difficult and, since 2010, there's been growing refinement with less malolactic fermentation and less new oak (see Try This).

Try this: Cloudy Bay Te Koko Sauvignon Blanc

Cloudy Bay's barrel-fermented Sauvignon Blanc is an alternative expression to the clean, crunchy, fruit-driven style that made the producer so famous. Hand picked and whole-bunch pressed, the proportion of new oak has steadily fallen in recent years and now stands at less than 10 per cent; malolactic fermentation is now down to 10 to 20 per cent (that figure stood at 100 per cent between 1996 and 2009). While it is impossible to rein in the natural flamboyance of Marlborough Sauvignon Blanc, its enthusiasm is curbed through these winemaking techniques. It remains aromatically rich, offering green capsicum, caramelized pineapple and a hint of struck match. The beauty of this wine is in its sumptuous texture and richness: mouthfilling and very satisfying, this is clearly a high-quality wine. Whether the flavour combination is your bag, however, is up to you to decide.

Visit

The cellar door is open from 10 a.m. to 4 p.m. daily. In summer, it opens an outdoor bar and visitors can enjoy a glass of wine and small plates in the courtyard, and challenge their companions to a game of pétanque or croquet on the lawn.

Dog Point Vineyard
Wairau Valley
dogpoint.co.nz

Founded in 2002 by former Cloudy Bayers James Healy, winemaker, nectarine lover and clarinetist, and Ivan Sutherland, viticulturist and Olympic rowing bronze medallist, Dog Point is an organic producer of Sauvignon Blanc, Chardonnay and Pinot Noir. Its white wines are sourced from its home vineyards on silty clays in the lower Brancott Valley (behind Blenheim airport!) while its Pinot Noir is produced from estate fruit and, since 2013, steep hillside vineyards on clay/loess: Settlement in the Omaka and Yarrum in the Ben Morven hills. The winery's most distinctive – and divisive – wine is Section 94. Produced using unclarified juice, this high-solids, wild-yeast, barrel-fermented and unfined Sauvignon is a world away from the classic fruit-driven Marlborough Sauvignon Blanc that put the region on the map. It is a highly textural wine with huge intensity from low yields but it is a Marmite wine – it is highly reductive in its youth, which is a love it or hate it character. However, put it in the cellar and open it seven, eight or nine years later and you'll be amazed how youthful it remains. The gunflint aromas are present in its Chardonnay and since its first vintage, the use of new oak has fallen to 15 per cent, producing a more harmonious citrus-driven wine that has vibrant acidity, a hallmark of the Mendoza clone. Dog Point's whites are perhaps the most impressive but with the inclusion of Southern Valleys fruit, its Pinot Noir is increasingly impressive, although it can be rather toasty in youth due to 35 per cent new oak.

Try this: Dog Point Vineyard Sauvignon Blanc
This is a pure, unadulterated expression of Sauvignon Blanc, made with a lot of TLC. The low yields are reflected in the high level of concentration in the glass; hand picking and whole-bunch pressing lead to a more elegant aromatic expression. Gooseberry, passionfruit and citrus flavours abound and a line of firm acidity provides a powerful conclusion.

Visit
There is no cellar door but tastings can be arranged by appointment. There is also a lovely bed and breakfast, The Bell Tower, on site.

Fromm Winery

Wairau Valley
frommwinery.co.nz

A Swiss-owned New Zealand winery, covering 8.5 hectares, Fromm is a superlative Pinot Noir purveyor, producing four different single vineyard expressions. Founded in 1992, Fromm farms its vineyards organically and the oldest plots are as near as dry farmed as you can get in the free-draining soils of the Wairau Valley. While it started off with parcels of Cabernet Sauvignon, Montepulciano and Sangiovese, these later ripening varieties have been given the nudge in Marlborough's cool climate although Malbec and Syrah survived the cull. In addition to its gorgeous Pinot Noir, it makes Sauvignon Blanc, Chardonnay, Riesling and Gewürztraminer. The winery's La Strada range, named after Fellini's Oscar-winning tearjerker, is a more affordable entry point to the Fromm range. Approachable on release, it is a non-vineyard specific range and it offers incredible value for money. Since it produced its first crop in 1994, Fromm has bought fruit from the Clayvin vineyard, the first close-planted hillside vineyard in Marlborough. While Giesen now owns the vineyard, Fromm continues to produce a complex Clayvin Pinot with depth, fruit richness and abundant tannin. In 2015, it added two single vineyard Pinot Noirs: Churton and Quarters Vineyards. It has also introduced Pinot Naturel: wild fermented with no additions, no fining or filtration, a portion of carbonic maceration brings lifted aromatics, which are pure joy in a glass. Fromm is also one of those Marlborough oddballs making Syrah. Hätsch Kalberer, the classical music-loving winemaker who has been at Fromm since day one, explains: 'Most benchmark wines are grown in marginal climates. Marlborough is marginal for Syrah yet it works every year. We have to be careful with our crop levels and allow more fruit exposure. In our vineyard Syrah is never overripe nor too alcoholic; we get a lovely flavour spectrum even at 19.5 or 20 Brix.'

Try this: Fromm Winery Cuvée H Pinot Noir
Fleshy and seductive with depth on the mid palate, this is a blend of its five single-vineyard wines. An abundance of lovely mouth-coating fine-grained tannins and long tea-leaf-like finish. Can be enjoyed when young but there's no rush to pull the cork. Yes, a cork. Fancy that!

Visit
The cellar door is open daily from 11 a.m. to 5 p.m. from October to April, and from 11 a.m. to 4 p.m. in the winter, from May to September. Private winery tours are also available by appointment. They've usually got some older library stock on hand as well as current releases.

Greywacke
Wairau Valley
greywacke.com

After twenty-five years making wine at Cloudy Bay, Kevin Judd wanted 'more time with the gumboots on and less time running reports'. But it meant starting from scratch again. He made his first Greywacke wines in 2009 with a little help from his friends: sourcing the fruit from friends and renting winery space from ex-Cloudy Bay colleagues at Marlborough producer Dog Point. Today, Judd, who was born in England and grew up in Australia, sources grapes from six growers and owns 2 hectares to produce seven wines: Sauvignon Blanc and Pinot Noir are at the heart of the Greywacke label. Since starting Greywacke, Judd has gone a bit wild: four of the seven wines in the range are wild fermented and the remainder have a hefty proportion of wild fermentation. The first of his Sauvignon Blancs is made along conventional lines: cool fermentation in stainless steel using mainly cultured yeast to produce a pure and aromatic expression. The Wild Sauvignon, as its name suggests, is wild fermented in old oak barrels (see Try this). The Chardonnay follows a similarly wild route and although it goes through full malolactic fermentation, the wine remains lithe and is never buttery. On the aromatic front, Greywacke Riesling – both off-dry and sweet – vintage dependent, always exudes a burst of sweet fruit like a ray of sunshine on the palate. His off-dry Pinot Gris is one of the most interesting expressions in New Zealand thanks to wild fermentation in old French oak barrels, time on lees and more than 50 per cent malolactic fermentation. Although white wine is the main event at Greywacke, Judd also sources fruit from the Southern Valleys to produce an increasingly soulful Pinot Noir. Judd is not only a talented winemaker, he is also a superb photographer – thanks for the cover shot, Kevin!

Try this: Greywacke Wild Sauvignon
Riper parcels of Sauvignon tend to end up in this barrel-fermented

Sauvignon. Winemaker Judd leaves the wine to do its own thing, which means fermentation can take up to two weeks to kick off and it can take a long time to finish fermenting – some barrels are still happily fermenting away a year after the grapes are picked so this is certainly not a quick-release Sauvignon. The result is a full-bodied, food-friendly wine. It shows struck-match characters, herbal, nettle and blackcurrant aromas but this is one Sauvignon that's not just about the aromas: there is a really interesting textural component. It is weighty, has a lovely, creamy lick and a fine grain on the finish. There's no doubting the complexity nor the quality of this wine but the style may not appeal to all.

Visits
By appointment only. Consult the website for contact details.

Hans Herzog Estate
Wairau Valley
herzog.co.nz
The Herzog family's wine heritage stretches back to the seventeenth century. Born in Switzerland, Hans Herzog followed the path his ancestors had forged and studied wine in Zurich. But the New World was calling. He travelled to California and Australia, but New Zealand's lure was too hard to resist. In 1998, Herzog and his wife Therese made their first wines and by 2000, the reality of working two harvests each year (in Switzerland and New Zealand) proved too much and they made the bold move to sell their vineyard and Michelin-starred restaurant in Switzerland and dedicate their lives to their new home in Marlborough. The stony vineyard sits in the northern part of the Wairau Valley, close to the Wairau river and the Richmond Range. Farmed organically since day one, the vineyard is home to twenty-eight different varieties, producing Sauvignon Blanc to Viognier, Pinot Noir to Cabernet Franc and, in 2018, celebrating his seventieth birthday, Herzog planted Carmenere. Vines are relatively close planted and yields are low – less than 1 kilogram per vine, making wine with intense concentration. The whites are typically fermented in 500-litre French oak puncheons while the reds are fermented slowly and then matured in barrel for between eighteen and thirty-six months. The wines are bottled with their vintage on the back label, de-emphasizing the seeming need of New Zealand

drinkers to have the newest, youngest wine on the table and underlining the Herzogs' long-term vision: 'For the Spirit [of Marlborough – a Merlot Cabernet Franc] and reds, our biggest market is New Zealand and no one has a really serious wine cellar at home so I do it for them. New Zealanders drink their wines too young. Everyone wants the newest wine every year but these wines need time.'

Try this: Hans Herzog Estate Viognier
Aged for eighteen months in puncheons, this is a full-bodied, ripe style, which caresses the palate. Intense level of fruit concentration with scents of apricot and elderflower. There's no oiliness and sufficient acidity to freshen the palate; and apricots and cream linger on the long finish.

Visit
Hans and Therese Herzog are a hospitality force in Marlborough. The cellar door is open every day with twice daily tours of the vineyard and winery; there is a bistro and restaurant on-site with a beautiful shaded veranda that makes it the perfect location to while away a summer's afternoon. It is also a wonderful place to stay for the weekend: its cosy country-chic vineyard cottage means you can enjoy all the delights of the restaurant without worrying about taxis; Hans will even bring breakfast to your cottage the next morning.

Mahi Wines
Wairau Valley
mahiwine.co.nz

Founded in 2001, Mahi specializes in single-vineyard wines from across the Wairau Valley. The irrepressible owner of Mahi, Brian Bicknell, has an in-depth knowledge of the Valley's nuances and expressions, which is expressed in liquid form. Mahi's focus is Sauvignon Blanc, Chardonnay and Pinot Noir. The approach to winemaking is gentle and low tech: whole-bunch pressing, wild fermentation, a high level of solids and no additions are standard practice for his whites off low-yielding sites. Bicknell is keen to reduce skin contact for Sauvignon Blanc in a bid to control the fruitiness of his wines: three of his sites are hand picked. The Boundary Farm Sauvignon Blanc, hailing from clay soils on a slope close to Blenheim, reflects its place with its much fuller palate weight and texture than those derived from river gravels. Barrel-fermented

Chardonnay is a major player at Mahi and the resulting wines – whatever the site – offer a high level of concentration, silken texture and flourish of acidity. The style of Pinot Noir is evolving at Mahi with earlier picking and more whole bunches providing sinew and spice to the piquant fruit.

Try this: Mahi Wines Twin Valleys Chardonnay
The Waihopai Valley meets the Wairau Valley, nearly 40 kilometres inland and at close to 100 metres altitude, providing a wider diurnal temperature range than by the coast. Here you'll find the 4-hectare Twin Valleys Vineyard, with 0.89 hectares dedicated to producing tiny berries of clone 95 Chardonnay. Whole-bunch pressed straight to barrel without any clarification, this is a full bodied and fully flavoured Chardonnay with a high level of savoury fruit concentration reminiscent of cream, lanolin and cashew. The wine sports a silken texture and a firm, lemony finish.

Visit
The winery and cellar door, which was the original base for sparkling wine producer Daniel Le Brun, sits at the base of an escarpment (fault line) to the west of Renwick. Tours and tastings at the cellar door are by appointment only, Monday to Friday, 10 a.m. to 3 p.m.

Seresin Estate
Wairau Valley
seresin.co.nz
Founded in 1992 by New Zealand cinematographer Michael Seresin, the brand made some changes in early 2018, selling the winery and surrounding vineyards west of the town of Renwick. Seresin's home patch is now Raupo Creek in the Omaka Valley, a 53-hectare vineyard established in 2001–02. While Sauvignon Blanc and Pinot Noir make up most of the plantings, you can also find Semillon, Pinot Gris, Chardonnay and even Viognier and Syrah. The brand continues to make its wine at the re-named Seresin winery, The Coterie, which has become a winemaking facility for small, quality-focused Marlborough producers. It's business as usual despite the sale: there remains a hands-off approach to vinifying its organic and biodynamically certified vineyards. Seresin makes Sauvignon Blanc that has little to do with the stereotypical Marlborough style: wild yeasts are used, there's usually

a proportion of juice that is barrel fermented and as much as 10 per cent Semillon can be included in the blend. The result is an out-of-the ordinary Sauvignon Blanc that sports talcum, floral aromas and an attractive salty lemon finish. Seresin's other main event is Pinot Noir. Its richest, most textural examples hail from its home base of Raupo Creek, its clay-rich hillside vineyard where vines are cropped low at a kilo per vine. There is no whole-bunch fermentation for Pinot Noir at Seresin but post-fermentation maceration can be as long as five or six weeks. The winery has taken its hands-off credentials to the next level with OSIP, a Sauvignon Blanc and Pinot Noir that have no sulphur added, at any stage. The pretty Pinot is eminently drinkable, pure and juicy.

Try this: Seresin Estate Sun & Moon Pinot Noir
Hailing from the clay soils of the Omaka, this is a spicy, mouthfilling and dense Pinot Noir. It shows sinew thanks to Marlborough's naturally fresh acidity and the clay-derived structured yet powdery tannins.

Visit
Tastings and visits can be arranged by appointment. Visit the website for contact details.

Te Whare Ra
Wairau Valley
twrwines.co.nz

Husband and wife winemaking team Anna and Jason Flowerday met while turning grapes into beautiful booze in McLaren Vale, Australia. Marlborough boy Jason lured South Australian Anna back to his homeland and the pair bought Te Whare Ra, one of Marlborough's oldest vineyards, in 2003. Established in 1979 by Allan and Joyce Hogan, the vines were grafted and survived phylloxera, which first appeared in Marlborough in 1984 and became widespread. As a result, the Flowerdays have some of the oldest – if not the oldest – vines in Marlborough.

The ambitious young couple have juggled the challenges that come with having two sets of twin girls while running an 11-hectare vineyard organically and biodynamically. While they buy some fruit from the Awatere Valley and the Omaka, wines labelled SV5182 signify that these are estate-grown wines – the code is their organic number, courtesy of certifying body BioGro. There were no Sauvignon Blanc vines when they bought the vineyard but there was a large block of Bordeaux varieties so there have been some changes under their ownership. However, Te Whare Ra remains an aromatic white specialist, producing taut and pure Rieslings from the home block in both dry and medium styles. It has also entered the world of Sauvignon Blanc, planting a little on the estate, as well as sourcing some fruit from the Upper Awatere. The home block Sauvignon (look out for that SV5182) is fermented in 600-litre used barrels. The result is an energetic, perfumed style with textural depth and mouthwatering acidity. On the red front, Te Whare Ra makes several serious Pinot Noirs and in warm, dry vintages its Syrah shows that the North Island does not have a monopoly on this variety.

Try this: Te Whare Ra SV5182 Toru
Meaning three in Māori, Toru is a blend of Riesling, Pinot Gris and Gewürztraminer. This Alsatian-inspired blend is co-fermented in a combination of stainless steel tanks and large format oak barrels. The Pinot Gris element brings texture, Gewürztraminer adds floral sumptuousness and Riesling brings line and length. It is an appetizing wine with plenty to keep your nose and palate occupied.

Visit
The cellar door is open weekdays from October until early March. During December and January it also opens on weekends.

Vavasour Wines
Awatere Valley
vavasour.com

The Vavasour family settled in the Awatere Valley in the 1890s and nearly a century later, in 1986, Peter Vavasour and partners developed the first vineyards in the region. Current winemaker Stu Marfell was at the first harvest in 1989 with his mother, brother and local farmers' wives. The vineyard now stretches to 85 hectares and was purchased by American-owned Foley Family Wines in 2009, but it has not strayed from its Awatere home.

Naturally cooler and windier than the Wairau Valley with lower fertility soils, Vavasour's Awatere grapes tend to be small and flavour packed, leading to wines with intense flavours, as well as deeper colour in the Pinot Noir. In addition to its pure, classic Sauvignon expression (see Try This), it also produces a characterful, whole-bunch pressed, barrel-fermented Sauvignon Blanc, Claudia's Vineyard. Staying with whites, Vavasour produces a zingy, barrel fermented Chardonnay, while single-site expression Anna's Vineyard is a step up in concentration and complexity.

The Pinot Noir fruit sourced from the 'Favourite' vineyard brings greater weight than river gravels thanks to soils with a clay loam content. It shows the cooler fruit profile of the region with bright, fresh fruit and lifted violet perfume. The wine spends around ten months maturing in 25 per cent new oak. Its entry level label is Dashwood, a blend of both valleys with the Awatere lending drive and structure to the Wairau's punchy aromatics.

Try this: Vavasour Wines Sauvignon Blanc
Vivacious with a taut citrussy profile, the 2010 vintage of this wine won the best Sauvignon Blanc over £10 at the Decanter World Wine Awards in 2011. Typically displaying oyster shell, nettles, lemon and even a hint of blackcurrant bud, this is pure and vibrant with a scintillating streak of acidity.

Visit
The Vavasour cellar door is situated at fellow Foley Family Wines brand Grove Mill, in the more popular tourist destination of the Wairau Valley. It is open seven days a week.

10

NELSON

'We are to the left of Blenheim in more ways than one.'
Judy Finn, co-founder, Neudorf Vineyards

It's an hour and a half's drive from Marlborough to Nelson. The journey takes you north and west (or left) through the tree-covered Richmond Range, past the shimmering waters of Pelorus Sound to the golden sandy beaches of Nelson. It is a region that attracts artists, hippies, naturists and liberal, left-leaning wine producers.

This is a wine region where small is beautiful. Most wineries are mom and pop operations that are focused on making wine in an idyllic region with a wonderful lifestyle. There's no burning desire to live out of a suitcase, selling wine to Europe, the Americas and Asia, as it would mean leaving this slice of paradise. The beauty of Nelson is hardly the best kept secret: the Abel Tasman National Park attracts 110,000 visitors a year to walk its trails, kayak its waters and spot the smelly seals.

Unlike Marlborough, Nelson is not carpeted in vines. Its moderate climate is perfectly suited to other crops from kiwi fruit and berries to hops, which supply the region's rapidly growing craft beer market. The region's evidence in support of a Geographical Indication (GI) explains that in recent times 'there has been an expansion of small artisan food producers growing and making an array of products from mushrooms to olives, to nuts, to cheese'. It is also home to the largest fishing port in Australasia, making it far from a monoculture. Its basket is truly flowing over.

LOOKING BACK

Forget grapes, Nelson's wine community has apples and pears to thank for attracting a pioneer of the modern wine industry. Austrian winemaker Hermann Seifried travelled to Nelson in 1971 to make apple wine for the New Zealand Pear and Apple Board. But it wasn't 'real' wine and he longed to plant grapes. So he started to look for land in Nelson and found a site in Upper Moutere, planting the first vines in 1974. At this time, many thought that the South Island was still too cold to be a reliable viticultural area but, over the Richmond Range, Montana was investing millions of dollars in land in equally cool Marlborough. And cool climate, wine-loving German speakers were here long before Seifried. Ruth Allan's *Nelson: a History of Early Settlement* describes how German emigrants who arrived aboard the *St Pauli* in 1843 included 'vine dressers [that] took vines with them with the intention of establishing vineyards and manufacturing wine in Nelson'. Upon their arrival, and hearing the news that they had found a hillside site suitable for growing grapes, the local newspaper *The Nelson Examiner* reported 'No emigrants are more valuable than the Germans and we hail the announcement of the intended cultivation of the vine with unfeigned pleasure.' Unfortunately their timing was pretty poor: relations between settlers and Māori were fragile and turned violent, throwing the settlement into disarray. The Germans soon upped sticks and headed for a more peaceful existence in Australia. It was another twenty years before F. H. M. Ellis and Sons set up Nelson's first winery, which operated continuously from 1868 to 1939. They were joined by several other grape growers in the following years, giving soon-to-be government viticulturist Romeo Bragato five vineyards to visit during his 1895 tour. 'From what I saw in Nelson I have no hesitation in advising the residents to plant vines on a large scale for wine-making purposes,' he reported. He was particularly taken with Upper Moutere, now home to producers including Neudorf Vineyards, Glover's Vineyard and Kahurangi Estate. He also thought it eminently suited to growing oak trees for barrel production, which seems a sensible idea – it would save the local industry the bother of shipping French oak barrels 19,000 kilometres.

Despite a glowing assessment, the vine took a long time to take root fully in Nelson. Viggo Dufresne was the first to give winegrowing in Nelson the attention it deserved in the second half of the twentieth century. In 1967, he was fermenting his first licensed crop of hybrid Seibel and producing Ruby Bay Red, despite the national viticultural station reporting that 'conditions in the South Island do not appear to favour grape growing for wine … wine production in the South Island [is] a difficult and doubtful proposition'. He persisted, and his tiny half-hectare vineyard on the edge of Tasman Bay produced a dry red that was the ultimate in minimal intervention. 'He refused any chemicals or even cultured yeasts. Old whisky barrels were tossed in the tide to deodorize them. The lips and teeth of Ruby Bay Red drinkers were the wine's only filter. '"Peasant's wine" he called it,' explains Jacqueline Haydn in *New Zealand Geographic*.

The peasant's wine wasn't drunk by peasants, however. There was a growing thirst for dry table wines in the 1970s and 1980s, and there were people willing to give it a go in Nelson. Hermann Seifried and his wife Agnes were joined by Tim and Judy Finn, who produced the first vintage of Neudorf in 1981, and David Glover, a mathematician who analyzed missiles coming out of submarines for the Australian Department of Defence before giving it all up for a Nelson vineyard. The region is still young and learning, however. Todd Stevens, the Neudorf winemaker, says: 'We only get to make wine once a year but as a chef you get to make dishes every night ten times. We are only forty vintages deep and we are one of the oldest [wineries] in Nelson so [in restaurant terms] we have not even reached closing time on the opening night. Wine is an incredibly slow learning curve.'

It has taken a while for Nelson to catch the wine bug but it has grown from 35 hectares in 1983 to 1,093 in 2017. The early years were a case of working out what to plant, trialling Italian and Bordeaux varieties as well as Chardonnay, white aromatics and Pinot Noir, which seem to be Nelson's highest achievers. In 1992, there were still just 81 hectares of vineyards but the 1990s brought a proliferation of new producers including Greenhough Vineyards, Brightwater Vineyards, Waimea Estates, Rimu Grove and Kaimira Estate. The early 1990s also gave Nelson its first wins at international wine competitions, raising awareness of Nelson beyond the Richmond Range.

GEOGRAPHY AND CLIMATE

The winegrowing area of Nelson sits on the edge of Tasman Bay, so called because Abel Janszoon Tasman sailed into the Bay in 1642 during a voyage of discovery for the Dutch East India Company. It is a sheltered spot: sitting on the waters of Tasman Bay, the region is cupped in a horseshoe of tree-covered mountains. To the east lies the Richmond Range, which separates Nelson from Marlborough; to the west the mountainous Kahurangi National Park acts as a barrier to the prevailing westerly winds. Hills rise to the south beyond the Waimea Plains and up to Nelson Lakes National Park where Mount Franklin stands tall at 2,327 metres. Its coastal location means frost is fairly low on the list of concerns for local grape growers and frost machines are uncommon. This is not a place of extremes due to the maritime climate: during the summer, sea breezes cool the days to peaks of around 25°C and mean minimum temperatures (i.e. night-time temperatures) remain pleasant in the low teens. 'We are always on the simmer, never on the boil,' says Stevens.

However, Nelson does have sunlight in spades: there's often a bit of debate between Marlburian and Nelson winemakers about which region receives the most sunshine, much as Australians and New Zealanders bicker over who invented the pavlova. The title can change hands on an annual basis, but the National Institute of Water and Atmospheric Research (NIWA) reports that the thirty-year average (1981–2010) in Nelson is 2,472 hours and 2,475 hours in the urban capital of Marlborough, Blenheim. I imagine those numbers won't settle the argument, and nor will the argument over the ownership of the meringue-based dessert be resolved.

Despite being relatively sheltered geographically, Nelson is the only New Zealand wine region on the western side of the country and is thus a little wetter than those sitting on the east coast: it receives around 960 mm annually (NIWA thirty-year average) compared with 704 mm in Marlborough. Summer brings the driest conditions and it can experience drought but April, a crucial month for harvest, is the third wettest month of the year. As a result, growers need to be on the alert for fungal diseases including botrytis and need to open up their canopies to allow ventilation. Recent wet vintages include 2016 and 2017 but Chris

Seifried remembers a particularly soggy year, 1995: 'I came home from university [where he was studying winemaking] and it rained every day and everything rotted; harvesters were stuck. There was lots of dilution, low sugar levels, it was an awful vintage.'

However, sufficient rainfall allows producers on the clay-gravel soils of the Moutere Hills to dry farm, which makes Nelson more sustainable than most. At Neudorf Vineyards, irrigation is only used to establish young vines; its older vines have to rely on nature for their water needs. Tim Finn, co-founder of Neudorf Vineyards in Upper Moutere, remembers the rather rudimentary irrigation system they first used. 'In the early years we didn't have irrigation so I put Judy [his wife] on the back of the tractor with a tank of water and a [spray] gun.' Judy is still talking to him and has no long-term injuries to report. The Waimea Plains are free draining and require irrigation, however: Andrew Greenhough of Greenhough Vineyards has also converted the estate to organic viticulture and, with more under-vine competition from cover crops, the vines need a little more water.

WHAT LIES BENEATH

The Waimea Plains

From the shores of Tasman Bay to the surrounding hills, the Waimea Plains area is low-lying land dominated by free-draining gravel soils deposited 18,000 to 25,000 years ago by two rivers: the Wairoa and Wai-iti, explains the region's GI application. The rivers have also left behind fine silty and clay loams in places, which retain some moisture. Fertility is modest and the vines require irrigation during dry summer periods. There are many producers based here – Seifried started in the Moutere Hills but is now firmly ensconced on the Plains. They are joined by producers including Brightwater Wines, Greenhough Vineyards, Richmond Plains and Waimea Estates. Both whites and reds are typically light to medium bodied and fresh with clear fruit expression.

The Moutere Hills

The Moutere Hills lie a few minutes' drive north west of the Waimea Plains. They form a series of gentle ups and downs that rise lazily from the plains. The vineyards don't sit at a great height: elevations of around 50 to 100 metres are most common so altitude doesn't play a significant role in the wine styles. It is what lies beneath that sets the hills apart from the plains. According to several reports by a Nelson-based soil expert, Dr Iain Campbell, a layer of gravel more than 1 kilometre thick was deposited by glacial movements millions of years ago. Since then, there have been a few geological happenings which have mostly involved fluvial erosion leading to the creation of these ups and downs. The alluvial matter left behind by the rivers has weathered to form clay-bound gravel with a topsoil of sandy loam. These soils are able to retain moisture, which is beneficial in the dry summer months, and they are low in vigour. The resulting wines tend to have more structure, weight and depth than on the plains. Here you'll find producers including Neudorf Vineyards, Kahurangi Estate and Alex Craighead.

Small is beautiful in Nelson: representing approximately 3 per cent of the nation's wine production, the average vineyard size is 9.8 hectares compared with a national average of 18.5 hectares. Across New Zealand, there are eighteen producers making more than four million litres of wine annually – and none of them are in Nelson. In fact, there are just three wineries in the region that produce more than 200,000 litres of wine each year and the majority make less than 45,000 litres. That's why there are a lot of small cellar doors selling their wines locally, and they are often manned by the owner or the bloke who tends the vines: they might have pruning shears in hand when they greet you. Chris Seifried says, 'Nelson is to Marlborough what Oregon is to Napa – wine production is more grass roots. When we go to Marlborough we always think "it's a bit flash!"'

WINE STYLES

Sauvignon Blanc is the most planted variety in Nelson despite the area considering itself a world away from Marlborough. It produces a dry and gentle expression of Sauvignon, which is neither exuberant nor thiol-laden, and alcohol levels can be refreshingly moderate. It could be the more clement, maritime climate or it might be the region's signature yeast: in 2015, a team of scientists discovered that the strains of *Saccharomyces cerevisiae* found in New Zealand's key Sauvignon regions produced distinct aromas and flavours, suggesting there is more to terroir than soil, climate and grape. The most distinct regional signature belonged to those wines produced by strains of yeast from Nelson, which contained particularly high concentrations of compounds that impart a sweet fruit and apple character to the wines. The more subtle, restrained character found in the region's Sauvignons can be found in its other Alsatian whites: Pinot Gris, Riesling and Gewürztraminer collectively account for around 15 per cent of Nelson's vineyards and offer the same restraint and purity you find in its Sauvignon Blancs.

Nelson made its name as a Chardonnay producer par excellence through the wine quality and international marketing efforts of Neudorf Vineyards. On the clay-gravel soils of the Moutere Hills, Neudorf produces high-quality, savoury Chardonnays with a high level of fruit concentration and richness on the mid palate sewn up by a fine line of acidity. Andrew Greenhough keeps Chardonnay lovers fulfilled on the Waimea Plains, producing delicate and finely constructed Chardonnays from his organically farmed Hope Vineyard. Based on this pair you'd think many others would have jumped aboard the Chardonnay train, but the variety represents less than 10 per cent of all plantings.

Pinot Noir is the main red variety in Nelson, making a range of styles. The plains tend to create a lighter style with lots of juicy red fruit and supple tannins. The finest barrel-aged examples offer concentration of fruit and finesse. On the hills, the clay-gravel soils produce a more structured, weighty expression. The most ambitious examples offer softness of plum fruit, often a savoury character, mouth-coating tannins and a fresh burst of acidity. There are also several newcomers who are bringing more daring techniques to Nelson Pinot Noir, such as 100 per cent whole-bunch fermentation and fermentation in amphoras, in addition to no fining and no filtration. It breaks with convention but it also questions the definition of what constitutes a 'regional style'.

Nelson doesn't have a signature variety and the styles that the gravels of the Plains produce are quite different to those from the Hills. Inevitably there is a range of quality levels and each winery has different ambitions for their wines and their lives. Some producers specialize in Chardonnay and Pinot Noir, others in Sauvignon Blanc and aromatic whites. Its eclectic nature makes it quite difficult to communicate what Nelson is to wine lovers around the world. Michael Glover, a recent returnee to Nelson after a long period making wine in Victoria, Australia, has an alternative view for Nelson's future: 'Why can't we be the area of the artisan? It's an area of potters and artists. This is the region you go to when you want to do what you want – making cool, quirky things on a small scale. Everyone else in Nelson is being quirky, why not wine producers?'

PRODUCER PROFILES

Alex Craighead Wines

Upper Moutere
alexcraighead.co.nz

Speak to people in the know in Nelson about who's new and exciting and the answer will invariably be Alex Craighead. Born in Sydney and raised in Christchurch, Craighead and his Argentinean partner Josefina left the windy climes of Martinborough behind for the Moutere Hills, purchasing Sunset Valley Vineyard in 2016. Originally planted in 1993 and farmed organically from day one, the 3.5 hectares provide the pair with Chardonnay, Pinot Noir, Sauvignon Blanc, Riesling, Gewürztraminer, Pinot Gris and Syrah. In 2017, they planted Gamay; Vermentino followed in 2018. The winemaking philosophy for both the Don and Kindeli labels is to make clean, technically correct wines without any additives. They develop wild starters for each vineyard and look to co-ferment varieties. New oak doesn't have a place here; inert vessels including amphoras, old oak barrels and former beer tanks are the modus operandi. From 2018, the Don label became a single vineyard Pinot Noir and Chardonnay specialist while Kindeli is a little more quirky. The range includes two *pétillant naturels*, a skin-fermented Chardonnay, and a Syrah produced with a high level of carbonic maceration. No fining, no filtration and no additives is a given in a bottle of Kindeli. If you're a classic claret drinker, these wines might be a little quirky for your liking.

Try this: Don Pinot Noir
As far away from classic Nelson Pinot Noir as you're going to get, but intriguing nonetheless. Craighead uses a high proportion of whole bunches; it is unfined and unfiltered and the result is a wine that speaks of its winemaking as much as its place. It is bright with a cool, fragrant nose bursting with fresh cranberry and red cherry fruit. A mid-weight expression with a fine precise finish. One to watch.

Visit
Cellar door visits are by appointment only. There is also vineyard accommodation available. Visit the Kindeli website for more details.

Greenhough Vineyards
Hope
greenhough.co.nz
Armed with a degree in art history, Andrew Greenhough was not suitably qualified for a career in wine but, after selling up a food business he ran with his chef brother in 1989, he wasn't sure what to do with his life and applied for a job in the cellar of Villa Maria in Auckland. From there Greenhough and his wife Jenny quit the big smoke for a quieter life making wine in Nelson. 'It was all reasonably naive and spontaneous, to be honest. We just wanted to start a new life in a new place and make some wine. We didn't cherry pick a region for wine; we wanted a lovely place to live.'

The pair bought an existing vineyard in 1990 from a keen amateur on the eastern side of the Waimea Plains. It was originally planted with Cabernet Sauvignon, Gewürztraminer, Müller-Thurgau and Riesling. More than a quarter of a century later, the 4-hectare adventure has expanded to 11 hectares; the Müller-Thurgau is long gone and the quality of Greenhough's wines clearly shows that the pair knows exactly what they are doing. Pinot Noir represents close to half of all Greenhough's plantings and the Hope Vineyard cuvée produces a delicate wine with a lovely core of ripe fruit and a fine sinewy conclusion. Sauvignon Blanc accounts for close to a third of the vineyards, making a restrained and highly successful barrel-fermented cuvée. The Hope Vineyard Chardonnay (see Try This) is joined by the rarely seen non-aromatic variety Pinot Blanc which offers a silken texture, appetizing almond and lemon flavours, and a fine line of acidity. It also has a tiny parcel of Riesling, including three rows on their own roots dating back to 1976. Since 2011 the vineyards have been certified organic; winemaking is hands off and all the ferments are wild.

Try this: Greenhough Hope Vineyard Chardonnay
Produced from two organically grown parcels, this Chardonnay can take months to ferment in barrel as wild yeasts slowly transform the sticky grape juice into a delicate white wine that has subtle nectarine fruit flavours and savoury nutty characters. It is a beautifully constructed wine, offering density of fruit within a delicate frame; a fine line of acidity sews up the outfit.

Visit
The cellar door is open during the summer months; check the website for opening times. Visits are by appointment only the rest of the year.

Kahurangi Estate
Upper Moutere
kahurangiwine.com

Hermann Seifried's original vineyard was purchased by Greg and Amanda Day in 1998. Sitting on Moutere clay, it specializes in aromatic whites and boasts the oldest Riesling vines in the South Island, dating back to 1973. The variety produces five different styles from dry to sweet. Its reserve range, Mt Arthur, is named after a 1,795-metre peak in the Kahurangi National Park. In addition to fruit from its home vineyard, it also sources fruit for its Estate range from the stony soils of the Waimea Plains.

Try this: Kahurangi Estate Dry Riesling
This wine is a piece of New Zealand history, being made from the oldest Riesling vines in the South Island. The Moutere clays give a touch of additional weight to this citrussy Riesling, which finishes dry and crisp.

Visit
The cellar door is open five days a week, Wednesday to Sunday, for tastings. There is a small charge which is refunded if wine is purchased. There is also vineyard accommodation on site. Visit the website for more details.

Mammoth Wines

Upper Moutere
mammothwines.co.nz

Outspoken, occasionally outlandish and out to make great wine, Michael Glover has finally returned to Nelson after a long absence. The son of Dave Glover, one of the early Pinot pioneers in Nelson, Glover Jr says 'Having made my career and reputation in Australia it is very humbling to return to New Zealand and hear "Oh, you're Dave Glover's son, aren't you?" Ha!'

Glover's Vineyard was founded on the clay gravel soils of Upper Moutere in 1984 with Sauvignon Blanc, Pinot Noir and Cabernet Sauvignon. Unsurprisingly the Cabernet Sauvignon didn't make the grade and was soon replaced with Chardonnay and Pinot Noir. While the vines were maturing in Glover's father's vineyard, Michael was off travelling the world making wine, including a ten-year stint (2005–15) at Bannockburn Vineyards in Victoria, Australia. Glover returned to make wine in Nelson and has started his own small label. He produces an alternative interpretation of Sauvignon Blanc (see Try This), as well as an intriguing Pinot Noir using 100 per cent whole bunches to maximize perfume. He also believes there is a rusticity in Moutere Pinot Noir, which whole berries can minimize. There's no destemming, no machinery and when he feels like crushing the grapes, he'll use his feet. Glover sources the fruit from his parents' vineyard and local organic growers who dry farm. He has taken over the stewardship of the family vineyard and intends to increase planting density to 10,000 vines per hectares. He will certainly shake up the Nelson wine scene with his personality as well as his wines.

Try this: Mammoth Rare White

It's a Sauvignon Blanc, but not as you know it. Inspired by a vintage in southern Italy making skin-fermented Fiano in acacia puncheons to the sounds of Charlie Parker, Glover has been making skin-contact whites for more than a decade in Australia. This Sauvignon Blanc undergoes carbonic maceration for fourteen days before being pressed and transferred to made-to-order 200-litre French oak vessels that emphasize the lees to wine ratio. The wine spends eighteen months on gross ferment lees before being bottled. While there's still varietal character here, this is a multi-layered, fascinating wine that offers another facet at every swig.

Visit

Mammoth's HQ is now at Glover's Vineyard. Visitors are welcome by appointment.

Neudorf Vineyards
Upper Moutere
neudorf.co.nz

An expert in animal behaviour and a journalist were two of the key ingredients in the Neudorf blend: founders Tim and Judy Finn started planting grapes in Upper Moutere, home to the country's oldest pub, and produced their first wine in 1981. In addition to Chardonnay and Pinot Noir, which turned out to be perfectly suited to their clay-gravel site, Cabernet Sauvignon, Cabernet Franc, Gamay, Müller-Thurgau and a fruit salad of other varieties were put on trial but didn't make the grade. Today, Pinot Gris, Riesling and Albariño have been given the official seal of approval by the Finns to sit alongside their precious Pinot Noir and Chardonnay vines. In addition to dry farming their vineyards, Neudorf has practised organic viticulture since 2010, achieving certification in 2016. The natural approach is pursued from grape to glass: all wines are left to ferment without the addition of packet yeasts (except the Sauvignon Blanc, which increases the proportion of wild fermentation year on year). Its inaugural wine was a barrel-fermented Chardonnay and the varietal continues to be the winery's crowning glory. In addition to its Moutere Chardonnay (see Try This), the addition of Rosie's Block in 1999 (named after their daughter and heir to the Neudorf throne), overlooking the home block, is more friendly in its youth, offering Neudorf's hallmark textural appeal, savoury thread and creamy allure. Best of all, it's good value. Also from Rosie's Block comes Twenty Five Rows Chardonnay. What started as an experiment inspired by the unoaked wines of Chablis has become an opportunity to taste unadulterated Neudorf fruit. Pure, sunlight filled and citrus led, it offers flesh on the mid palate and a linear finish. Neudorf's other calling card is Pinot Noir. Its Moutere Pinot Noir and Tom's Block – a neighbouring paddock which was purchased and planted entirely to Burgundy's red grape in 1999 – offer an unfiltered, savoury interpretation with smoky charcuterie-like flavours, broody plum and spice. They are round and gentle but the cool climate of the South Island is always in the background providing a flush of tightening acidity in conclusion. Its

aromatic whites – Riesling, Pinot Gris and the recent addition, Albariño
– offer purity of fruit, fragrance and precise acidity.

Try this: Neudorf Vineyards Moutere Chardonnay
Produced entirely from the hen and chicken-prone Mendoza clone,
the Moutere Chardonnay is tightly wound in its youth. The wine is
always focused with innate power. A high level of solids feeds the wild
yeasts that drive this barrel fermentation along and, when coupled with
extended lees ageing and *bâtonnage*, the result is a savoury Chardonnay
with richness on the mid palate. Give it time to blossom fully.

Visit
The farmhouse-style cellar door at Neudorf is open daily from 11 a.m.
to 5 p.m. during the summer. In the winter months of July and August
it is closed. There is no restaurant but antipasto-style food is available.
Check the website for full details and opening times.

Seifried Estate
Appleby
seifried.co.nz

Austrian-born Hermann Seifried, an incredible hulk who could outwork
any man on a vineyard, planted his first vines in Upper Moutere in
1973. He had travelled to New Zealand to work for the country's Apple
and Pear Board but armed with a winemaking degree, he soon yearned
to make wine in his new home. He met his Kiwi wife, Agnes, on the
local ski slope and the pair, soon with three children in tow, built the
Seifried vineyards and wine brand to become Nelson's biggest producer.
Seifried planted a fruit salad of varieties in the virgin land to see what
was best suited to the area, but it soon became clear that aromatic whites
and Pinot Noir were the best way forward. The company grew and grew
and, in 1992, bought a piece of land on the Waimea Plains on the main
road from Nelson to Abel Tasman National Park. Today, they have nine
vineyards covering 300 hectares from free-draining river gravels to clay-
based slopes. The winery put itself on the world map by winning the
1994 International Wine and Spirit Challenge Sauvignon Blanc trophy,
but its most famous wine is perhaps Sweet Agnes Riesling, a late-harvest
dessert wine whose trophy cabinet is overflowing with domestic and
international awards. There is a large number of wines made under the
Seifried umbrella. Its four ranges are Seifried, Winemakers Collection,

Old Coach Road and its premium range, Aotea. The latter now includes a Pinot Noir/Chardonnay 'traditional method' sparkling wine, which spent four years on lees. Hermann and Agnes's children all work in the business and when two grandchildren were born fifteen hours apart in April 2011, the sparkling wine was conceived to celebrate the births.

Try this: Seifried Estate Sweet Agnes Riesling
An unctuous late harvest Riesling hailing from a free-draining stony site about 12 kilometres from the coast. The concentrated, shrivelled berries provide intense orange and floral fruit characters and a high residual sugar level – it usually sits in the high 100s. Thank goodness for Riesling's high natural acidity to cut through such sweetness.

Visit
Seifried is perfectly situated close to Nelson on the main road out to Abel Tasman. The cellar door is open seven days a week and, this being a family winery, children are very welcome: there is a playground and non-alcoholic grape juice to drink.

Spencer Hill
Upper Moutere
spencerhillwine.com
One of only three Nelson wineries producing more than 200,000 litres of wine annually, Spencer Hill specializes in Chardonnay, oak-aged

Sauvignon Blanc and kosher wine. It has 20 hectares of vines planted on the clay gravels of the Moutere Hills, which are mostly dry farmed. It was founded by Philip Jones, a San Francisco businessman who sold up and moved to Nelson in the late 1980s, producing his first vintage in 1992. Its most affordable range is Latitude 41˚C, which offers a gentle yet fresh Sauvignon Blanc sur lie, a delicate yet round barrel-fermented Sauvignon Blanc and a structured clone 5-dominant Pinot Noir. The Spencer Hill label is a selection of its best parcels of fruit, which are bolder in terms of winemaking inputs such as solids, oak and lees. Its kosher label Goose Bay is sold in the United States. Staying Stateside, the family also own a winery in Oregon. Pacifica is situated closer to the border with Washington state.

Try this: Latitude 41˚C by Spencer Hill, Small Batch Pinot Noir
Made in one-tonne batches, this Pinot Noir offers plenty of ripe fruit on entry but the core of this wine is spicy and gutsy with unexpected structure on the finish. Oak-derived vanilla supports the fruit.

Visit
Tastings are by appointment only. Visit the website for contact details.

Waimea Estates
Richmond
waimeaestates.co.nz
Founded by Trevor and Robyn Bolitho on the Waimea Plains in 1993, the winery was acquired in 2017 by Wellington-based superannuation fund Booster. The deal was spearheaded by Louis Vavasour, the founder of Awatere River Wine Company, in which Booster has also taken a stakeholding. In 1997 Waimea produced its first wine, which was awarded the title of 'Best Sauvignon Blanc' in Australasia by *Winestate* magazine; the variety continues to be one of its signature styles. It excels at aromatic whites and, in addition to the usual suspects, Waimea has expanded its mind and vineyards to lesser-known varieties that are well suited to the sunny maritime Nelson climate including Grüner Veltliner and Albariño. Both have been received with critical acclaim. Its classic Riesling consistently provides a fine and balanced citrus expression with a line of fresh acidity. In addition to aromatic whites, it also produces a balanced, fruit-led Pinot Noir that offers a touch of sensitive new

French oak that brings complexity without becoming the main event. Its second label, Spinyback, is named after a native lizard, the tuatara.

Try this: Waimea Estates Albariño
First produced in 2014, Waimea has done a great job of harnessing the beauty of this Galician native from the off. The wine is fermented at cool temperatures in inert vessels to preserve the variety's ripe apple, peach fruit and floral characters. It offers depth on the mid palate with mouthwatering acidity on the finish.

Visit
The cellar door and cafe are both open daily. Check the website for opening times.

11

CANTERBURY AND NORTH CANTERBURY

Take a class of Master of Wine students, add a week of gruelling seminars and then give them a quiz at the end. Inevitably, brain cells will be fried and confidence battered but they should be able to name the four major wine producing regions of New Zealand's South Island, right?

Wrong!

It took a New Zealand resident (me) to remind everyone that (North) Canterbury existed. Marlborough, Central Otago and Nelson were all ticked off without worry but the fourth region – what could it be?

If this is the state of play for MW students, who should have a mastery of wine general knowledge at their fingertips before even embarking upon the course, then where does that leave the rest of the world? Eyes down, look in and get to know North Canterbury, because this is a region that remains relatively undiscovered but, true to its slogan 'the coolest little wine region in the country', this is the hottest place to be right now.

Those who remember Central Otago and Marlborough in the late 1980s and early 1990s compare it to North Canterbury today. It is still a small, rural area with a strong sense of community between the producers. Many of the key players are in their forties and they socialize together, their children go to school together, and they are happy to not only promote their wines but also the region. They look outward not inward, and their future is bright.

LOOKING BACK

Canterbury's first encounter with vines was as early as the 1840s. Frenchmen were given free transport and just over 2 hectares of land in Akaroa on Canterbury's Banks Peninsula as long as they stayed in the colony for five years. In *Canterbury, Grapes and Wines: 1840–2002* the vinous history of the region is told fully. Those who took up the offer of the Nanto-Bordelaise emigrant company were offered half of any land that they cleared and, in exchange for produce, could buy agricultural equipment. While a Marist priest is thought to have carried vines with him to Akaroa, there were no vignerons on board – though there was a shoemaker, a blacksmith, a gardener, and a locksmith. Nevertheless, vineyards did flourish alongside other crops despite the cool, windy conditions that had initially concerned newcomers. A writer from Christchurch newspaper *The Press* who travelled aboard the first carriage journey from Akaroa to Christchurch reported that upon reaching Akaroa in February 1872 he saw the cottages of French settlers 'each with their little vineyard dotting the hillside, and making a pleasant feature in the landscape'. But as the initial settlers died, so too did their vines. By the time Romeo Bragato arrived in New Zealand to survey the country's vineyards in 1895, Akaroa's early promise had not been fulfilled. In his report, Bragato says 'It would seem that the pioneer French settlers of Akaroa failed to communicate to their offspring even a small percentage of that enthusiasm over the cultivation of the vine which they were in such a large measure possessed of, or it may be their descendants suspended work by reason of the vines becoming attacked with oidium, thus causing the disappearance of vineyards which had been to their forebears as a bit of the fatherland.' Although he tasted some Chasselas and Muscat of Frontignan and noted that fine Rhine-like wine might be made here, it was clear that humans were an essential part of the terroir, and they were the missing part of the equation.

Today, there are a few vineyards in the Akaroa area but the town is now more famous for its dolphin-watching tours than its wine. The French fire still burns, however. Renan Cataliotti, a native of Antibes on the Mediterranean coast, heard about the French history of Akaroa while backpacking in New Zealand. A one-day visit turned into a six-week stay and the start of his new life: he met his now wife, Joey, they have since had two children together and he undertook a viticulture and winemaking course. He now manages French Peak Wines in Akaroa and leases a 3-hectare vineyard at French Farm, farming organically

The modern history of Canterbury's wine production begins in a car park. *Canterbury's Grapes and Wines* explains that in the 1960s, Graham Thiele, a lecturer at the local agricultural college, Lincoln, suggested that Canterbury could be a successful wine region and 'he arranged for the planting of an experimental row of grapevines … They did not flourish, appearing to be affected by a virus. The principal of the day, Dr Malcolm Burns, ordered their removal.' While the vineyard is now a memory and the land is used as a car park at Lincoln University, a lecturer in fruit production – David Jackson – turned up just in time to see the vines. With the help of Czech-born winemaker Daniel Schuster, Jackson started seminars and workshops in grape growing and winemaking and successfully applied for a grant to study grape growing in Canterbury. His research found that wind, frost, birds and wasps were challenges for growing grapes here – and they still are. Emboldened by their seminars, several vineyards were planted around the Christchurch area. Robin Mundy planted St Helena and employed Danny Schuster as winemaker. Its 1982 Pinot Noir won a gold medal at the Air New Zealand wine competition and suddenly Canterbury was back on the winemaking map.

Further north in the Waipara Valley, five vineyards were planted in the early 1980s. Sheltered from the cold easterly wind by the Teviotdale hills, this area grew rapidly and is now the dominant voice in the Canterbury wine choir, representing 90 per cent of the region's vineyards. Pioneers have even ventured inland to Waikari. In the 1880s, an Alsatian woman, Sophie Glasman, considered that the area's limestone had the potential to make great wines; more than a century later, Bell Hill and Pyramid Valley Vineyards fulfilled her vision with exceptional results. Today, the term North Canterbury seeks to embrace growers from Waikari and Waipara under one banner. It is easier to pronounce than Waipara and won't be confused with Wairarapa. Let's hope Master of Wine students have now got North Canterbury on their radar. They'll be missing out, if not.

GEOGRAPHY AND CLIMATE

It was a sad day at Greystone Wines on 15 November 2014: the vineyard team lost its mobile tearoom to caravan heaven. Sitting on the summit of the vineyard, the caravan provided much-needed shelter on cold days; it was a place to brew a cup of coffee or eat lunch and warm up frozen pruning fingers. On this particularly gusty day the caravan was swept to its end. Blown from its home and down a gully, the caravan and well-used microwave could not be saved. Lesson learned, and now even the vineyard loos are tied down to prevent an unsavoury incident.

The caravan episode is an illustration of one of the major challenges for Cantabrian grape growers: wind. The focal point of the region's wine industry is now centred around the sleepy town of Waipara, about forty-five minutes' drive north of Christchurch. Waipara Valley is protected from cold easterly winds by the Teviotdale hills, which rise to heights of more than 500 metres at their zenith. Nestled close to the hills' protective shield, the vines take shelter, but wind is still considered one of the major challenges here. Across Canterbury, the drying north-westerlies, known as norwesters, streak through the region in spring and summer. If you look to the sky and see streaky clouds over the Southern Alps, hold on to your hats, portaloos or caravans: the hot, moistureless wind races across the plains and can batter shoots, leaves and cause water stress, particularly on warm summer days. Rows of trees known as shelter belts are common in a bid to slow the pace of these ferocious norwesters. Ivan Donaldson, founder of Pegasus Bay Winery, remembers the new owner of a neighbouring vineyard wanting to chop down the trees that stood between their vineyards because they attracted hungry grape-loving birds. Donaldson refused: he knew that nets could stop the birds from eating the fattening berries, but only the trees could slow the wind. Needless to say, the trees are still standing tall.

North Canterbury is a cool climate. With 1,288 growing degree days it is not dissimilar in its heat summation to Marlborough (1,241), which is 250 kilometres north of Waipara. The winters can be very cold. Nick Gill, the founding viticulturist at Greystone Wines, was acclimatized to the heat of his native South Australia and the bitter winters were a shock to his system: 'I had never done cool climate Canterbury viticulture – I had never seen snow before I came here!' But since his arrival in the early 2000s, snow has been known to fall to sea level, and he witnessed a low of -15°C in the vineyard, killing buds on the vine before they had had a chance to burst. In the spring, frost remains one of the biggest worries for growers and, if the vines negotiate the freezing nights, cold weather and rain during flowering can be equally problematic. Many wineries in the region reported poor yields in 2005, 2007, 2012 and 2015 as a result of rain at flowering. This inherent variability between seasons is part of the North Canterbury terroir. 'Crop levels can alter significantly: one year you might make enough for eight months' supply of wine and the next vintage, you might make fifteen months' worth of wine,' says Pegasus Bay's marketing manager, Edward Donaldson.

Despite concerns about rain at flowering, North Canterbury is actually rather dry, thanks to the rain shadow provided by the Southern Alps which form the South Island's spiny backbone: just 623 mm of rain falls annually, which is less than Marlborough, with the majority falling in the winter and early spring. In combination with the low summer rainfall and the warm, drying norwester, vines can become stressed and require irrigation during the growing season. That said, autumn rainfall can deal a sharp blow to growers, as they wait for their grapes to ripen. Nicholas Brown, winemaker at Black Estate, explains the dry and wet sides of North Canterbury: 'I grew up in Christchurch and would drive through here on my way to Hanmer Springs [a spa and skiing village]. It was just a dry and arid place.' However, as harvest approaches, rain and the tail end of wet tropical storms have a tendency to find their way to New Zealand. 'In 2014, I remember looking at the Home Vineyard and it was amazing: there was so much fruit there but we only ended up getting one-third of it off [the vines] because the rains came,' he explains. The pain of losing two-thirds of the harvest followed by the aha moment that they didn't need to hang the fruit out as late as they thought to achieve ripeness has been a hard-learned lesson. 'We don't need massive ripeness if you work hard through the season, you can get the fruit ripe with lovely freshness,' he says.

WHAT LIES BENEATH

The wine-producing areas of North Canterbury have many distinctive soils but the three that are of most interest to Waipara wine drinkers are

Glasnevin Gravels, Awapuni clay loam and Omihi clay loam. For those that are interested, a group of soil scientists based at Lincoln University and Landcare Research compiled a comprehensive study on the region's geology and soil in 2015. Stretching to more than 200 pages, it is almost as complex as applied mathematics.

Having distilled the information, the long and short is that the Glasnevin Gravels are free-draining gravelly sandy loams. The Waipara river left sand, silt and loam particles behind in varied proportion in the vine-rich flatlands of the valley. The Pinot Noir styles from this area are lighter in style with juicy, fruit-forward appeal. A number of wine producers on these soils seek to make more serious styles, including Pegasus Bay, which attributes its structural framework to the Swiss clone 10/5 (10 bar 5).

The most exciting area in Waipara for fine wine sits to the north and east of the town in the Omihi valley. The vineyards sit on fan slopes facing north and north-west, with Awapuni clay loams merging downslope with Omihi soils. The Omihi soils have calcium carbonate in the subsoil overlying calcareous sandy gravels whereas there is no calcium carbonate in the Awapuni soils. Higher, on the adjacent hill slopes, Waikari soils are developed on the limestone bedrock but most of the finest vineyards in this small jewel of North Canterbury sit on Awapuni or Omihi clay loam. Both the Awapuni and Omihi soils give greater density, weight and savoury character to Pinot Noir, which you don't find in the fruit grown on the Glasnevin Gravels. Wine estates that have their homes here include Greystone, Muddy Water, Mountford, Black Estate and Fancrest.

If you're driving north to Marlborough you'll pass by these vineyards, but many cars turn off State Highway 1 a little earlier at Waipara and head west for Hanmer Springs. After negotiating the Weka Pass, there is a small town called Waikari and there's little reason to stop there unless you are a wine geek, or wish to board a vintage steam train to take you back to Waipara. This is hill country and there are sizeable slices of Waikari limestone that lie underfoot. Here you'll find Pyramid Valley and Bell Hill, which is planted on a former lime quarry.

WINE STYLES

Waipara Valley Pinot Noir was characterized by 'greater barnyard, herbal and violet aromas and in-mouth fruit density/concentration' in Dr Elizabeth Tomasino's thesis on New Zealand Pinot Noir, which was part of her doctorate at Lincoln University. Sitting between Marlborough and Central Otago both geographically and in wine styles, its Pinots have a density somewhere between a serious Marlborough Pinot and a robust Central Otago style. The herbal and violet character is certainly apparent throughout the wines of the region and there are a large number that are savoury, with those wines grown on the clay loams bringing depth and structure.

The warm, sunny days of summer coupled with cool nights and a long growing season provide mid-weight expressions with a complex array of aromatics and fresh acidity. There is plenty of ambition among the producers and vines are cropped fairly low both to ripen the fruit fully and produce a wine with sufficient fruit intensity to mature over a year or longer in high-quality French oak barrels.

Despite the lack of attention it receives, Sauvignon Blanc remains the number one white grape variety in the region, making crisp and pure whites with vibrant acidity. However, North Canterbury's most interesting whites are arguably Riesling and Chardonnay. Riesling is the third most popular variety, accounting for 20 per cent of all plantings, and this region may become known as the Riesling capital of New Zealand. If only it sold as prolifically as Sauvignon Blanc. From dry to sweet and sometimes botrytized, the Rieslings of the region are pure and highly fragrant with scintillating acidity. Winemakers tend to preserve the pristine fruit by fermenting in inert vessels but there are adventurous individuals playing with partial barrel fermentation and long lees contact. The most complex dry and off-dry styles display a high level of fruit concentration (orange is a common descriptor here) and a savoury edge with a spicy botrytis influence.

Staying with the Alsace-inspired varieties, Pinot Gris has also spread its roots far and wide in North Canterbury. It might not be the most interesting of grapes but the dry, cool climate allows this early ripener to gain some more aromatic interest and retain freshness. Most winemakers tend to adopt a neutral approach to winemaking, fermenting at cool temperatures in stainless steel tanks to preserve fruit but there are a number of quality-oriented producers who are happy to play with skin contact, old barrels and lees work to add texture and weight.

Chardonnay is a small but significant player in the North Canterbury region with a handful of exceptional wines gaining a reputation on the world stage. The close-planted, limestone-based slopes of Pyramid Valley and Bell Hill just outside of Waikari should stop white-Burgundy lovers in their tracks, and quality-oriented producers around Waipara including Pegasus Bay, Greystone and Black Estate are taking Chardonnay to new heights. Fruit is not front and centre in the best North Canterbury Chardonnays – texture, shape and tension are the name of the game.

PRODUCER PROFILES

Bellbird Spring
Waipara
bellbirdspring.co.nz

Having worked in the UK wine trade, Guy Porter decided he wanted to make the stuff and, after a stint working in Australia, studied winemaking at Roseworthy College, Adelaide. His parents had lived in New Zealand in the 1970s before returning to the UK in 1978 but the lure of Aotearoa proved too much and they all returned in 2002, buying land in rural North Canterbury. The first vines were planted in 2002 and they sold the fruit to local wineries until 2008 when Porter crafted a white field blend. The range has grown steadily since then and now includes 'aqua vitae', a clear pot still brandy, a flor-aged Pinot Gris (see Try This) and an homage to the Vin Doux Naturels of southern France. Bellbird Springs has two vineyards. The home block sits on the free-draining Glasnevin Gravels while Block Eight, which is home to Porter, his wife Leigh, two young children and a family of Wessex saddleback pigs, is a rather isolated spot in the north-west of the Waipara Valley, sitting at 120 metres above sea level on clay-loam soil. In 2016, the vineyards achieved organic certification.

The range includes two Sauvignon Blancs. The Pruner's Reward cuvée is a crisp, grassy example with its edges rounded by a portion of barrel-fermented wine, while Block Eight is a richer, textural fully barrel-fermented style. Its River Terraces Pinot Noir is grown on the gravelly home block creating a fresh, light-bodied expression with a gentle tannic grip.

Try this: Bellbird Spring Sous Voile
Made from Pinot Gris, this is a rare flor-aged wine. It's not fortified, unlike the wines of sherry, but it tips the scales at around the 15 per cent alcohol mark, which is in the same ballpark as a Fino or Manzanilla. The wine was fermented in old oak barrels. After the fermentation, winemakers normally top-up barrels to prevent oxidation but Porter didn't, and a layer of yeast grew, feeding on the alcohol and glycerol in the wine. The result is a dry, round and nutty-flavoured wine and it's fair to say that this is the most interesting New Zealand Pinot Gris I've ever had.

Visit
Bellbird Spring does not have a cellar door but it does welcome visitors by appointment.

Bell Hill Vineyard
Waikari
bellhill.co.nz

Sherwyn Veldhuizen and Marcel Giesen, one of three brothers behind the hugely successful New Zealand brand Giesen, founded Bell Hill Vineyard in 1997 in an area that had never before seen a single vine. They found their spot 15 kilometres north-west of Waipara via the Weka Pass toward the Southern Alps, close to the tiny town of Waikari. On its outskirts, a former limestone quarry provided the calcareous soils that are so prized in Burgundy. The pair's fine-wine ambitions were clear from the outset, planting at densities between 9,250 vines and 12,500 vines per hectare on steep slopes, and the effort has paid off: the vineyard has become one of the most exciting wineries in New Zealand since producing the first Bell Hill Pinot Noir in 2003, and the inaugural Chardonnay in 2004. There are plans to create single block wines. The Shelf, a very close-spaced Chardonnay and Pinot Noir block of less than 0.5 hectares, is likely to be the first candidate. Since the spring of 2007, the vineyards have been managed according to organic and biodynamic principles and the estate has been certified organic since 2015. The winemaking is hands off: wild yeasts are handed fermentation duties and, to retain all the goodness from the vineyard, the wines are not fined and only given a very light filtration, if needed. Bell Hill releases its wines three and a half years after the grapes were picked to allow the wines to unfurl. For those who want to try Bell Hill but don't have $120 to spend on a bottle, it also produces a Chardonnay and a Pinot Noir under the Old Weka Pass Road label, a barrel blend which hails from the vineyard's high-density limestone slopes and receives the same amount of TLC in the vineyard and winery – for around half the price.

Try this: Bell Hill Vineyard Pinot Noir

If you know a Pinotphile who remains unconvinced that New Zealand has the magic ingredients to make superlative Pinot Noir, you need to pour them a glass of this. One of those rare wines that elicits an emotional response and reminds your weary palate why you fell in love with wine in the first place, Bell Hill offers innate power in a delicate core. It has a sense of energy and a fine thread of acidity and chalky tannins that weave across your palate.

Visit

Bell Hill is not open to the public but appointments can be made. Visit the website for more details.

Black Estate

Waipara
blackestate.co.nz

Planted by Christchurch restaurateur Russell Black in 1994, Black Estate was acquired by winemaker Nicholas Brown, his high-flying lawyer wife Penny Naish, and her parents Rod and Stacey in 2007. Brown had been working with pioneering Czech Danny Schuster in the region and had been on the hunt for a property in the area, which Black agreed to sell after a year of discussions. The vineyard seemed perfect: it was planted on its own roots on a north-facing hillside. Since taking over at the helm, Black Estate has converted to organic viticulture and biodynamic practices and, in 2011, added 1 hectare of Chardonnay and 2 hectares of Pinot Noir. Brown, a fan of the Loire, also added Cabernet Franc and Chenin Blanc to the mix and, tasting the results, the gamble has truly paid off. The dynamic duo of Nic and Pen have taken Black

Estate to new heights in a short space of time, and they have expanded their holdings to the Pinot Noir and Riesling vineyard Damsteep. Having bought fruit from these 2.2 hectares previously, they knew that the site brought density and richness to the resulting wines. The most recent acquisition was Netherwood, a 0.8-hectare vineyard established with no irrigation by Black and Schuster in 1986 on a rare south-facing sandstone hillside. There is minimal intervention in the winery with the fermentation yeast propagated in the vineyard. Crushing may be done by feet; there are low levels of sulphur, and no fining or filtration.

Try this: Black Estate Damsteep Pinot Noir
Sourced from nine different parcels on this organically and biodynamically grown vineyard, the grapes are fermented separately before blending. The clay soils create a suave and mellifluous wine, which shows classy fruit and delicate handling. The tannins are textural, almost chalky. In the cool climes of North Canterbury, the fine acidity zips this wine up on the finish. The Riesling off this vineyard is similarly impressive: dry, savoury and incredibly satisfying.

Visit
In 2012, Black Estate opened a tasting room and then expanded their on-site offering to an eatery which focuses on local produce. It was named Winery Restaurant of the Year 2017 by New Zealand food magazine *Cuisine*, taking the title from nine-time champions, the fellow North Canterbury winery Pegasus Bay. It also has a one-bedroom cottage on site. For more details and opening times, visit the Black Estate website.

Greystone Wines
Waipara
greystonewines.co.nz

'Our dads make the best Pinot Noir in the world,' read the homemade signs, captured on camera and sent out to that world. Behind the children holding the signs were Greystone's award-winning fathers: viticulturist Nick Gill, accountant-turned-winemaker Dom Maxwell and general manager Nik Mavromatis. The team were celebrating winning the International Pinot Noir trophy at the Decanter World Wine Awards with their flagship wine The Brothers' Pinot Noir 2012. It has been a heady ascent to global stardom. While New Zealand brothers

Peter and Bruce Thomas own Greystone Wines, Gill and Maxwell have been the faces of the estate since planting the first vines in 2004 in the clay limestone hills of Omihi, a few minutes north east of Waipara township. The first wines were made in 2008 and the trophy cabinet has quickly been filled; it is regularly named one of the finest Pinot Noir producers in the country with the Pinot blocks sitting high on the limestone-rich upper slopes. The vineyards have been farmed organically since 2014 and the winemaking philosophy looks to capture what this virgin land has provided. All the grapes are hand picked, wild yeasts are used and, in 2012, the team trialled fermentation in the vineyard rather than the winery. The wines are neither fined nor filtered. When it comes to whites, the intense, savoury Erin Reserve Chardonnay, from a limestone-rich block high in the vineyard, is highly regarded. However, aromatic varieties are its trump card. Planted on the lower, flatter sections of the vineyard on clay and gravel, the cool climes of North Canterbury imbue Gewürztraminer, Pinot Gris and Riesling with a sense of vibrancy. Its range of Rieslings from dry to sweet – and sometimes botrytized, if nature permits – are invariably pure and citrussy with a fine line of spine-tingling acidity.

Try this: Greystone Wines Sea Star Riesling
A dry, savoury style that also has bright orange elements. It is a powerful expression with lipsmacking acidity and a hint of phenolics providing

drive on the finish. The style has become less creamy on the palate since 2013, as a result of abandoning lees stirring. An ageworthy example.

Visit
The cellar door is open daily throughout the year, costing $5 per person which is refunded against purchases. Guided tours of the vineyard and winery run daily and include a barrel tasting and a sharing plate. There is also accommodation on the vineyard in a glass-walled eco-cabin. The Greystone Purepod (purepods.com) is a perfect place to get back to nature, turn off your mobile phone and watch the stars.

Mountford Estate
Waipara
mountfordestate.com
Mountford was founded in 1991 by Michael and Buffy Eaton. C. P. Lin, the Taiwanese-born blind winemaker at Mountford Estate from 1997 until 2013, reportedly got the job after telling the founders that their wines were 'crap'. Under his stewardship, the winery's single vineyard Pinot Noirs, The Gradient and The Rise, became highly regarded. However, its star faded in the years surrounding Lin's resignation; he very publicly announced he would be leaving and criticized the approach of the then owners. Mountford entered a fresh, new era in May 2017, when New Zealand's Overseas Investment Office approved the purchase of the brand, its vineyards and winery by Takahiro Koyama. The Japanese-born, New Zealand-trained winemaker first worked at Mountford in 2004 as a cellar hand while attending Lincoln University, and joined the company in 2007 as assistant winemaker under Lin. He established his own label, Koyama Wines, while working at Mountford and left in 2012 to focus on the project. However, in 2017 he was able to purchase Mountford with investment from Japan.

The vineyard is 9.3 hectares in total with Pinot Noir accounting for more than half of all plantings. In 2000, two steep hillside blocks – The Gradient and The Rise – were planted with Pinot Noir. In the same year a tiny 0.4-hectare block consisting of Riesling, Pinot Gris, Muscat Blanc à Petits Grains and Gewürztraminer was also established, producing Hommage, an Alsatian-inspired co-fermented field blend that may spend a few hours on skins, depending on the vintage. In 2008, the vineyard was expanded to include Chardonnay, Riesling and more Pinot Noir.

Try this: Mountford Estate The Rise Pinot Noir

At its best, The Rise can offer incredible perfume and a fine line of acidity that weaves across the brooding palate with masses of concentration. There is something, dare I say, mineral about this wine. It will be interesting to see how the wine expresses itself under new ownership: the new team has set out to allow wild ferments with gentle hand plunging followed by a week or so of post-fermentation maceration before spending twelve to eighteen months in French oak. The 30 to 60 per cent whole-bunch regime for both The Rise and The Gradient will be retained by the new owners, while its 'estate' Pinot Noir is fully destemmed.

Visit

The tasting room is open by appointment only.

Muddy Water

Waipara
muddywater.co.nz

Muddy Water, a translation of the word Waipara, was founded by Jane and Michael East in 1993. It was the first organically certified winery in the region, starting a wave across the Waipara Valley. Retiring in 2011, the couple sold the property complete with winery to the owners of winery-less Greystone Wines. The two brands remain separate, despite fermenting in the same tin shed – with a resident rooster Rodney waking up the cellar hands sleeping on-site at an unreasonable hour. Winemaking is hands off, allowing the ferments to kick off naturally and the wines are bottled unfined and unfiltered. Under the young, dynamic winemaking team, a skin ferment Chardonnay/Pinot Gris blend was also introduced in 2016, producing a highly floral, attractively phenolic dry white. The 12-hectare vineyard sits across clay loam and, as the slope rises, this gives way to clay limestone. Pinot Noir is the main event with three, separate bottlings hailing from individual blocks. Its 'estate' Pinot Noir is blended from younger vines grown on own roots and is an elegant, mid-weight style with both savoury and floral characters (see Try This). Its flagship Pinot Noir, Hare's Breath, is planted at higher density than other blocks; the result is a savoury, earthy style with robust structure that demands bottle age. A parcel of ungrafted Riesling named 'James Hardwick' produces a medium-dry, savoury Riesling. And for some reason the Easts thought it was a good idea to plant Pinotage. Apparently it's very popular – even at $60 a bottle.

Try this: Muddy Water Pinot Noir
An elegant, mid-weight style with savoury complexity, the estate Pinot Noir is the perfect bottle to open to understand the Muddy Water philosophy and style. Planted between 2000 and 2002, the vines produce just a kilo of fruit per vine, producing a balanced wine with plenty of mid-palate density. The wine is matured in around 30 per cent new French oak, giving vanilla and spice aromas in youth, sitting alongside dried herbs, earthy notes and plum fruit. The site and climate gives the wine lots of sinew and a taut finish. Unfined and unfiltered.

Visit
Muddy Water shares its cellar door with Greystone Wines and is open daily throughout the year. Check the Greystone website for opening times.

Pegasus Bay Winery
Waipara
pegasusbay.com

After a year's sabbatical in London, neurosurgeon Ivan Donaldson and his wife Christine returned to Christchurch in the late 1970s and became involved in a hobby vineyard. Deciding it was too cold to grow grapes in Christchurch, they shifted their attention to the area around Waipara and having 'looked at every piece of land that was for sale for two years, decided we were going about it the wrong way. We found a piece of land that we wanted and made an offer.' Pegasus Bay was formed in 1986 but Donaldson kept up the day job until 2001. Their four sons have also joined the business, making this a real family concern. The 40 hectares of Pegasus Bay vineyards are nestled in the lee of the Teviotdale hills on a series of free-draining stone and gravel terraces. Riesling and Pinot Noir are Pegasus Bay's most important varieties, with each accounting for a third of total plantings; the remaining third is planted with a range of varieties, including Chardonnay, Pinot Gris, Sauvignon Blanc and Semillon. Its other varieties are associated with Bordeaux rather than Burgundy: Cabernet Sauvignon, Cabernet Franc, Malbec and Merlot. The Riesling is produced in a range of styles from dry to sweet with a portion of botrytized fruit appearing across the spectrum, when nature permits. The wines always display a distinctive orange-zest character and vivacious acidity, cleansing the palate, even the medium-sweet Aria or the fully sweet, botrytized Encore. Pegasus Bay's Sauvignon/Semillon blend and Chardonnay are both partially barrel fermented with high solids and lees work generating textural styles that often display a struck-match character. Its top Chardonnay, Virtuoso, is a barrel selection only made in the best vintages from ungrafted vines dating back to the 1980s. When it comes to Pinot Noir, Pegasus Bay is undergoing an evolution in style, becoming less muscular and increasingly elegant in recent vintages. That said, the flagship Pinot Noir, Prima Donna, from the oldest vines on the estate remains robust, spicy and ageworthy. There is also a red Bordeaux blend, which isn't the average in North Canterbury but usually manages to pull it off with grace. All the Pegasus Bay wines rest in bottle for at least twelve months prior to release. Main Divide is Pegasus Bay's more affordable range and consistently offers some of the best value Riesling, Chardonnay and Pinot Noir in the country.

Try this: Pegasus Bay Winery Bel Canto Riesling
A dry Riesling with pure, savoury expression. Bel Canto is only made in years when there is botrytis, and can include as much as a third botrytized fruit. A slight spritz in young examples brings liveliness on entry. When it comes to aromatics, there's often orange peel, spice and marmalade. The finish is powerful with phenolic grip and linear acidity hinting at a Batman-like fight scene: 'Pow!'

Visit
Sitting in grounds still tended by Christine Donaldson, the pink terracotta, just-stepped-out-of-Tuscany winery houses the nine-time-winning Winery Restaurant of the Year. It is open Thursday to Monday for lunch. The cellar door, open daily, has a long window allowing you to peer into the barrel cellar while you taste through the range.

Pyramid Valley Vineyards
Waikari
pyramidvalley.co.nz

In 1999, Mike and Claudia Weersing bought a sheep farm in a remote part of North Canterbury and planted a 2.2-hectare vineyard with a staggering 12,000 plants to the hectare. Situated west of Waipara through the Weka Pass leading to the small town of Waikari in the foothills of the Southern Alps, Chardonnay and Pinot Noir vines sit pretty in a clay-limestone amphitheatre. The vineyard was farmed biodynamically from day one and almost all of the original vines were ungrafted (2 per cent of vines were planted on rootstock 420A – the only lime-tolerant rootstock available at that time, explains Claudia Weersing). The first Pinot Noir was produced in 2006 with Chardonnay following in 2008. The wines are made with minimal intervention – there are no packet yeasts here, gravity is used to move wine, and there is no fining or filtration. As a result of the tender loving care in both the vineyard and winery, the wines display incredible texture; they are seamless and capture density of fruit without weight. There are two Chardonnays from the home vineyards: Lion's Tooth hails from lime-rich soil providing a mid-weight style with fine texture and savoury characters, while Field of Fire Chardonnay hails from heavier clays producing a round, more expansive wine, which remains delicate and tends to show quince and chamomile aromas. In 2012, clay vessels were introduced for the Chardonnay ferments. There are also two unadulterated Pinot Noirs: Earth Smoke (see Try This) and Angel Flower. The more delicate of the pair, Angel Flower, would be an American Smooth if it were a dance: it is seductive and floats ethereally across your palate. It is always a complex wine that offers violet top notes with savoury, smoky, paprika bass notes. The tannins are always finely pixellated.

In 2017, the vineyard was acquired by US billionaire and philanthropist Brian Sheth and his wife Adria in partnership with New Zealand-based Master of Wine Steve Smith. Under new ownership, the vineyard is set to expand – there are sides of the natural amphitheatre that have not yet been planted – and there are plans to produce more Chardonnay and create a sparkling wine. The functional winery will be renovated and improved (the fruit was hand destemmed under the Weersings), and there are plans in place to build accommodation on site.

Try this: Pyramid Valley Vineyards Earth Smoke Pinot Noir
Call it the power of suggestion, but this Pinot Noir is smoky and broody. Mellifluous and delicate, it is an unadulterated, ethereal wine with no fining or filtration. Fine chalky tannins provide an attractive phenolic grip that imbues it with the potential to develop in bottle.

Visit
Check the website for the most up-to-date information on Pyramid Valley visits and accommodation.

Tongue in Groove

Waipara

tongueingroove.co.nz

On 22 February 2011, a 6.3-magnitude earthquake hit Christchurch, felling large parts of the CBD and killing 185 people. Roseworthy graduate and marketing maestra Angela Clifford had travelled to the city centre from the vineyards of Waipara that day and realized how lucky she was to escape unharmed: 'It was a carpe diem moment.' Having toyed with the idea of launching her own wine brand, she seized the day indeed and launched Tongue in Groove with winemaking goddess and self-titled 'Pinot dominatrix' Lynnette Hudson. The pair specialize in small volumes of Riesling (see Try This) and Pinot Noir, throwing in a little skin contact Pinot Gris and Gewürztraminer blend because they are the bosses and granted themselves permission. The Pinot Noir hails from the Cabal Vineyard, a north-facing hillside producing a savoury, complex red that ranges from floral high notes to the earthy iron-inspired taste of blood (in a good way). The cool climes of North Canterbury provide cleansing acidity and the mid-weight palate is wrapped in a structured framework of chalky tannins.

Try this: Tongue in Groove Riesling

Waipara has long been associated with Riesling, and the Robard & Butler Amberley Rieslings of the 1980s were one of the reasons Angela Clifford fell in love with this wine region. The Tongue in Groove offering is a dry, savoury Riesling with lovely concentration of fruit reminiscent of clementines and quince. There's spice here too in botrytis years, adding an extra layer of complexity. A slight phenolic grip and fine orange-laced acidity provide a dazzling finish.

Visit

There is no cellar door at this small operation but you can keep up to date with Clifford's latest adventures in North Canterbury through Instagram: @TheFoodFarmNZ

12

WAITAKI VALLEY

Marginal climates can produce some of the world's most scintillating wines: the world of fine wine would be a lesser place without the wines of the Mosel Valley, Champagne, Chablis – and now you can add Waitaki Valley to that list. Its wines vibrate with nervous tension, a nervousness that is a reflection of the grapes' annual race to the ripening finish. The wines – aromatic whites and Pinot Noir – have a truly distinct character that separates them from the rest of New Zealand, and which has intrigued a few adventurous wine lovers to seek out the home of these wines. Visitors have soon discovered that Waitaki isn't just a marginal viticultural region; radio and telephone signals are intermittent in this remote, sparsely populated area; the local cattle look quizzically at passing cars on the rural roads as if vehicles rarely pass by.

It's not just the cows and sheep that are rather perplexed: people continue to look befuddled when you mention the name Waitaki, despite its Pinot Noirs winning international trophies and critical acclaim. It's in North Otago, in case you were wondering, 180 kilometres northeast of Central Otago's Cromwell and, despite its short history, it has been one hell of a ride.

HISTORY

The journey started with Dunedin businessman Howard Paterson, who developed the first vineyards in the area at the turn of the new millennium. He was behind Doctors Creek, which was named the best New Zealand Pinot Noir at the 2012 International Wine Challenge. He was also behind the Waitaki Valley Estates on Grant's Road. Marlborough-based wine producer Dr John Forrest made the journey to North Otago and produced the region's first wine in 2003 from the Doctors Creek site but Paterson did not get to taste the fruits of his labour: in July 2003 he choked on a chip in a hotel in Fiji and died, aged fifty.

The early 2000s also witnessed the arrival of Jim Jerram. After twenty-nine years as a general practitioner in New Zealand (and as far afield as Kunde hospital on the trail to Everest Base Camp), Jerram founded Ostler Vineyards on a limestone slope above the village of Duntroon in 2001 with his brother-in-law, Jeff Sinnott, who was then winemaker at Central Otago winery Amisfield. Intrigued by the wines that these pioneering sites produced, others decided to try their hand at viticulture in the region including Antonio Pasquale. Leaving northern Italy for New Zealand in 1997, Pasquale saw the potential of Waitaki, and its offshoot, the almost unpronounceable Hakataramea Valley. 'The cool climatic edge here, along with the limestone soils, is ideal for wines of crispness, concentration and lasting minerality,' predicted Pasquale, adding 'Great wines can be made here.' He planted over 100,000 vines in the valley and, in 2009, built and equipped the area's first and only winery before putting it up for sale in 2013, citing the high costs.

American-owned Craggy Range also released some impressive crisp whites in 2008 and 2009 under the Otago Station label, but soon pulled the plug, explaining that the company had decided to focus on its home vineyards and Te Muna Road property. While the quality had been evident, Steve Smith MW admitted that the yields had been unviable and making it work commercially was one of its biggest concerns.

Yet Waitaki gained momentum and, by 2012, vines covered more than 100 hectares. However, Pasquale's Hakataramea vineyard was pulled out and lots totalling 65 hectares, part of the original subdivision by Paterson, were disposed of by mortgagee sale. Murray Turner, a Waitaki man who helped develop the early vineyards with his brother and worked for Pasquale before setting up his own label, River T, explains the reduction in the vineyard area: 'One of the big [vineyard] developers went broke and a local farmer bought it and they [the vineyards] have gone back to pasture,' he says. 'It was not because the vineyard wasn't any good but there was a genuine reason why those things happened: developers were trying to make a buck out of unsuspecting people.' Indeed, a number of wealthy individuals bought the land, including celebrity chef Peter

Gordon, and many became absentee landlords, unaware of the attention these vineyards needed. It was hardly an ideal start and has slightly tarnished the region. As a result, the vineyard area had reduced to just 56 hectares in 2016. There are several vintners from outside the region – Marlborough-based John Forrest and Central Otago's Grant Taylor – who have successful businesses that can support their love of Waitaki. However, those that are left, 'the hardcore' as Turner calls them, are truly dedicated to the region and, somewhat unsurprisingly, have one thing on their mind: making truly fine wine with a sense of place.

GEOGRAPHY AND CLIMATE

Waitaki Valley – or North Otago – is rather different to Central Otago despite lying on the same latitude of 45° S. While Central Otago is encased by mountains and is characterized by a semi-continental climate, the Waitaki winegrowing region begins 40 kilometres from the Pacific. The vineyards face north on the southerly banks of the Waitaki River, which forms the boundary between Otago and Canterbury and flows out into the cold seas. It is the cooling easterly breezes off the ocean that keep Waitaki cool on summer days when Central Otago vineyards are basking under the sun's sultry rays. Follow the river upstream and further inland toward Lake Waitiki and the maritime influence diminishes, making the summer days noticeably warmer. Registering just 850 growing degree days versus 1,100 for Central Otago's Cromwell Basin, it is immediately evident that Waitaki is significantly cooler. It is perhaps more useful to compare the Waitaki climate to Gibbston, which sports 910 growing degree days; the heat summation of both of these areas would fail to reach the lowest threshold for Californian Albert Winkler's climate classification. Waitaki also has fewer sunshine hours than Central: 1,800 hours versus 2,270 hours respectively. Thankfully, autumn temperatures don't fall off a cliff in Waitaki, giving growers the opportunity to let their fruit hang for longer. Moreover the influence of the sea means autumn frosts are not a problem here, unlike the Central Otago frosts which can snatch the grapes from the pickers' baskets at the eleventh hour. 'Waitaki has warmer temperatures in the late autumn which equals longer hang time allowing the tannins to ripen,' says Jeff Sinnott, Ostler's winemaker. 'This is right on the edge of possibility. A lot of people will follow the line of least resistance but that isn't available for Waitaki winemakers. I'd say in terms of difficulty, Central would be an 8 and the Waitaki would be a 9.5.'

While spring frost was once considered a threat for Waitaki growers, it can be nipped in the bud by installing frost protection, which Ostler did in 2014. However, the biggest challenge in spring and early summer is successful flowering and fruit set. Achieving a large crop is rare, as straggly Pinot Noir bunches often weigh as little as 60 or 70 grams. In the spring of 2006, barely a berry was harvested in the valley due to cold and wet weather, while spring 2011 brought hard frosts. Yet 2016 saw a warm flowering, pine-cone-like bunches laden with berries and, in 2017, Turner reported bunch weights as high as 180 grams. Grant Taylor, founder of Valli in Central Otago, purchased Blue House Vineyard in 2017 after thirteen years of buying fruit in Waitaki. 'It's hard to get 3 tonnes to the hectare but the vines are getting older now and it's just a matter of perseverance,' he says.

Site selection is key to success: there are pockets that are frost prone and warmer sites which are more likely to set and ripen consistently. At least the area does not have to worry about rainfall, which is just as well as picking can still be taking place in late April or even early May. The region registers an average of just 380 mm of rain a year – similar to Bendigo in Central Otago. As a result, irrigation is necessary but that's something Turner knows a lot about: in addition to running his 4-hectare vineyard, he has a day job as managing director of Waitaki Irrigation Management.

WHAT LIES BENEATH

The initial excitement surrounding Waitaki was, in part, due to the limestone soils in the region, formed in the Oligocene era, around 22 to 30 million years ago when New Zealand was underwater. Burgundy lovers understand the significance of such calcareous soils. Take a closer look at the soils and there are ancient marine fossils to be found at Clos Ostler or Doctors Creek. However, it's not all limestone. Alluvial soils play an important role on the valley floor close to the Waitaki River, while further upstream, towards the Southern Alps, mica schist appears in the soil composition.

WINE STYLES

Meet the heartbreak variety in a heartbreak region. Covering close to half of all plantings, the risks involved with growing Pinot Noir in Waitaki are great but the rewards are greater. Negotiating spring frost and fruit set, the long, cool growing season allows for slow flavour development, bringing a complex array of red fruit, savoury and floral characters. The cool climate allows for acid retention and reins in sugar development, keeping alcohols modest, while the long hang time brings all-important phenolic ripeness. Yields are low, providing intense concentration and good colour. The resulting wines are highly fragrant, elegant and finely structured. In this marginal climate, vintage variation produces fantastic vertical tastings. John Forrest, whose 2009 Waitaki Pinot Noir won the best New Zealand Pinot Noir at the International Wine Challenge 2012, explains that Waitaki's unique personality needs to be allowed to shine and winemaking needs to be hands off: 'I joke somewhat seriously to my staff in the winery that if I see them putting the Waitaki Pinot Noir in the Mercurey barrels we put the Central Otago wines in, they will get sacked! We don't want to cram it with sweet toasty oak or too much whole berry: with all the Waitaki wines we are trying not to overpower the personality. It has a distinctive signature that seems to resonate with visiting Pinotphiles from overseas.'

The most planted white variety is Pinot Gris, representing around a quarter of all vineyards. In Waitaki's cool climate, this early ripener takes its time to get to the finish line. It offers purity of fruit, restraint and elegance. Prone to low acidity and high alcohol, the Waitaki climate offers a refreshing interpretation. Riesling is a small but important part of the varietal mix in Waitaki: having a similar number of growing degree days to the Mosel, Germany, the resulting wines are bright and full of energy with palate-cleansing acidity. The long growing season allows full phenolic ripeness to be achieved with modest alcohol levels. Intense and citrussy, the wines are often bottled with some residual sugar to balance the powerful acidity.

PRODUCER PROFILES

Forrest Wines
Marlborough
forrest.co.nz

While John Forrest has been making wines in his native Marlborough since 1990, he has been a supporter of Waitaki from the off. He produced the region's first Pinot Noir from the Doctors Creek vineyard in 2003, which his friend the late Howard Paterson developed. Impressed by the results, Forrest and his wife Brigid, along with the help of wine-loving friends Rob and Pip Robertson and Dave and Lynne Knappstein, bought land and planted a vineyard in the area. They picked a 28-hectare site, 5 kilometres east of Kurow with an elevation of 200 metres on north-west facing limestone terraces and, most importantly, surrounded to the south and east by an escarpment that protects the vineyard from the cold winds blowing in off the ocean. Named TattyBogler, the block was planted in 2004 with Pinot Noir, Chardonnay and Pinot Gris totalling 3.65 hectares and, according to Forrest, it has a specific microclimate: frost free and warmer, allowing for earlier ripening and consistency. Forrest has expanded its holdings in Waitaki, adding a 12-hectare parcel of land in a cooler site close to Clos Ostler in Duntroon. The Carluke vineyard has since been planted with Pinot Noir and Chardonnay, totalling 1.5 hectares. The Waitaki wines are vinified in Marlborough and bottled under the TattyBogler range and the John Forrest Collection label, whose 2009 Waitaki Valley Pinot Noir took the title of best New Zealand Pinot Noir at the International Wine Challenge 2012.

Try this: John Forrest Collection Waitaki Pinot Noir
Always complex and elegant, this Waitaki Pinot Noir is pure, focused and restrained with a core of plum fruit, violets and savoury earthiness overlaid with clove and cinnamon spice. Very gently handled with very subtle oak influence, the tannins are fine, almost chalky in texture, and the marginal climate provides fine acidity that brings tension and purpose to the wine.

Visit
Forrest Wines' cellar door is in Renwick, Marlborough and is open seven days a week for tasting. It is both child and dog friendly and

offers a great place to relax while tasting. There are always three wines open to taste for free or, if you want to linger a while on the picnic benches or bean bags, you can also buy a six-wine tray to savour with a cheeseboard. The Waitaki wines are not usually in the line-up but may be opened on request.

Ostler Wines
Kurow
ostlerwines.co.nz

Many doctors give up their career to concentrate on improving their golf swing and playing with the grandchildren but Jim Jerram is not your average medicine man. He moved to grape growing in 2001 in a venture with his brother-in-law, Jeff Sinnott, then Amisfield's winemaker. Their mission was to make Pinot Noir on limestone and they bought a site on an escarpment above the valley floor near the village of Duntroon, naming it Clos Ostler, which provides the fruit for their flagship Pinot Noir, Caroline's. In retrospect, they admit that their climate analysis of the area was on the optimistic side but experience has taught them that site selection is key to succeeding in the valley and, if possible, to spread the risk across several parts of the valley rather than in one place. The label has attracted much attention with unsuspecting international wine critics and Burgundy experts astonished at the restraint, purity and structure that its Pinot Noir displays. In addition to Pinot Noir, Ostler also produces two Pinot Gris, including a savoury and textural part wild-yeast barrel-fermented cuvée Audrey's. The 'Lakeside Wines' in the range are sourced from Sinnott's father's vineyard close to Lake Waitaki, a warmer site than Clos Ostler sitting on alluvial soils, while its Blue House range has been discontinued since the purchase of the Blue House Vineyard by Valli's Grant Taylor in 2017.

Try this: Ostler Wines Caroline's Pinot Noir
Always alluring, pure and highly fragrant, Caroline's manages delicacy as well as density, indicative of the naturally low yields that Waitaki's climate provides. The wine caresses the palate, and the naturally fresh acidity of this cool climate combined with the chalky tannins gives this wine a tautly wound structure. Always elegant, complex and long, it is wine that unfurls with bottle age.

Visit

The former post office built in the 1930s in the small town of Kurow has been transformed and is now home to Ostler's cellar door and offices. Known as The Vintner's Drop, it is open weekdays and, during the summer, it is also opened on weekends. There are simple tasting plates as well as wine tastings and they also have a local craft beer on tap to cleanse your wine-weary palate. Consult the website for opening times and more information.

River T

Kurow
rivertestate.co.nz

Murray Turner has spent forty years in the Waitaki Valley growing fruit and launched a small label with his partner Karen Tweed in 2016. He manages the valley's irrigation schemes as well as the 4-hectare vineyard. You will struggle to find anyone who knows the Waitaki vineyards as well as Turner; he had a viticultural business with his brother and has 'been involved in planting nearly every vine in the region'. The vines were planted in 2007 and, until 2016, his fruit was destined for Valli's Waitaki wine label. Grant Taylor continues to make Turner's Pinot Noir and Riesling, which is bottled under the River T brand while the Pinot Gris and rosé is vinified by Anthony Worch at Alexandra Vintners, Central Otago. The first vintage shows the elegance of Valli's pre-2016 Waitaki Pinot Noirs (see Try this) while the citrus and floral Riesling has a lick of residual sugar to counterbalance the vivacious acidity. Its Pinot Gris is an off-dry, easy-to-like, fruity style with modest alcohol and an appetizing line of acidity. You'll notice a pair of cowboy boots on the labels – Turner's son Ben has been a Pro Bull rider in Canada.

Try this: River T Pinot Noir
Light in body with fine tannins, this is taut and lively with an intriguing combination of savoury and floral characters. There's a fine line of acidity that weaves through this wine.

Visit
The cellar door is open seven days a week from September to May and there is a self-guided vineyard tour available, in addition to tasting and platters.

Valli Vineyards

Gibbston, Central Otago
valliwine.co.nz

Central Otago-based Valli founder Grant Taylor has been making wine from grapes sourced in Waitaki since 2004. He took the plunge to buy the Blue House Vineyard on the appropriately named Grants Road in 2017. The Pinot Noirs have always shown their coolness of place with a delicacy, linearity and herbal thread. Since making Waitaki Riesling for the first time in 2013, the styles have ranged from off-dry to fully sweet and botrytized. Taylor says he lets the 'vineyard lead the dance'. The volumes produced are tiny.

Try this: Valli Vineyards Waitaki Pinot Noir
A cool expression of Pinot Noir with its light body and fine acidity that floats across the palate. Dried herbs combine with violets, followed by a fine, dry, smoky finish.

Visit
The Central Otago winery is situated in a rather unglamorous building in Cromwell but visits take place in the much more scenic setting of its

Gibbston vineyard. If you wish to visit, contact the winery directly to make an appointment.

13

CENTRAL OTAGO

'We are at the end of the world and the challenge is different every year. I have not experienced two vintages that were the same, not even close.'

Paul Pujol, Prophet's Rock

Central Otago has provided rich pickings since the discovery of gold in 1862 attracted fortune-seeking newcomers to the region. While many left empty-handed, two million ounces of gold were extracted from its soils and rivers by 1867, transforming this region from nowheresville to the richest in New Zealand. One of the original gold prospectors was a Frenchman, Jean Desiré Feraud, who remained in the region after the gold rush, planting fruit trees and vines as well as becoming the first mayor of the Clyde area. His wines, cherry brandy, and lemon and peppermint syrup won medals in shows in Melbourne and Sydney before he sold up and moved to Dunedin in 1882 but by then, he had already staked his place in the region's vinous – and political – history.

But he was not the first to plant vines. That title goes to an almost-forgotten Frenchman, Jacques (James) Bladier. An expert in Central Otago history and lecturer at Lincoln University, Dr Lloyd Carpenter, is keen to set the record straight: Loire Valley-born Bladier, who had made wine in Victoria's Bendigo region before moving to Central Otago, imported 600 vines from Australia with financial help from the government. The *Otago Daily Times* reported on 30 July 1864 that its 'mild and equitable climate' which was 'not nearly so severe as it is in many portions of the south of France' might grow 'delicate and fruitful' grapes. However, Bladier never made any wine from his vines, which is perhaps why his role in Central Otago's wine history is overlooked: he sold his property to his neighbour, Feraud, in June 1865 before heading to the west coast and eventually sailing back to Victoria to make wine.

In the next decade, other settlers had a crack at growing grapes and making wine at the bottom of New Zealand. Some of those efforts were recorded in 1895 by the soon-to-be-appointed national head of viticulture Romeo Bragato in his *Report on the Prospects of Viticulture in New Zealand*. Having landed in Bluff, a town now famous for its oysters, on 19 February, he took a train and a steamer to Queenstown. While he noted the 'low temperature throughout the year' he believed viticulture was possible in certain parts of the region where a suitable north-facing aspect could be found. His first glass of wine in New Zealand was provided by a lady named Mrs Hutchison of Arrowtown: 'although made after the most primitive fashion, it reflected great credit, and need not be despised by any one.' While this was hardly glowing praise, he went on to find ripe grapes in Cromwell on 25 February, 'a convincing fact to me that the summer climatic conditions here are conducive to the early ripening of the fruit. This and the Bannockburn district are pre-eminently suitable for the cultivation of the vine, both of wine-making and table varieties.' He did note that 'these districts are very dry' and discussed the benefits of irrigation – he was a man ahead of his time.

While Bragato acknowledged Central Otago as having great potential for Pinot Noir and Feraud had early success, it would be another century before commercial winemaking resumed. The pioneers of Central Otago's modern era were an unlikely bunch including a nurse (Ann Pinckney of Taramea) and an Irish journalist, Alan Brady. In his autobiography, *Pinot Central*, Brady writes: 'What arrogance to assume that I, a refugee from city life, could produce wine in this remote and rugged mountain valley at latitude 45° S in a part of New Zealand inhabited mainly by merino sheep and rabbits.' But it had been done before and it would be done again. The so-called 'first five' included Alexandra-based Verdun Burgess, 'a pipe-smoking Southland carpenter with a smile as big as his bushy moustache', and Sue Edwards at Black Ridge, Bill Grant in Dunstan Road, as well as Rolfe and Lois Mills at Rippon near Wanaka. The quintet were widely dispersed, planting in what are today considered the coolest (Gibbston), wettest (Gibbston and Wanaka) and most extreme (Alexandra) parts of Central Otago.

There were no vineyards around the town of Cromwell when the first wines (1987 vintage) were released from Gibbston Valley, Taramea and Rippon. Grant Taylor, who has been making wine in the region since 1993 and founded Valli Vineyards in 1998, says, 'The cooler examples showed the real potential of great Pinot Noir but people realized that they needed to make a living and in the slightly warmer areas you would up your chances of making wine.' As a result, around 70 per cent of Central Otago's vineyards are now situated around the Cromwell Basin. However, when the modern pioneers first planted their vines, Cromwell was not the town it is today. Many parts of the town and former orchard-covered river terraces are now submerged under the waters of Lake Dunstan, which was created as part of the controversial building of the Clutha Dam. The 26-square kilometre lake was filled in 1992 and 1993, providing essential irrigation for a wave of vineyards which rise up from its shores. It also gives jet skiers and speedboat drivers – sometimes referred to by disapproving locals as 'water bogans' – a new playground to visit during the summer holidays.

Since 1990, and with the arrival of a much-needed water source two years later, vineyard plantings increased from 19 hectares to almost 2,000 hectares today. When Austrian-born Rudi Bauer, the founder of Quartz Reef, arrived in Central Otago to make wine at Rippon in 1989, he was making many different varieties in tiny quantities: '70 litres of Riesling, 140 litres of Osteiner, 40 litres of Pinot Gris and three barrels of Pinot Noir'. In the early days, there was even a Merlot/Cabernet/Syrah blend named after Rolfe and Lois Mills' son Nick, now the winemaker at Rippon. While the Osteiner (a Riesling and Sylvaner cross) is still in production, the red blend has not survived – Central Otago is a land of Pinot Noir, which represents more than three-quarters of all plantings.

GEOGRAPHY AND CLIMATE

Located at 45°S, Central Otago is the world's most southerly grape-growing region, and it is a challenging place in which to grow them. At the end of the earth, next stop Antarctica, you can visit a penguin colony in the morning and enjoy a wine tasting in the afternoon – how is that possible? Paul Pujol, winemaker at Prophet's Rock, calls it a 'bubble': sitting in the middle of the South Island surrounded by mountains, conditions in Central Otago are semi-continental, which is why slapdash vintage reports for New Zealand need to be taken with a pinch of salt – when the east coast of New Zealand, which is the home of the majority of New Zealand's vines, gets hit with rain, Central Otago producers can be sitting on their sun loungers eating ice cream.

The story of Central Otago's dry climate starts on the wet west coast where the Milford Sound meets the Tasman Sea. The rain-bearing westerlies dump more than 6 metres of rain here annually, according to the National Institute of Water and Atmospheric Research (NIWA). Rainclouds have to traverse three ranges, the Darran, Humboldt and Richardson Mountains, before even getting to Queenstown, the adrenaline capital of New Zealand. By this time, the climate is getting drier – around 740 mm of rain. Drive eastward out of Queenstown on State Highway 16, almost hugging the Kawarau River, and a slither of vineyards appears, sandwiched like a thin piece of cheese between dramatic craggy peaks. This is Gibbston, which receives a similar amount of rainfall to Queenstown and is the coolest of all the subregions. Continue eastward to Cromwell and you'll be greeted by a giant fruit sculpture, which isn't dissimilar to Carmen Miranda's hat. Erected in 1989, the statue could do with updating, as both grapes and cherries – the area's most famous crops – are conspicuous by their absence. It is getting increasingly dry here; annual rainfall has now fallen to 437 mm. Heading south-west along the controversial Clyde dam to Alexandra, the climate becomes even more sheltered and drier: just 363 mm of rain falls each year. Conroys Gully, close to Black Rock, is the driest place in New Zealand. It is unsurprising that irrigation is necessary in Central Otago: in Alexandra, one producer explained that he irrigates every second day at the height of the summer, giving 15 litres of water to each vine a week on the driest sites.

At the start of the season – and sometimes in its dying throes – frost can be a major challenge for growers; sleep can be in short supply for viticulturists. Not only does Mike Wing, vineyard manager at Two Paddocks, have three young daughters to keep him awake at night, in a bad season he can 'get up to twenty or thirty frost-fighting days'. Frost can strike late: in the 2012–13 season, it made an unwelcome appearance in November, while snow has been known to fall in January (the summer holidays), and can strike while the grapes are being picked, as in 2015. In Central Otago winemakers have to expect the unexpected. It's lucky that most of them are laid back.

In cold springs, it is not surprising that the vines experience poor flowering and set. However, in abundant years, growers have to manage crop size to ensure the fruit on the vine ripens fully. With the days shortening as summer descends into autumn, temperatures falling and the threat of frost rising, it can be a nail-biting finale. 'In 2001, the crops were too heavy and we ran out of time and in 2011 it was pretty much the same thing – but with the extra experience we had in 2011, we were able to make a good job out of it,' says Bauer.

The summers in Central Otago, however, can be much hotter than you'd anticipate so far south. It's not unusual for peak temperatures to rise above 30°C, yet within hours the night-time temperatures can drop to just above freezing. The wide diurnal temperature range is thought to assist in the development of the deep, soulful hue of Central Otago's Pinot Noirs and the amplification of aromas. It also means campers have to pack bikinis and woolly hats on their summer holidays to Central. And, for those baring all on vacation, sunscreen is imperative. The levels of ultra-violet (UV) radiation in Central Otago could burn you to a crisp. Dr John Harris, an academic and co-founder of Māori Point Vineyard, has written a paper on the effects of UV radiation on grape growth in Central Otago. He notes that Central Otago has 'around 40 per cent more UV radiation' than its latitude suggests, due in part to its low level of air pollution, clean air and a hole in the ozone layer above New Zealand. As a result, this could enhance the colour, aromas and flavour compounds in Pinot Noir, and turn your skin magenta. Viticulturists have to manage their canopies carefully to ensure that vines and bunches get the Goldilocks effect when it comes to the sun: not too much, not too little, it has to be just right. Based on the vines running north–south, the side of the vines that receives the weaker morning sunlight (the east) is subject to a more thorough leaf plucking than on the afternoon side (the west), when the sun is more intense and, at this latitude, doesn't set until 9 p.m. – or later, in the summer months. A balance is required. Open the canopy too much and it can potentially lead to sunburned, dehydrated grapes, but open it too little and it can reduce airflow and promote disease. Surrounded by mountains, some vineyards find themselves in the shadows first thing in the morning or late in the day but Blair Walter, winemaker at Felton Road, wonders whether or not that is a positive attribute. 'Some of the vineyards under the Pisa range [the westerly edge of Lake Dunstan] lose the sun in the late afternoon and maybe that's not a good thing. On the other hand, we have a lot of sun in Central Otago and that will reduce the amount of heat.'

Wind can also pose challenges to successful grape growing in some sites. Between lifting fruiting wires and applying biodynamic preparations on the steep slopes of Burn Cottage Vineyard, Shane Livingstone, vineyard manager, is busy planting poplar, olive and cypress trees to act as windbreaks. 'Whenever we are trying do something like put shoots or wires up, or the [bird] netting, the wind blows!' he says. In the southeast of Central Otago, growers in the sub-region of Alexandra are most affected by cold winds blowing up from the Southern Ocean. The prevailing winds in the region are the norwesters, which can be dry and hot. In extreme cases, the vine leaves shut their stomata to prevent water loss through transpiration but this also stops photosynthesis. 'Your leaves are your engine for ripening,' says Wing, 'and it slows everything up.'

WHAT LIES BENEATH

The story of the region's soils involves crocodiles and snakes. Dead ones: fossils of creatures you wouldn't want to meet up close and personal. Central Otago was once a landscape of low, rolling hills that enjoyed a tropical climate, unrecognizable in contrast to the dramatic mountainscape that attracts skiers across the Tasman Sea today. Around 120 million years ago the region went through a period of mountain building which then stopped and, over the ensuing 80 million years, the mountains were eroded leaving behind this gentle landscape that was home to crocs and serpents rather than snowboarders.

Rather sadly for this tale, the age of dangerous reptiles in Queenstown plays a small role in Central Otago viticulture. The modern story of vineyard soils in Central Otago starts 650,000 years ago with a series of glacial advances and retreats, leaving huge gravel deposits behind and creating flat plains which would later become terraces as rivers cut through them. Each glaciation advance was smaller than the previous one, meaning the highest terraces you find in and around the Cromwell

Basin are the oldest, such as Chinaman's Terrace in Bendigo. During the next glaciation, around 400,000 years ago, the valley was filled up again but not to the same level, leaving the School House terrace in Bendigo as well as the Bannockburn high terrace. Around 150,000 years ago, another advance came and went, leaving behind its debris, and there were later advances too – the last finishing only 14,000 years ago. Remnants of these terraces are found all around Central Otago area so neighbouring vineyards may be on different terraces formed tens (or hundreds) of thousands of years apart in time.

For those who are time poor and find geology confusing, Central Otago's soils are, in short, glacial derived and schist is the parent rock. The soil types around the region are a blend of free-draining gravels, loess often peppered with sparkling schist and quartz pebbles and, in some areas, clays. Soil types can change rapidly even within a small area: Felton Road's Block 3 planted to Pinot Noir sports a 40-cm loess topsoil on top of silt and gravels, whereas on the other side of the driveway, just metres apart, Block 2 has proved to be a more suitable site for Chardonnay and Riesling with schist gravels visible on the surface. Throughout the region, the soils are generally low in organic matter and low in vigour, and growers need to work hard to improve this with compost and cover crops.

For those who like to indulge their inner soil nerd, read on. It might come as a surprise to hear that Central Otago soils, particularly the older soils, can have a high lime content. Carbon dioxide dissolved in water in the soil meets up with calcium released from the parent material as it weathers and is chemically broken down, explains Roger Gibson, local soil scientist and founder of local winery Lowburn Ferry. 'This weathering process happens very slowly in Central Otago as the climate is so dry. When the two – calcium and dissolved carbon dioxide – get together they react to form calcium carbonate, and normally this is washed right through the soil profile and down into the ground water in a process called leaching. But in the dry environment of Central Otago it is very rare for enough rain to fall for this to happen, so leaching is incomplete and the lime accumulates.' This doesn't happen overnight; it takes tens of hundreds of thousands of years and is a feature in the older soils of Central Otago. This 'Pedogenic lime' is not formed in the same way as limestone, but chemically there is no difference.

WINE STYLES

While gold was discovered in Central Otago more than 150 years ago, the region's vineyards are now better known as a source of liquid gold in the form of densely fruited Pinot Noir. The red variety accounts for more than three in every four hectares planted in Central and, despite its relatively small size, Central represents around one-quarter of all Pinot Noir vineyards in New Zealand.

Kiwis started sitting up and paying attention in the early 1990s when Wanaka-based Rippon started winning awards for its Pinot Noir, but it took another decade for the rest of the world to wake up to its charms. There was a rapidly growing wine community and a group of twenty-two producers under the banner of the newly formed Central Otago Pinot Noir Ltd (COPNL) took their deeply coloured, fruity, bold wines from the 2002 vintage to London. 'The ripe, deep fruit – perhaps now I look back at it was over the top but it was so easy to understand: full bodied, technically correct Pinot Noir. It was such a vintage that everyone was able to achieve that character of Pinot pretty easily,' recalls Walter.

Since then, Central Otago has been on a journey of self discovery. The big, deep Pinot Noir style with sweet cherry fruit, liberal oak and high alcohol put this mountainous region at the end of the world on the wine lovers' map but it also created a 'caricature' style that the region is now eager to correct. Nature imbues Central Otago's Pinot Noirs with a wealth of colour, fruit and richness that it cannot deny. Walter says, 'Sometimes our wines are so fruity and pure. That is seen as a negative but that's just what nature gives us.' The large diurnal swings during the summer months and the high levels of UV light contribute to its characteristically deep hue (although depth of colour can and does differ from wine to wine, producer to producer), aromatic intensity and brightness of flavour.

The long, warm summer days and the dry autumns with little disease pressure allow grapes to reach full flavour and physiological ripeness. However, this can lead to grapes with high Brix levels and consequently high alcohol levels, which tends to dull some of the brightness of fruit and overpower its finer aromatic detail. There are moves in some camps to pick earlier – Burn Cottage Vineyard and Felton Road, for example, are leading the way with earlier harvest dates, which is prompting others to reconsider their perception of ripeness.

SUBREGIONALITY AND PINOT NOIR

Subregionality within Central Otago has been a theme played out by the region's producers since I arrived in New Zealand in 2009 but it has left me – and others – scratching our heads. I was starting to wonder if I was missing something but it seems other people, including the local producers, were wondering if this division of wines was actually useful at all.

This was apparent when a group of sommeliers and buyers toured the region and were flummoxed by the lack of clear, subregional characters on a tour of these areas, explains Walter. 'Traditionally we'd present a tour of the subregions – go to Alexandra and taste the wines there, go to Bendigo … I was always uncomfortable with it. At the end [of the tour], people said "We are more confused than ever now, having been around these subregions". Winemaker style is just as influential and the wines off heavier soils can outweigh the influence of subregion.'

Duncan Forsyth, of Mount Edward, who owns vineyards in Bannockburn, Lowburn and Gibbston agrees: 'We look at wines from different subregions and they can have a lot of similarities. You get tied up in knots. People – people like us – have rapidly been going away from talking about subregions and looking at similarities between the wines [across subregions] and why these similarities exist.'

Growing disillusionment with subregionality in Central Otago inspired a masterclass at the region's annual Pinot Celebration in 2015. Leading the masterclass was Roger Gibson. In his half-hour whistlestop speech, Gibson set out a new way of thinking about the development of the soils of Central Otago and their relationship to the glacial history of the landscape that has turned subregionality on its head. Subregionality was 'probably not well thought through,' says Gibson. 'To follow almost the Burgundy model where you've got nice tight appellations – I think people assumed here we would do the same – we could put nice circles without stopping to think about what is sometimes a huge variation in soils within each area.'

It is in the soil that Gibson has sought answers, as the climate is fairly similar throughout the Cromwell Basin around Lake Dunstan: hot and dry, as the locals' sun-baked faces and visitors' cracked lips attest. The basin includes the 'subregions' of Cromwell, Lowburn, Pisa, Bendigo and Bannockburn and accounts for around 70 per cent of Central Otago's wine. While Bendigo is 'possibly the warmest of all the subregions' according to the region's wine trade association, COPNL, the differences between these defined areas are marginal and can vary from year to year. Paul Pujol of Prophet's Rock attests to that: 'In some years, Bendigo will be warmer than Bannockburn and Pisa, but at other times it will be cooler and we'll pick later.'

While there's a question mark over the usefulness of carving up Central Otago, there are some areas that have a distinctive personality. In the coolest subregion, Gibbston Valley, the Pinot Noirs evoke descriptors like ethereal, transparent, pretty, floral and herbal; Gibbston is typically the last place to harvest its grapes – it can even be as late as May – and yet alcohol levels rarely breach 13.5% abv and acidity is mouthwatering. However, frost – in both spring and autumn – is Gibbston's enemy number one and in some years, there is no harvest: in 2012, frost put paid to any wine at Two Paddocks' Gibbston vineyard. Many wineries based in the Valley such as Gibbston Valley and Mount Edward source the majority of their fruit from the more reliable Cromwell Basin.

Alexandra also sits apart from the rest of the region both geographically and stylistically. While the harvest is typically before Gibbston, it is often later than vineyards in the Cromwell Basin. Producers who have vineyards in both Alexandra and Bannockburn report that picking dates are one to two weeks later in Alexandra, despite it often reaching the highest maximum temperatures during the days. The overnight lows tumble, however, giving wines that offer a ripe red-fruited and thyme character which retains distinctive acidity and a mineral streak on the bony hillside sites.

At the north-eastern end of Lake Dunstan, about fifteen minutes' drive from the town of Cromwell, lies Bendigo Station. The home of Shrek, a sheep which evaded shearers for six years and became famous for his 27-kilo fleece, the station is also the site of many fine hillside vineyards including Quartz Reef, Prophet's Rock and Chinaman's Terrace. Bauer was the first to plant on Bendigo Station in 1991. It was a dry, dusty, scrub-laden piece of dirt pocked with rabbit holes when he bought it; today, it is a biodynamically certified north-facing vineyard – with fencing to keep the rabbits out, of course. Bendigo is characterized as having a natural generosity of tannin and muscular frame, and tannin management is key to success. And yet, try Prophet's Rock's wines, made on a steep terrace high above Quartz Reef, and the Pinot Noirs are increasingly silken, almost seamless. Winemaker Pujol plunges his Pinot Noirs just once, not once a day but once during the entire fermentation process. 'I quickly worked out that I didn't need to go hunting for structure [in Bendigo]. I think a lot of that [structure] is how people make the wine – is Bendigo really more tannic than Bannockburn?' Only time will tell.

The story that seems to be emerging from the latest chapter in Central Otago's short history is that there are blurred lines when it comes to splitting Central Otago into neat geographical areas. Producers are each seeking their sense of place, and that place is not a subregion, it is their vineyard. In Central Otago there are so many variables within subregions, and then people intervene with their own philosophy on viticulture and winemaking, and produce their interpretation of a site – which can be very different. For example, Burn Cottage and Valli have operated a 'fruit swap' since 2014 in a bid to better understand the interpretation of site: Valli gives Burn Cottage some grapes from Gibbston and Valli receives some in return. They each decide when they want to pick: Burn Cottage typically picks earlier than Valli and then the decision over whole clusters, oak, time on skins is up to the winemaker. It is a delight to taste them side by side, although there isn't much of it made so you have to get in quick. Claire Mulholland, Burn Cottage general manager, worked alongside Valli founder Grant Taylor at Gibbston Valley many moons ago. 'Now people [in Central] feel more confident making wines from individual sites,' she says. 'I guess that is time and experience.'

It is encouraging that attitudes toward viticulture and winemaking are becoming increasingly sensitive. The dry climate with low humidity means that it is possible to farm organically without having a nervous breakdown: around 20 per cent of the region's vineyards were in conversion or were already certified organic at the last count. With experience, winemakers are making better decisions when it comes to picking dates and handling their fruit: across the region, extraction is becoming much gentler. Oregon-born winemaker Jen Parr has been in Central Otago since 2007 and has seen a change in the region's approach: 'When I arrived everyone did three punch downs a day because that's what they did, but now quite a few of us do one or two a day. Rarely would we do three.' There's an ongoing debate about cold soak, whole-bunch fermentations, wild yeast and the length of time on skins but that's hardly unique to Central Otago winemakers.

IT'S NOT ALL PINOT NOIR

Believe it or not, Central Otago isn't just Pinot Noir, Pinot Noir and more Pinot Noir. Aromatic whites excel in pockets of Central Otago and Chardonnay has its feet – albeit a small pair – firmly in the region's glacier-derived soils.

The most-planted white variety in Central is Pinot Gris, representing around 12 per cent of all plantings. It is actually a colour mutation of Pinot Noir so it's not straying too far from home. Styles vary widely from sweet and lush to dry and taut. However, the wide diurnal swings in Central Otago and its cool climate (1,070 growing degree days versus 1,631 in Hawke's Bay) elongate the cycle of this early ripener, preserving acidity and restraining alcohol levels. As a result, it produces some of the finest – and most interesting – Pinot Gris in the country: try Prophet's Rock and Misha's Vineyard for starters. Pinot Gris is typically produced in stainless steel to preserve its delicate aromatics but the region's winemakers are maturing alongside their vines and now they are happy to use wild yeast, ferment the wine in barrels and leave it on lees to build aromatic and textural interest. There's even an orange Pinot Gris produced by Valli, which spends up to three weeks on skins and is a Campari-lovers' wine.

Central Otago whites get even more interesting when it comes to Riesling. The coolest subregion, Gibbston, records a heat summation of 910 growing degree days putting it between the Mosel and the Rheinhessen – two of the world's most renowned Riesling producers – while the Cromwell Basin (1,100 GDD) is more akin to Baden in the south of Germany. The styles in Central Otago, as in Germany, can range from dry to sweet but botrytized wines are a rarity in this dry, arid climate. However, there's no consensus on what Central Otago Riesling is: there is an array of stylistic interpretations even within one winery. Felton Road, for example, produces a dry Riesling and a pair of sweet, low-alcohol, luscious styles. What's more, the quirky seasons in Central Otago also have their say in the final wine styles. There is a common thread that links Central Otago's Rieslings: they are sewn together by a scintillating line of acidity that pulls the wines through to a precise finish. You can expect clean lines, crystalline purity, citrus and floral aromas and an intensity of fruit on the palate. Felton Road, Misha's Vineyard, Mount Edward, Prophet's Rock, Rippon, Two Paddocks, and Valli's Rieslings never fail to impress.

Aromatic whites are most common in Central Otago but Chardonnay also makes a guest appearance. It is often the first variety to be picked and winemakers seek to preserve its purity of fruit flavours, going easy on the new oak. The cool climate expresses itself in the Chardonnay style: clean and crisp, offering apple, nectarine and lemon-like fruit flavours, often with mineral grip on the finish. Start your Central-meets-white-Burgundy journey with Carrick's pair of Chardonnays or one of the three cuvées made at Felton Road. This non-aromatic variety is also grown in partnership with Pinot Noir to make *methode traditionelle* sparkling wine blends. Leading examples include Akarua, Quartz Reef and Amisfield (a *blanc de noirs*).

Central Otago is the adventure capital of New Zealand, so it's inevitable that the wine producers in this region are getting a bit more adventurous with their varieties. Rippon started with Osteiner, which has survived the Pinot expansion and continues to make a crisp aromatic white today but there are now others who are giving new varieties a go. There's Gamay and Gewürztraminer, Grüner Veltliner and Chenin Blanc. And, this being New Zealand, there's a smattering of Sauvignon Blanc. The style is more restrained in its expression than Marlborough; as clean and pure as the Central Otago air. But make no mistake, Central Otago might be on the same island as Marlborough but it is a world away.

PRODUCER PROFILES

Amisfield

Lake Hayes/Pisa
amisfield.co.nz

Having failed to properly consult a map as a young backpacker, I set off on a failed mission to cycle around Central Otago wine country. I soon hired a car when the distances became glaringly apparent. However, Amisfield is the first winery cellar door and restaurant on the road out of Queenstown, and is easily accessible by bike or by car. Its 90 hectares of organically farmed vineyard are situated further afield under the Pisa range, producing Pinot Noir (60 per cent of plantings), Sauvignon Blanc, Pinot Gris, Riesling and, rather curiously, Chenin Blanc. The story goes that the South African vineyard manager wanted a taste of home and so found what seemed to be the only Chenin vine at the Otago Polytechnic, grafted it himself, propagated it, grew more and surreptitiously started planting it around the edges of the vineyard, hiding it where possible!

Amisfield was founded in 1998 by Alan Darby, a Queenstown architect and qualified viticulturist. The main event has always been dark, fleshy Pinot Noir. The style has gradually evolved as the vines and the winemakers have matured. From using commercial yeast and plunging intensively, the wines are now wild fermented and the cap is not worked as intensively during the fermentation; instead the wine spends up to four weeks on skins. Its flagship Pinot Noir RKV has also evolved from a barrel selection to a site selection: a consistently over-performing rocky ridge on a north-facing slope has proven to be the killer Pinot parcel. Since 2013, it has started fermenting a portion of the wine in the vineyard: DNA sequencing has shown that more than 60 per cent of the yeasts were not previously known. *Saccharomyces*, yes, but yet to be identified, meaning this is a real expression of place.

In addition to its Pinot Noir, it has built a reputation for its Brut-style vintage *blanc de noirs*. A solitary hectare of Chardonnay nestled above the winery was used in the blend until 2017 when it was used to produce the company's first varietal Chardonnay.

Try this: Amisfield RKV Pinot Noir
The flagship wine now partially fermented in the vineyard is becoming

increasingly complex and interesting. A dark, broody and textural wine with powerful fruit and savoury layers.

Visit
The cellar door is open seven days a week from 10 a.m. to 6 p.m. The bistro is open for lunch between noon and 3 p.m.; dinner service runs from 5 p.m. until 8 p.m.

Burn Cottage Vineyard
Cromwell Basin
burncottage.com

In 2002, the Sauvage family, which runs a US-based fine wine distributor and also owns a wine estate in the Pfalz, Germany, purchased a 24-hectare property in Lowburn, a stone's throw from the township of Cromwell. Marquis (pronounced Marcus) Sauvage, who heads up the family business and looks more heavy-metal than soft Pinot, convinced Ted Lemon of Littorai Wines in Sonoma to join the team. Lemon insisted that the site should be farmed biodynamically from day one, making it the first vineyard in Central Otago to follow the waxing and waning of the moon and spray teas on its vines from inception. The focus is naturally Pinot Noir. The hillside vineyard is an amphitheatre divided into blocks. There are ten Pinot Noir clones across the site and most blocks have a selection. Claire Mulholland of Burn Cottage says the aim 'is to pick and ferment each block individually, which requires the different clones and rootstocks to be managed carefully to reach desirable maturity. We are looking to learn from each vineyard block as we focus on expressing our terroir.' From its first vintage (2009), it was clear that Burn Cottage was going to be a special vineyard. In addition to its estate Pinot Noir, it now makes a more affordable cuvée Moonlight Race, blending fruit from three Cromwell Basin subregion sites (one being Burn Cottage), as well as growing Riesling and Grüner Veltliner on the home block. Since 2014, it has operated a fruit exchange programme with Valli, making a small amount of Gibbston Valley Pinot Noir, and Valli picking and making the same amount from Burn Cottage. In early 2018, it added a 5.8-hectare vineyard (planted in 1999) in Bannockburn.

Try this: Burn Cottage Vineyard Pinot Noir

Burn Cottage tends to pick earlier than many of its fellow Central Otago producers and it achieves ripeness without weight and heaviness. It always captures the beautiful cherry fruit of Central Otago in an elegant and detailed package with pixellated tannins.

Visit

Tastings are held by appointment, Monday to Friday, at the winery in Cromwell.

Felton Road Wines

Bannockburn

feltonroad.com

Felton Road was first established by Stewart Elms in 1992, later selling to British businessman Nigel Greening. Since taking ownership, Greening has slowly expanded the estate which now comprises four vineyards covering 32 hectares across Bannockburn. Long-serving winemaker, pilot and driver of his Messerschmitt bubble car, Blair Walter joined Felton Road in 1996, having been Elms' lab partner at Lincoln University. This Pinot-focused producer has managed its vineyards organically and biodynamically since 2002, achieving Demeter certification in 2010. The winery sits in the middle of The Elms Vineyard, which comprises thirteen different blocks, and is home to Jancis the cat (mark 2 – Jancis the first was killed in a possum trap in 2010; Oz the goat found his way to the lunch table and has not been replaced). The vines extend from the roadside and ascend steeply behind the winery to 335 metres altitude. Both the MacMuir (purchased 2010, planted 2012) and Calvert Vineyards (leased since 2001, purchased Aurum, Willows and Springs blocks in 2013) lie along Felton Road while Cornish Point has the rather unusual position of sitting on a promontory surrounded by the waters of Lake Dunstan. There are five different Pinot Noirs to choose from, opening with the not-so-entry-level 'Bannockburn' cuvée: a blend of all the sites, offering a taste of both the subregion and Felton Road with its pure fruit and spice, silken texture and fine tannins. Hailing from the original Elms Vineyard comes Block 3 (see Try This) and Block 5. The latter offers a more broody, dense expression with more classical structure and detail than Block 3. Head a kilometre down the road to the Calvert Vineyard and you'll find a site that produces elegant Pinot

Noir with an innate sense of power. It can be a little shy in youth but is always concentrated and pure. Meanwhile Cornish Point doesn't seem to get the attention it deserves: it is fragrant and often has a savoury spiciness, sporting a dense, juicy core and fine stone-licking tannins. Keep an eye out for its trio of juicy, spine-tingling Rieslings and its fine Chardonnay.

Try this: Felton Road Wines Block 3 Pinot Noir
Hailing from one of the original blocks in front of the winery, the deep soils at the base of the hill imbue this complex, ageworthy Pinot with richness. It is highly scented, offering layers of black cherry fruit, florals, spice and chocolate. Always seductive and texturally enigmatic.

Visit
Visits are by prior appointment only, from Monday to Friday, closed on weekends and public holidays. Contact the winery through the website.

Gibbston Valley Winery
Gibbston
gibbstonvalley.com

Founded by Irish journalist Alan Brady, Gibbston Valley Winery is one of the pioneering producers of Central Otago's modern era. Brady planted Gibbston's first vineyard in 1983 and made the first commercial wine in 1987. A winery was built in 1990 and, with the addition of a restaurant and an underground wine cellar blasted out of a schistous rockface behind the winery, Gibbston Valley became a major tourist attraction. It continues to lure visitors 25 kilometres outside Queenstown today but Gibbston is no longer its main source of grapes. While it retains its vineyards in the coolest of Central Otago's subregions, it owns more hectares in the warmer, less frost-prone – and thus more reliable – Bendigo area. The brand has four tiers but its single-vineyard Pinot Noir wines are the most complex and interesting. They hail from the elevated School House and China Terrace vineyards in Bendigo while Glenlee and Le Maitre, a homage to Brady, are Gibbston-grown.

Try this: Gibbston Valley Winery Glenlee Pinot Noir
This hails from a close-planted vineyard (in New Zealand terms, that is) at 6,000 vines per hectare, sitting on a former sheep station and, when it doesn't get frosted (there was no 2015 vintage), it creates a

finely scented, elegant and incredibly smooth wine. The winemaking is sensitive, allowing the fruit to shine; oak plays an unobtrusive supporting role. Vivacious acidity on the finish provides the brightness and line that is so attractive in Gibbston.

Visit

The cellar door and neighbouring cheesery is open seven days a week. Tours around the winery and wine cave run up to five times a day; prices depend on the tour and wines tasted. The restaurant opens for lunch every day and the winery can organize transport from Queenstown, if required. A bike-hire centre is on-site providing access to various trails around the region. For more information, visit the website.

Maude Wines

Wanaka
maudewines.com

Leaving behind their high-flying winemaking roles in Australia's Hunter Valley, Sarah-Kate and Dan Dineen moved back to Central Otago in 2005, where Sarah-Kate's parents planted a small vineyard on a steep slope close to Wanaka in 1994. The 4-hectare Mount Maude Vineyard is the source of the winery's finest cuvées: its eponymous Pinot Noir, which is typically a whopping 100 per cent whole-cluster fermented, is fragrant yet sinewy and benefits from cellaring. This illustrious site also produces some fine Riesling: the East Block is a pure and finely constructed Riesling that tends to be medium sweet but offers crystal-clear acidity that dances across your palate. The vines have their feet in deep clay-based gravels, created by the last advance of the Hawea glacier 14,000 years ago, and have been dry farmed for more than a decade. The small size of the Mount Maude Vineyard means that the Dineens source fruit from Queensberry and their Sitting Bull Vineyard in Lowburn for the Maude Pinot Noir, Pinot Gris and Chardonnay, while there is also a Marlborough Sauvignon Blanc in the portfolio.

Try this: Maude Wines, Mount Maude Vineyard EMW Pinot Noir
EMW, standing for East Meets West, refers to the orientation of two parcels of old-vine Pinot Noir that combine to produce this wine. With no crushing, plunging or pumping, the whole bunches are combined to produce this non-interventionist style, creating a seamlessly textured

wine with no hard edges in sight. The flavours are unadulterated and intriguing: herbal notes meet Christmas spices, dark cherries and orange peel. This wine seduces you and then surprises you with its abundant yet resolved tannins which, combined with bags of mouthwatering acidity, make for a deeply satisfying finish. Delicious early on, better with age.

Visit

Maude is a small, family-run operation and its tasting room is open Thursday to Monday, from noon to 5 p.m.

Misha's Vineyard
Cromwell Basin
mishasvineyard.com

After sixteen years living in Asia it was time for Andy and Misha Wilkinson to head to New Zealand and pursue their dream of owning a vineyard. Having finally settled on a piece of land in Bendigo above the eastern shores of Lake Dunstan, their first vines were planted in 2004. The vineyard now stretches over 26 hectares on north-west-facing slopes at heights ranging from 210 to 350 metres, and is planted to Pinot Noir and aromatic whites. The wine names have a theatrical or musical theme – Misha's mother was an opera singer and Misha a dancer – so you'll find The High Note Pinot Noir, Dress Circle Pinot Gris and Limelight Riesling in the range. Winemaker Olly Masters plays with wild fermentation and older barrels to bring additional aromatic and textural interest to the aromatic whites. The Pinot Noir spends its post-fermentation days in French hogsheads (300 litres) rather than barrels and is released three to four years after the harvest. The approach to the vineyard and winemaking has evolved since day one: the vineyard was treated as one unit in the early days but, with experience, cropping levels and fruit exposure have been adjusted to suit individual parcels. Older vines have also given Olly Masters the ability to include more whole berries and bunches in the ferments. Its flagship Pinot Noir, Verismo, hails from three different blocks each planted to a single clone. It is almost Brunello-like in its release date: the wine does not go on sale until five to six years after picking the grapes.

Try this: The High Note Pinot Noir
A supple and full-bodied Pinot Noir that still maintains an elegant stance. It typically has an abundance of tannin providing a male baritone to the female soprano.

Visit
The tasting room is located on the outskirts of Cromwell. Its range of aromatic white wines and Pinot Noirs is available to taste daily.

Mount Edward
Gibbston
mountedward.co.nz

Gibbston pioneer, the Irish journalist Alan Brady, started another local winery, Mount Edward, after resigning from Gibbston Valley Winery in late 1997. In 2004, a Dunedin-born, Bermuda-based businessman John Buchanan teamed up with local winemaker Duncan Forsyth to acquire the brand. While the winery is based in Gibbston, its major vineyard holdings are in the more reliable Bannockburn and Lowburn areas. All of its vineyards are farmed organically and the winemaking is increasingly hands off, producing more transparent wines. Forsyth is far from a beige winemaker: he sports T-shirts declaring that the son of God was a Riesling drinker and throws legendary parties which inevitably end in a dressing-up bonanza – a whole room in his house is dedicated to fancy dress costumes. He is also becoming more experimental with every year that passes, producing an unsulphured 95 per cent whole-berry Gamay, a *pétillant naturel* and a Vermouth based on Riesling and Chenin Blanc. What has this got to do with Central Otago Pinot Noir? Becoming more daring in the winery has given the team the confidence to apply their learning to its more conventional wines, whether it's using more whole bunch, eliminating winery additions or reducing the use of sulphur dioxide.

Try this: Mount Edward Muirkirk Vineyard Pinot Noir
Hailing from a site on Felton Road, the dense clay loams and the Bannockburn climate create a Pinot Noir with flesh and depth while retaining an aura of elegance. In cooler years, it offers a more nervy, translucent expression that can develop beautifully over five to ten years.

Visit

If you're driving along State Highway 6 and are suddenly overcome by the urge to drive up Coal Pit Road to Mount Edward, you can chance your arm and see if there's anyone willing and able to show you around and open a few bottles. The better-organized visitor should make an appointment in advance. Contact details can be found on the website.

Prophet's Rock

Bendigo
prophetsrock.co.nz

Founded in 1999 by Mike and Angela Mulvey, the couple sold the business to six New Zealanders in 2013. Winemaker Paul Pujol has been the face of the company since joining in 2005 and has played a pivotal role in determining the Prophet's Rock style. The home vineyard sits high on Bendigo Station, reaching 383 metres altitude at its zenith. It also has another vineyard – Rocky Point – which lies a few kilometres along the eastern shores of Lake Dunstan. The fruit from this rock-hewn site is a more affordable entry to Prophet's Rock. Since working the 2009 vintage at the ethereal Chambolle-Musigny producer Domaine Comte Georges de Vogüé, Pujol has developed a friendship with its poetic winemaker, François Millet. This has resulted in a Burgundy–Central Otago winemaking collaboration: Millet travelled to Prophet's Rock in 2015 to make the first Cuvée aux Antipodes. Pujol's approach to extraction has also changed dramatically since his first vintage in 2006: from three punch downs daily, he quickly worked out that he did not need to seek out structure in Bendigo fruit, and now he plunges once per ferment and does not rack the barrels. The resulting Pinots are so silken you might go weak at the knees. Prophet's Rock has a policy of releasing its reds a little later than most and it launched an aged cuvée in 2015: Retrospect is its reserve Pinot Noir, released after five years.

Try this: Prophet's Rock Dry Riesling

Having spent three years as the chief winemaker at Alsace's Kuentz-Bas – the first non-family winemaker since the house was founded in 1795 – Pujol knows how to make mighty fine Pinot Gris and Riesling. The latter is pure, dry and light bodied, yet also intense and powerful. Fermented in old barrels and having spent ten months on lees, it might have the line of an Olympic skeleton champion but it also has texture.

And, whenever anyone asks me for a recommendation for New Zealand Pinot Gris, Prophet's Rock is always my first response: it is always precise, concentrated and fine.

Visit
There is no cellar door at Prophet's Rock and visits are by appointment only.

Quartz Reef
Bendigo
quartzreef.co.nz

Rudi Bauer, an Austrian-born winemaker, worked in Hawke's Bay before answering a job ad to become the first trained winemaker at Rippon Estate in 1989. In 1996 he founded Quartz Reef, becoming the first to plant on Bendigo Station's dry and dusty north-facing slopes. Today, verdant rows of Pinot Noir, Pinot Gris, Chardonnay and Grüner Veltliner line his 30-hectare biodynamic vineyard. Its highly acclaimed non-vintage Pinot Noir/Chardonnay sparkling wine is made by the 'traditional method' and spends twenty-four months on lees before disgorgement. The Pinot Noir component brings a dark red fruit aroma and powerful structure while the Chardonnay, combined with no malolactic fermentation, brings a crisp, citrussy line of acidity on the finish. The vintage cuvée is even more refined, thanks to the high proportion of Chardonnay in the blend and time on lees extending to almost four years.

Try this: Quartz Reef Single Vineyard Pinot Noir
The muscle of Bendigo is evident in the generous structured frame of this fresh Pinot Noir. The cherry fruit filling the frame is charming, with oak-derived nutty nuances in a supporting role.

Visit
Quartz Reef is probably the only tasting room which offers a former rocket launcher cartridge from Afghanistan as a spitoon. Its cellar door is not in Bendigo but at the functional winery in Cromwell. The cellar door is open Monday to Friday, noon to 4 p.m., and vineyard tours can also be arranged by appointment.

Rippon Vineyard

Wanaka
rippon.co.nz

Sitting beside the shores of Lake Wanaka, Rippon (pictured below) is probably the most photographed vineyard in the world. Rolfe and Lois Mills were pioneers in Central Otago's modern wine-producing era. Rolfe (1923–2000) grew up on the property, trying to find out what would grow best on this isolated farm (as well as serving on submarines in the Second World War). In the 1970s he started planting vines, and the first 'commercial' block was born in 1982. At this time, no one knew that Pinot Noir was going to be the red grape of Central Otago and that's why, in the early 1990s, you could buy Rippon's Nicolas – a red blend of Merlot, Syrah and Cabernet Sauvignon named after their then-teenage son Nick Mills, who became the winemaker in 2003.

There are still six varieties planted on its sloped schistous sites including Riesling, Gewürztraminer, Sauvignon Blanc, Gamay and Osteiner. The vineyard is now certified biodynamic and around 80 per cent of the vines are grown on their own roots rather than grafted on American rootstocks. Its 'Jeunesse' wines are made from younger, irrigated vines; Mills considers his Pinot Noir vines 'mature' when they hit fifteen years old, and his Riesling at twelve years. He does not consider the phenolics to be as ripe nor fine in younger vines and consequently does not include any whole bunches in the young red ferments. The named vineyards of Tinker's Field and Emma's Block are both based on schist gravels, although Emma's Block is closer to the lake and sports 'sausage-like' lenses of clay. Being so close to this mass of water, the diurnal temperature extremes experienced at Rippon are less pronounced and, as the closest subregion to the Main Divide, Wanaka tends to experience more cloud and rainfall than Cromwell or Alexandra. This contributes to a more restrained, mellow and textural style of Pinot, as does the hands-off winemaking.

Try this: Rippon Vineyard Tinker's Field Pinot Noir
Sourced from biodynamically farmed vines on a north-facing slope consisting of coarse schist gravels, Tinker's Field typically produces seamless wines that are pure, fine and have great depth without heaviness. Unfined and unfiltered, this is an unadulterated Pinot Noir.

Visit
Rippon's cellar door, overlooking the vines that cascade toward Lake Wanaka, is open daily from 11 a.m. to 5 p.m.

Valli Vineyards
Gibbston
valliwine.co.nz

Otago-born winemaker Grant Taylor was lured back to Central after more than a decade in California by Alan Brady, the founder of Gibbston Valley Wine. Taylor founded Valli Vineyards in 1998 and planted his first vines in Gibbston in 2000, making the first wine in 2003 while also remaining at Gibbston Valley Wines until 2006. Valli specializes in singular expressions of Central Otago producing a Gibbston, Bannockburn and Bendigo Pinot Noir. In 2014, Valli added a Lowburn-sourced cuvée, as part of a fruit exchange project with Burn Cottage. It's wrong to say that they are subregional expressions of Central Otago; they are single-vineyard expressions. It's not all Pinot Noir at Valli: the Gibbston vineyard, Taylor's first purchase in 2003, produces poised Pinot Gris. In 2015, Taylor went from hippie to hipster with his Pinot

Gris, and his long beard: the Real McCoy spends up to three weeks on skins and is a Campari-lovers' wine; dry and phenolic with flavours reminiscent of bitter orange and rhubarb. Valli is not solely a Central Otago producer. In 2017, after thirteen years buying fruit from Waitaki (North Otago), Taylor took the plunge in this marginal area and bought Blue House Vineyard. The site is limestone based with overlying gravels, and the Pinots from the region are savoury with a spiny acidity bringing a nervous tension, while the Rieslings are citrus-led with lipsmacking freshness.

Try this: Valli Gibbston Vineyard Pinot Noir
From the coolest subregion, Gibbston is the last place to reap the harvest in Central Otago. It can be nerve-racking but it's worth the wait. The resulting wine is delicate, elegant, aromatic and pure with lifted floral characters and a textural, drawn-out finish.

Visit
The winery is situated in a rather unglamorous building in Cromwell but visits take place in the much more scenic setting of the Gibbston vineyard. If you wish to visit, contact the winery directly to make an appointment.

PART 4
CONTEMPORARY NEW ZEALAND

14

CURRENT ISSUES

INNOVATION

New Zealand is a young and innovative wine-producing country. It does not have centuries of tradition nor a rigid appellation system, meaning producers have artistic licence in their vineyards and wineries. There is a lack of fear when it comes to trialling new ideas and methods based on a can-do attitude and a desire for continual improvement. Kiwi ingenuity is known as the 'No. 8 wire' mentality, referring to the 8 mm wire that was used imaginatively to fix more than fencing on farms. At the bottom of the earth, New Zealanders have long had to be resourceful and find solutions for problems – and that stretches to all aspects of life and wine, even the packaging.

Screwed over

Fed up with failing cork, New Zealand producers put their No. 8 wire mentality to good use. Following the lead of a bunch of Clare Valley Riesling producers, who had ditched cork for screwcaps in 2000, Kiwi producers saw what was happening across the Tasman Sea (otherwise known as the 'ditch') and formed their own group after each writing off hundreds or even thousands of cases of wine because of failed corks. The New Zealand Screwcap Wine Seal Initiative was born in 2001 with thirty-two members. Journalist George Taber explains in *To Cork or not to Cork* that Kim Crawford was first in the race to release the 2001 vintage under screwcap at a midnight party in Auckland for local hospitality staff: 'Each sommelier was given a bottle of the Riesling that had attached to it a condom with a note that said the screwcap was there to protect the wine from TCA [the compound responsible for the musty smell known as cork taint] and the condom was there to protect the sommelier.'

In August 2001, the screwcapped wines were launched to local wine media and soon after some of its founding members – and a local parson – held a much-publicized funeral for the cork. It was all too much for some. An article in *The New Zealand Herald* following the launch suggested 'For the traditionalist, it is all too much. Wine bottles with screw-cap tops instead of corks? Why not go the whole way and introduce fine dining at McDonald's?' While many producers continued with cork alongside screwcap in the early days, Villa Maria decided in a thirty-minute meeting that it was going totally cork free, and that even its finest reds were going to be closed with aluminium – a step too far for many screwcap-using producers today. It was considered an act of madness by some. 'We got a lot of abuse to begin with – we took the brunt from the US and England when we went cork free,' says George Fistonich. In his autobiography he recalls receiving a letter from a New Zealand expatriate, which read: 'I've lived in America for ten years, and I have been proud of the New Zealand wine industry, but I am ashamed about Villa Maria trying to destroy the great reputation of New Zealand wine by using screwcaps.'

The launch of the Screwcap Initiative coincided with a large-scale study by the respected Australian Wine Research Institute (AWRI), which highlighted the benefits of screwcaps and provided evidence that they weren't going to ruin the country's wines or their reputation. Adoption occurred quickly: in 2001, screwcap producer Stelvin 'sold 2 million screwcaps to New Zealand; in 2002, 11 million; and in 2003, 25 million. The first year 1.6 per cent of New Zealand wines were in screwcap, but in the third year the number had jumped to 34.5 per cent,' notes Taber. Celebrating its ten-year anniversary, figures showed that more than 90 per cent of New Zealand wine was under screwcap. Such is the dominance of screwcaps that a New Zealander now looks like a rabbit in the headlights when they're asked to locate a corkscrew from the back of their kitchen drawer. While New Zealand wines under screwcap have reproduced as quickly as the Central Otago rabbit population, the cork industry has since revolutionized its processes but it seems to be too little too late for New Zealanders. Nevertheless, the cork remains the global leader, sealing 11.5 billion – or 64 per cent – of the 18 billion bottles of wine produced every year, according to Portuguese cork company Amorim (2016). Meanwhile, screwcaps account for 4.5 billion or 25 per cent of the closures market with synthetics making up the remainder. Closures are the last piece of the wine puzzle, ensuring the wine gets to the consumer's glass as the winemaker intended, but New Zealand innovation starts in the vineyard.

In the vines

No-one expects to see machine harvesters in the vineyard in late spring and early summer. There are no grapes to harvest, yet they can be seen driving up and down the rows as a result of industry research, which found that shaking the vines can reduce botrytis. Marlborough viticultural consultant Mark Allen was involved in a four-year mechanical thinning study, which found that not only did the process lower yields as desired, but it also had another positive effect: it lowered the botrytis levels by removing the 'floral trash' that remains in the bunch after flowering, which includes stamens, unset berries and flowers. The industry magazine *New Zealand Winegrower* reported that Allen subsequently wanted to find out if botrytis incidence would fall when he shook a vine without thinning the crop. It did. By 50 per cent or more. While there was concern that the vines would be damaged during the process, it actually appears that it does the vines no harm. Now there are rods or arms attached to machine harvesters, which would otherwise be sitting idle in sheds until harvest, giving the vine trunks and area above the fruiting zone a shimmy in spring. This also allows older harvesters and inexperienced drivers an opportunity for a run out before the main event. 'Botrytis is the most significant limiting factor to cool-climate grape growing. We have very few cultural opportunities to control it apart from leaf plucking and manipulating canopies. I believe that if growers can reduce the dependence of spraying options for botrytis, it could, as estimated in the Mechanical Thinning Trials save the industry overall $8 million. So the cost savings are starting to add up,' Allen told *New Zealand Winegrower*.

It is estimated that 50 per cent of Marlborough has since adopted the technique. Dr Damian Martin, group science leader with Plant

& Food Research, says 'Successful innovation is about uptake by the industry. Where New Zealand is successful and where we have that flexibility and willingness, people are willing to try new things at every level, but the end result is adoption at the producer level.' His colleague Mike Trought, a Birmingham-born scientist who left England for New Zealand in 1978, adds: 'I visited the Côte d'Or recently where you have a vast area of grape vines but ownership changes every few rows so it's difficult to innovate – can you imagine someone trialling a Scott Henry system there?! The laws wouldn't allow it. It's more difficult to innovate under appellation regulations but also in Marlborough we have biggish blocks – you can take a 4-hectare parcel and innovate. If the findings are favourable, you can start to adopt it on a larger scale.'

Another British scientist involved in New Zealand wine-science research is Dr Matt Goddard, who has been instrumental in understanding the ecology of the vineyard. In 2015 he was part of a team which published research showing that there was a microbial aspect to terroir. 'I first started exploring yeast with Michael Brajkovich [Kumeu River]. We wanted to know if yeasts differed from vineyard to vineyard and what they did in the winery. That was the first science to show yeast in a wild ferment actually derived from the local environment – nobody had ever shown that before.' This led to a larger Sauvignon Blanc trial at the University of Auckland funded by the university, the national wine association and the government. Firstly, the team identified and isolated six major strains of *Saccharomyces cerevisiae* present in six New Zealand wine-producing regions. The researchers then inoculated these thirty-six strains individually into the same batch of sterilized Sauvignon Blanc juice (so that there were no other yeasts present) to begin fermentation and followed the wines through their journey from must to wine. The trials showed that the regional strains produced distinct aromas and flavours, suggesting there is more to terroir than soil, climate and grape. The most distinctive regional signature belonged to those wines produced by strains of yeast from Nelson, which does tend to display a different Sauvignon Blanc profile from the rest of the South Island.

Now Goddard is working on another project involving microbes and other organisms invisible to the naked eye. Vineyard Ecosystems is a $7 million research project that ties in with the wine industry's sustainability ethos and is funded by the national wine association and the government. The aim is to improve the longevity of vineyards, reduce chemical inputs and disease. 'The industry cares about sustainability: they want to leave their vineyards to their kids and it's good marketing. They are innovative too – that's why they want to understand the effects of pesticides in the vineyards,' explains Goddard. 'We are going to measure everything we can in the vines across twenty-four vineyards over six years: half the vineyards are farmed conventionally and half are farmed organically so we will see the difference. People believe you would see more biodiversity in an organic vineyard, but after two years the preliminary results show there isn't a huge effect.'

There's also the lighter wines programme, which has the aim of making New Zealand the world's top producer of lower-alcohol and lower-calorie wines. Thus far, many people don't want to drink lower-alcohol wines, as they're perceived to taste inferior: if you pick early, the wines taste green and austere while reverse osmosis machines strip the wine of more than just alcohol. 'I've heard very few negative comments,' says John Forrest who has been at the forefront of developing low-alcohol wine in New Zealand with The Doctors' Range, which includes a 9.5% abv Sauvignon Blanc, rosé and even a Pinot Noir. Admitting that many low-alcohol wines didn't taste very good in the past, he decided to do something about it: 'The eureka moment was when I realized that the fifteen leaves on a vine don't have the same photosynthetic ability so if you can identify the ones that create the most sugar and remove them, the plant just doesn't have the horsepower,' he explains. 'It doesn't seem to impinge on flavour, acid or phenolic ripeness because the hang time is identical.' His work is being further developed in the seven-year lighter-wines project that has been funded by the government and national wine industry. The aim is to find ways to naturally reduce alcohol in the final wine in both the vineyard and winery and make New Zealand the go-to country for lower-alcohol wines. However, the answer to reducing alcohol intake seems obvious: don't have the third glass, or make a spritzer; there are also plenty of 8.5% abv Rieslings to enjoy but they come with sweetness and calories. Whether or not a 9.5% abv Sauvignon Blanc can be as enjoyable as its 13% abv equivalent, the scientific findings can only enhance the country's knowledge base further.

SUSTAINABLE NEW ZEALAND

Sustainability is a word you'll hear at any event run by New Zealand Winegrowers, the national wine trade body. In 1995, it launched a pilot programme, Sustainable Winegrowing New Zealand (SWNZ) and, in 2007, set a goal for all New Zealand wine to be produced under independently audited environmental programmes by 2012. The aims are to reduce the use of chemicals, energy, water and packaging, and wherever possible reuse and recycle materials and waste. There are measurable standards for members to meet. By 2016, 98 per cent of the country's vineyards, equivalent to more than 35,500 hectares, were certified as sustainable.

Seven 'pillars' were identified as part of the programme: biodiversity; soil, water and air; energy; chemicals; by-products; people; and business practices. The first – biodiversity – encourages growers to create a more diverse ecosystem of plants and animals in the vineyard. Tony Green, Villa Maria's Gisborne viticulturist, explains how it has changed his vineyard. 'In the early days of SWNZ, we used to do a count of our species in the vineyard and we would get to one. Now we can count into double figures.' There are now various flowers, clover, thistles, barley grass, rye and more flourishing between the vines; bees buzz happily, butterflies flutter. In Marlborough, there are also attempts to regenerate the endangered native falcon population to keep the hungry birds off the grapes; visitors to Brancott Estate can meet one of them on the vineyard's falconry tour.

When it comes to soil, the cover crops improving biodiversity are also improving the organic matter and structure of soils. Members are encouraged to reduce chemical inputs such as herbicides. While there are still plenty of bare landing strips to be seen under vines, they are fewer in number with under-vine mowing increasingly common: 83 per cent of vineyards retain permanent inter-row crops throughout the year and some like to use sheep to do their mowing. Water is also a precious resource. While New Zealand has more than forty rivers, 700 lakes and plentiful rainfall (particularly on the west coast), the availability and cleanliness of water is an issue facing vineyard owners of the future. That's because 85 per cent of the vineyard area is irrigated, and water is an essential tool for cleaning wineries. Without water, Gimblett Gravels would not be viable and, in 2017, Hawke's Bay wine producers had to legally challenge a Water Conservation Order on the Ngaruroro River, from which 65 per cent of its growers draw water.

In the vineyard, reducing the use of chemical inputs is one of the key goals, using them only when needed rather than spraying out of habit. The New Zealand wine industry has invested heavily in research to look at better ways to manage pests and diseases through smarter viticulture and this is filtering through to the day-to-day duties of vineyard teams. Between 2001 and 2016, SWNZ members have reduced the use of insecticides by 50 per cent, and 99 per cent used non-chemical cultural controls as part of their pest and disease strategy. There are many more strands to reducing the impact of winegrowing on the local environment from reducing spray drift to improving waste-water disposal.

Sustainability isn't just about saving the environment, it is about making sure the industry is sustainable from a business perspective, ensuring the long-term health of its vineyards, people and companies. The list of rules and recommendations is mind boggling and it sets a high bar for the entire industry. And yet there are some elements of the New Zealand wine industry that aren't particularly environmentally friendly, like the gallons upon gallons of diesel that need to be used to power frost fans, the huge amounts of water needed to irrigate free-draining vineyards and the polystyrene packaging in which some members still send their wines. But there is no such thing as perfection.

While the programme is voluntary, wineries that want to enter the national wine competition or participate in any industry event have to be sustainable, providing a very real push to participate. Given the extra work involved in gaining accreditation and the annual fee of around $700 a year (excluding sales tax) needed for a 5-hectare vineyard and winery to be certified, there are a minority of small producers who feel it is yet another cost and another layer of paperwork that a one-man band can't face.

Going organic

The move to organic viticulture is a natural next step for those who have dipped their conventional toes into sustainable waters. Around one in ten wineries in New Zealand is organically certified, with many more on their way to full certification. Some of the largest wineries in the country, making millions of litres every year, have some vineyards that have converted to organic viticulture. Organic Winegrowers New Zealand (organicwinenz.com) has a list of wineries and vineyards that are certified and also offers a mentor system for those interested in becoming organic. The certification process takes three years and, as you drive through the gates of an organic vineyard, you'll see a 'BioGro' sign with the winery's membership number. BioGro is the largest and best known organic certification body in New Zealand. Te Whare Ra is so proud of its organic status that its certification number, 5182, now adorns the labels of its estate wines. And, showing how long they've been practising organics, Millton Vineyards – which is also a hub of biodynamics – has the number 99.

Organic cultivation seeks to grow grapes without recourse to synthetic pesticides, herbicides and fertilizers. The aim is to reduce inputs in order to boost the soil's life and improve the plants' resistance to pests and diseases. Copper sulphate and sulphur sprays are still permitted to combat fungal diseases but at lower levels compared to conventional viticulture. Cover crops are encouraged, which can help to fix nitrogen in the soil, prevent erosion and attract predators. For example, Felton Road in Central Otago plants buckwheat to attract a parasitic wasp that eats the light brown apple moth which can cause bunches to rot.

There are some New Zealand regions where organic viticulture is easier to practise than others: in the arid climate of Central Otago, particularly the Cromwell Basin and Alexandra areas (annual rainfall is 437 mm and 363 mm respectively), fungal disease is uncommon, making it easier to manage vineyards without synthetic products. In the warmer, wetter and more humid climes of Gisborne, Auckland and Northland, fungal-disease pressure is much higher, making organic viticulture more challenging – but not impossible, as a number of growers have demonstrated.

There is a growing thirst for organically grown wines. 'I'm constantly fielding phone calls from established wine companies and new wine companies looking to purchase organic fruit, because they're seeing and being asked for it in markets around the world, and the supply is not there,' says Bart Arnst, an organic viticultural consultant based in Marlborough. A growing interest in organic grapes and wines is not unique to New Zealand: organic vineyards covered 330,000 hectares of the earth in 2015 (FiBL-IFOAM). In Spain, Italy and France, the total hectares of vineyard farmed organically in each country is far greater than the total vineyard area in New Zealand. While the land devoted to organic viticulture in New Zealand is fairly small in global terms, organics seems to fit with the 'clean and green' image that has been stamped on the national psyche; the '100% Pure New Zealand' tourism campaign, which launched in 1999, has captured the perception of New Zealand's unpolluted, relatively untouched land. However, the uptake of organic products within New Zealand has been strangely slow, reports Dr Geoffrey Jones, a professor at Harvard Business School. In a 2016 study, published in *Business History*, he explained that this imagined greenness of New Zealand, 'whose government had long run marketing campaigns that it was a natural paradise', retarded the advancement of organic food [and wine] domestically, as 'the development of an organic agriculture sector threatened to undermine the brand value of New Zealand's conventional agriculture, which rested heavily on the country's image. On the other hand, retailers encountered resistance from consumers who were confident of their existing food and natural environment.'

Internationally, the organic wine sector is a growing and popular market, particularly in Germany and Scandinavia. The Swedish monopoly Systembolaget set a target for organic wines to represent 10 per cent of total sales by 2020, which it surpassed five years early. A working paper written by Harvard's Jones and Emily Grandjean estimated that the global organic wine market was worth more than US$3.4 billion in 2015 and it is forecast to continue growing, albeit at different rates according to each national market. New Zealand's organic wine producers will be hoping for a slice of that wholesome pie.

Biodynamics

Growing grapes and producing wine according to lunar cycles or putting horse manure in a cow's horn and burying it in the vineyard sound crazy to some conventionally reared individuals, but biodynamic viticulture has a growing band of proponents in New Zealand. First adopted by the Milltons in Gisborne in the 1980s, its Crazy by Nature label is a tongue-in-cheek nod to doubters. Biodynamic cultivation adopts the no-synthetic pesticides and no-herbicides approach for the same soil-improvement reasons as organics. Likewise, copper and sulphur sprays are permitted, although discouraged, and cover crops encouraged.

However, organics seeks to reduce inputs whereas biodynamics actually makes additions to the vineyard. The biodynamic philosophy, based on Austrian philosopher Dr Rudolf Steiner's tenets, views the vineyard holistically as a whole or a farm, with animals encouraged to live on the estate. Working by the phases of the moon, stars and planets is an important part of biodynamics, which is not used in organic (or any other) viticulture. Some properties find it is not practical to work by the phases of the moon, particularly at vintage time, and have to adapt it to commercial reality. The other crucial difference is the biodynamic preparations used for compost. There are a number of preparations involved in biodynamics – the first two, 500 (cow manure fermented in a cow horn) and 501 (silica mixed with rainwater), are sprayed on the soil and plants respectively while preparations 502 to 507 are applied to the compost and include oak bark fermented in an animal's skull (505), which must be inserted into the compost to 'dynamize' it. The philosophy also states that you cannot grow vines under power lines.

While there has been no definitive scientific study on the effects of biodynamics, many of the producers that have adopted biodynamic practices are convinced of its positive effects on their farms, on the vines, the wines and the people. It would be difficult to argue with the results when some of New Zealand's finest wine producers are certified by the global biodynamic body Demeter. They include Felton Road Wines, Millton Vineyards, Pyramid Valley Vineyards, Quartz Reef, Rippon Vineyard and Seresin Estate. There are other eminent vineyards that have adopted its principles or are in the process of certifying.

COMING OF AGE

'Remarkable, quite remarkable. One would not have thought it would have kept this long. This really is quite good, there is not the slightest trace of acidity or vinegar. No sign of decay at all. A very mellow wine.' These words were uttered by the French-born English wine merchant and author André Simon in 1964 when tasting Hawke's Bay winery Te Mata's 1912 red blend. More than half a century after it was first made – in the same year as the sinking of the Titanic – the red wine was still very much alive, so why has New Zealand not developed a reputation for making ageworthy wines?

Two words: Sauvignon Blanc.

The New Zealand wine industry is dominated by a grape variety that is typically fermented and put into bottle within months – or even weeks – of being harvested. 'Picked, pressed and pissed before Christmas' is the life cycle of Sauvignon Blanc in some winemakers' view. Why wait for Christmas when you can drink the wine before Easter? Moana Park winery has released a Sauvignon Blanc on 1 April and that was no April Fool. If the previous vintage has been small and stocks are running low, a few blocks might be picked early to produce a wine to bridge the gap between vintages, such as Villa Maria's Early Release Sauvignon Blanc.

New Zealand Sauvignon Blanc, sold in supermarkets alongside toilet rolls and frozen pizza, has become a fast moving consumer good (FMCG). There has been an attitude that if you're selling a bottle of Sauvignon Blanc two years after the vintage, there's something wrong with the wine or the sales team. However, there are a growing number of smaller, quality-focused producers who are holding back their Sauvignon Blancs before releasing, giving them time on lees and time in bottle instead of releasing babies on to the market to be consumed within a day of purchase. Having tasted some of Marlborough's finest Sauvignon Blancs at seven or eight years old, drinkers need not be in such a hurry. But putting the brakes on wineries releasing wines doesn't help their cash flow and, with grape growers to pay and bank repayments due, accountants can overrule winemakers, putting the onus on drinkers to put the wines in their usually non-existent cellars.

It is partly a matter of wine culture: New Zealand does not have a long-standing tradition of making and drinking wine; it is not yet sewn into the fabric of its people. It is a young country in terms of wine production and wine consumption. Having rejected Prohibition in 1919, the country continued to operate under a cloud of abstemiousness promoted by restrictive licensing laws. Until 1961, New Zealanders couldn't enjoy a glass of wine with a meal in a restaurant. Previously, wine lovers had to drink a BYO bottle covertly, sometimes decanting the wine from the bottle into a teapot to avoid arousing suspicion. The 1960s brought licensing change with more and more restaurant licences granted and a rise in the number of wine shops, while a rise in tax on beer and spirits in the 1958 'Black Budget' gave wine an encouraging bump. The 1950s witnessed the birth of aspirational winemakers and pioneers seeking to move away from fortified wine and hybrids to quality table wine made from *Vitis vinifera*, which gained increasing momentum, culminating in legislation outlawing a sugar and water culture and a state-sponsored vine pull in the 1980s. In the 1970s, regular wine columns appeared in several newspapers, catering for an educated population who had done their 'OE' (overseas experience), travelling around Europe, experiencing wine and food culture in France, Spain and Italy. From just 174 ml of wine per capita in the early 1960s, wine consumption had increased to 5.3 litres by the end of the 1970s. In 2016, the figure stood at 20.2 litres but it has remained stagnant for a decade with imported wine sales rising. Domestic wines account for around 60 per cent of Kiwi intake.

Red wines in New Zealand, like whites, are all too often released early and consumed early, meaning there are few older vintages available to purchase and enjoy. There are relatively few wine collectors and fine-dining restaurants with cellars and mature stocks of New Zealand wine, and thus some wineries are starting to take responsibility for ageing their wines until they approach their drinking window. Judy Fowler, owner of Puriri Hills Vineyard in Clevedon, Auckland, which specializes in Bordeaux blends, has a Brunello di Montalcino approach to releasing her reds. 'My late-release policy is based on the fact that we attempt to produce Bordeaux-blended wines made in the longstanding traditions of Bordeaux. The great Bordeaux wines generally benefit from ageing five to ten years or longer. Ours are built to age well. However, we are a small, newer vineyard [established 1998] with perhaps another 300 years to earn the reputation for quality that the grands crus of Bordeaux have. As such, we do not expect our customers to want to wait for five or more years to taste our wines at their best, so we do the ageing here at the vineyard before release.'

Fowler is not alone. Central Otago's Prophet's Rock launched Retrospect Pinot Noir, taking the responsibility for maturing the wine in-house. Five years after the grapes are picked off its home vineyard in Bendigo, the limited production – around 720 bottles – is released, with fine dining in mind: 'If restaurants want to list it, it has not been sitting by the glass washer for the past five years, it's been stored well.' The sentiment is echoed across the fine wine producers of New Zealand; one of the country's largest producers has even unveiled a pre-aged wine collection. Starting with the 2009 vintage, Villa Maria began selecting several reds for cellaring and released its first Library Release wines in 2017 to demonstrate both the ageability of New Zealand wines and the rewards of patience.

However, most wineries don't apply the release-when-ready-to-drink policy across the entire range, as it can leave suppliers wine-less and raise the prospect of delisting. However, if you are family owned, have been in operation for more than thirty years and have a loyal fan base, it can smooth the transition. The Donaldson family of Pegasus Bay in the Waipara Valley made the decision to give all the wines a minimum twelve months in bottle before release. 'People look at New Zealand wine as largely an early drinking proposition; they know about Sauvignon Blanc but there are a range of premium producers making wines worthy of putting down in a cellar for a good number of years. We were sick of the wines starting to drink well just when they were sold out and we didn't want to change the wines to make them ready to drink earlier,' says marketing manager Edward Donaldson. 'Yes, we had a few gaps between vintages but we made the sacrifice and after two years we are able to release everything a year after vintage.' What's more, as early as 2006, the family started looking to the future, putting Pinot Noir and Riesling in the cellar with the aim of releasing it ten years later. In 2016, they released the first decade-old wines – which sold out within a month.

It is difficult to judge the ageability of New Zealand wines with so little precedent. In the past decade, young vines have matured, viticulture has evolved, winemaking has become more refined: a Pinot Noir produced ten years ago from young vines by winemakers who were still getting to know their site will be quite different today from a current vintage opened in a decade's time. When asked to provide drinking windows for a recent Central Otago Pinot Noir or Hawke's Bay Cabernet Sauvignon, it is a case of pinning the tail on the donkey. Unlike Bordeaux or Burgundy, there aren't decades of historic vintages to reference.

However, there's no doubting that the country's best wines have the components to age gracefully: intensity of fruit, richness of ripe tannins, acidity (and pH), alcohol and magic all play their part in the development of a red wine. In whites, high levels of acidity and flavour precursors elongate their shelf life. There's also a small matter of the closure: screw-caps are omnipotent in New Zealand. Although a small but significant number of producers continue to seal their top Bordeaux blends under cork (while putting the rest of their range under screwcap), it is likely that the wines will age more slowly because of the lower rate of oxygen ingress compared with a natural cork. That said, screwcap manufacturers have developed different liners to provide more than just a hermetic seal.

What is clear, is that far too many New Zealand wines are being consumed before they are out of nappies. It's time to let them grow up.

Drinking windows for New Zealand wines

Whites

Sauvignon Blanc
Drink entry-level wines aged six months to two years for their vibrant fruit and zesty freshness. Wild yeast and barrel-fermented examples are often released around a year after the grapes were picked and are ready to drink upon release but will continue to drink well for up to five years from the vintage.

Chardonnay
Fresh, fruity, unoaked examples destined for the supermarket shelf are ready to drink as soon as you are. Mid-range examples should be drunk within five years while top-flight wines can be enjoyed as early as three and savoured at eight years old (and occasionally longer).

Pinot Gris
There are just a handful of producers making Pinot Gris with any level of seriousness. With its relatively low acidity levels and soft mouthfeel, New Zealand Pinot Gris is grown and produced to drink within one to four years of the harvest.

Riesling
In the right hands, Riesling's naturally scintillating acidity and stunningly low pH give this white variety interminable ageing potential. New Zealand Rieslings are full of fruit and vigour in their youth and slowly take on honeyed, lime marmalade and kerosene notes as they develop. The botrytized examples have the additional benefit of sugar to preserve them for a decade or more.

Reds

Pinot Noir

Fresh, juicy, unoaked examples cropped high on alluvial sites are made for early drinking – within two or three years. While the New Zealand climate provides Pinot Noir with a natural fruitiness, making even the most serious cuvée approachable in youth, vine age is imbuing the wines with greater seriousness and an abundance of ripe tannins. Most vintages in the noughties are past their peak but, in good vintages, ambitious producers are making wines that enter a sweet point at six to eight years old. In the future, this drinking window is likely to grow and grow.

Merlot/Cabernet

Juicy and fresh in youth, there are plenty of New Zealand Merlots that offer a whole lot more fun than a Saint-Émilion Grand Cru at the entry level. They should be enjoyed from two to five years. Serious examples that include Cabernet Sauvignon in the blend need at least four years to shed their youthful vigour. It will take several more years before they lose their primary characters and develop secondary and tertiary flavours. There is no reason why you can't age fine New Zealand Merlot/Cabernet blends for the long term if the late André Simon was impressed with a fifty-year old example back in 1964.

Syrah

New Zealand's distinctive expression of Syrah can be enjoyed in its youth for its fleshy blackberry-like palate and black-pepper spice. However, in its Hawke's Bay heartland, the variety is capable of producing deeply coloured wines that are rich in flavour and offer mouth-coating tannins. After four years, the finest wines (hailing from a good vintage such as 2013, 2014 and 2015) are still far too young for any serious wine collector to want to pull a bottle out of the rack. Give them six to ten years to enable Syrah's savoury delights to appear.

10 must-have ageworthy wines for your NZ cellar

- Ata Rangi Pinot Noir, Martinborough
- Bell Hill Vineyard Pinot Noir, Waikari, North Canterbury
- Dog Point Section 94 Sauvignon Blanc, Marlborough
- Dry River Wines Pinot Noir, Martinborough

- Kumeu River Maté's Vineyard Chardonnay, Kumeu
- Millton Vineyard Clos de Ste. Anne La Bas Chenin Blanc, Gisborne
- Pegasus Bay Encore Noble Riesling, Waipara Valley, North Canterbury
- Sacred Hill Deerstalkers Syrah, Hawke's Bay
- Te Mata Estate Coleraine, Hawke's Bay
- Villa Maria Ngakirikiri, Hawke's Bay

THE GENERATION GAME

Baby Boomers were responsible for the modern New Zealand wine industry we know and love today. The irrepressible energy of youth gave rise to the vineyards of Marlborough, Martinborough, Central Otago and more in the 1980s and, while there are a fair few who have yet to grow up, they are getting older and need to look to the future of their businesses. The high cost of entry, rising land prices and arrival of wealthy overseas investors mean it is more difficult for the next generation of young dreamers to get a foot on the New Zealand wine ladder which is a sad irony, and yet there are plenty of new faces with considerably fewer wrinkles launching new (albeit often vineyard-less) wine brands across the country while holding down a day job and juggling the demands of a young family.

For those in their twenties and thirties who do want to become chief winemakers at established wineries, it's a long road that requires patience. Winemakers know when they're on to a good thing and thus relatively few opportunities come along. What's more, a number of small wineries have been incorporated into larger entities, resulting in fewer top jobs. Being both frustrated and motivated, fledgling wine labels are being established by those who want to take the big decisions when it comes to what goes in the bottle. The previous generation were operating in a New Zealand with relatively few established wine brands, but there are now more than 670 wineries. The intense competition and high costs of entry today mean these new labels – such as Julianne Brogden's Collaboration, Alex Craighead Wines or Dan Brennan's Decibel Wines – are made with the help of family and friends and launched without fanfare, building a niche fan base at home or overseas. In many instances, but not all, the new generation of young winemakers don't own vineyards but buy grapes from local growers and vinify the wines while they build the brand. Like any new business, it is a labour of love.

When it comes to the pioneers of the modern industry who are approaching or have passed retirement age, there are a surprising number who have not yet implemented a succession plan. Auditing company Deloitte undertakes an annual financial survey of the New Zealand wine industry and succession is low on the lists of winery concerns. In its 2017 report, its authors expressed surprise at its low ranking 'given, anecdotally, we understand many view this as an important issue in the wine industry, similar to other agricultural industries in New Zealand. With the age of the country's farmers sitting at an average of 48 and with 15 per cent over 65, it is worth considering the extent to which this also impacts the wine industry. While consolidation in the industry can have positive effects, we see the potential for many business owners having to settle for less (lower sale prices) in unplanned succession events, as opposed to those [which] are planned early and properly.' With lucrative acquisitions by local and international investors in recent years, it would seem only sensible for those getting to retirement age to start taking the steps to get their house in order. However, it is not considered a priority by many producers, who are more worried about short-term issues such as the exchange rate, sales margins and distribution channels.

A lack of succession planning is not just a wine problem. The New Zealand arm of professional services firm PricewaterhouseCoopers found that 51 per cent of Kiwi family-owned businesses haven't made these decisions: 'that's a huge problem, especially as the current generation of owners aren't getting any younger and need to consider how they will transition to the next generation,' it reported in its 2016 Family Business Survey. That said, there are a number of family wine businesses that have transitioned successfully from generation to generation: David Babich, born in 1968, is the third generation to run the family wine business after acquiring an oenology degree, a commercial degree and spending seven years with pharmaceutical firm Glaxo. His commercial experience beyond wine brought a new skillset to the business and he soon tightened business processes, accounting and forecasting, making it fit for the demands of selling New Zealand wine in the twenty-first century. Similarly, George Fistonich appointed his daughter Karen to the Villa Maria board after her successful career in the banking sector while also appointing experts to key board positions. In February 2018, he stepped down from his CEO role after fifty-seven years running the business. There are many other family business that are preparing the next generation for their future roles in the business, both within the company and externally, and ensuring that the essence of the family is not diluted.

Ones to watch: New Zealand's emerging talent

- Alex Craighead, Alex Craighead Wines, Nelson
- Ben Byrne, Byrne Wines, Northland
- Braden Crosby, On Giants' Shoulders, Martinborough
- Daniel Brennan, Decibel Wines, Hawke's Bay
- Francis Hutt, Carrick, Central Otago
- Joel Watson, Luna Estate, Martinborough
- Jordan Hogg, Seresin Estate, Marlborough
- Julianne Brogden, Collaboration Wines, Hawke's Bay
- Laura Swift, Ash Ridge Winery, Hawke's Bay
- Rosie Finn and Todd Stevens, Neudorf Vineyards, Nelson
- Samuel Millton, Millton Vineyard & Winery, Gisborne

There are some wineries with the issue that there is no one to take over, or no one willing to do so. Alwyn Corban, whose Lebanese great grandfather Assid Abraham Corban was one of the country's early wine pioneers, has a son – but he did not want to take over the business, instead establishing a digital marketing company in Napier. Having co-founded Ngatarawa Wines in the Bridge Pa area in 1981, Corban sold the brands to fellow Hawke's Bay winery Mission Estate in 2017. 'You can look at succession plans in two ways,' Alwyn Corban explained to *New Zealand Winegrower* magazine. 'One is passing on to family, and that's very European in its approach. But the other is to pass the brands on to someone who is going to be in stewardship of them and I think that is equally valid.'

New Zealand is certainly attracting an increasing number of foreign owners, lured by the beauty of its wines, the beauty of its land and its remoteness. While New Zealand's Overseas Investment Office has to approve purchases by non-New Zealanders, around a third of New Zealand wine production is controlled by foreign owners. With an unsullied reputation for making premium wines, it is unsurprising that wealthy individuals are looking to New Zealand rather than overpriced Burgundy or Bordeaux to buy a piece of dirt. In March 2018, Martinborough's Escarpment Vineyard was purchased by American-owned Australian winery Torbreck, while in 2017 American tech billionaire Brian Sheth joined forces with New Zealand Master of Wine Steve Smith to buy Waitaki's Pyramid Valley, Central Otago's Lowburn Ferry and 4 hectares of land in Hawke's Bay. Another super-wealthy American, Bill Foley, acquired Central Otago winery Mt Difficulty in 2018 to add to his collection of New Zealand wineries, which include Vavasour and Te Kairanga. They join the United Nations of New Zealand wine: a young grape-growing country shaped by newcomers with a dream.

15

TOURISM

New Zealand's immigration authorities received a surge in registrations from American citizens in the week following Donald Trump's election as the 45th President of the United States. Under the rather sensational headline 'Trump apocalypse', *The New Zealand Herald* reported that 13,000 Americans – more than seventeen times the usual number – had shown an interest in waving goodbye to the land of the free for the land of the long white cloud.

While New Zealand is a country of two rather shaky islands, earthquakes seem to be a minor concern for rich Americans buying up parts of New Zealand as a secure getaway from the craziness of the modern world. Citing government statistics, *The New Yorker* reported that in the first ten months of 2016, foreign buyers purchased 'nearly fourteen hundred square miles of land in New Zealand, more than quadruple what they bought in the same period the previous year', with tech billionaire Peter Thiel beating them to the party with the purchase of a 193-hectare property in Central Otago a year earlier.

The country's remote location and the safety that this brings is part of the lure in uncertain times. A minimum twenty-four-hour flight from London and twelve hours from San Francisco, New Zealand isn't a destination you visit for a long weekend. Its major attraction is undoubtedly its natural beauty. From the sailing mecca of the Bay of Islands, four hours' drive north of the country's biggest city, Auckland, to the snowy peaks of the Southern Alps forming the jagged spine of the south island, this is a country that does breathtaking views in large gasps.

Nature and wildlife are also high on visitors' list of things to do, with whale and dolphin watchers heading for Kaikoura, an easy drive south from Marlborough's main town of Blenheim. Others come for the glow worms and the unique birdlife that comes with being an island that's at the bottom of the earth – where else could a flightless bird, the kiwi, manage to survive? There's also plenty of opportunity to get your penguin fix the further south you head. Forget the aquarium, New Zealand has three species of penguin including the world's smallest, the korora or little blue penguin, and they can be spotted in a number of locations including near the university town of Dunedin or on Stewart Island.

The country's waters don't just offer a chance to spot sea life. Surf breaks dot the coastline whether it's the black-sand beaches of west Auckland made famous by the triple Academy Award-winning film *The Piano,* or the remote waters of Gisborne. While the more sedate pastimes of sailing, golfing and walking (known as tramping in New Zealand) are available in large dollops, New Zealand has made its name as the place for high-octane activities. Want to jump off a bridge with a piece of elastic tied to your ankles? They've got that covered – and hopefully your travel insurance has too. Want to raft down rushing rapids, jump out of a plane, take a helicopter to a remote mountain and ski down or fly down a zipwire? Head to Central Otago, settling your frayed nerves with a glass of powerful Pinot Noir.

The heady mix of extreme sports and a once-weak New Zealand dollar made this country a mecca for backpackers, but with a stronger economy and a more sophisticated tourism sector, there is an increasing number of operators catering for high-net-worth individuals: fine dining, luxury lodges and helicopter hire are all commonplace for those who have the means to enjoy it. Play golf overlooking the Pacific at luxury resort Cape Kidnappers in Hawke's Bay, and relax with a spicy Syrah after the eighteenth hole or fall in love with Wharekauhau Lodge – as the current owner US wine mogul Bill Foley did in 2009 – while sampling the savoury Pinot Noirs from nearby Martinborough.

You don't come to New Zealand to visit the cities. The capital Wellington and the country's most populous urban centre, Auckland, can't really compete with London, New York or Paris when it comes to historic buildings, high culture or retail therapy, but it is inevitable that you'll fly into one or both cities during a stay. Overnighters should take in Te Papa, the country's national museum on Wellington's waterfront for a succinct introduction to the nation's history and culture. The compact city is also a hotbed of coffee that will have you reeling off superlatives, as well as fine food and hidden cocktail bars. If you're pressed for time, give Auckland's CBD a miss and jump on a commuter boat, or hire your own, to Waiheke Island. Once a place for hippies, it is now a hideaway for Auckland's millionaires and home to ever-improving wine producers.

And when you pack your bags, remember that the band Crowded House weren't joking when they sang 'Four Seasons in One Day' – pack for all conditions and don't forget the factor-50 sunscreen. Kiwis have long been reminded to 'slip slop slap', meaning slip on a shirt, slop on the sunscreen and slap on a hat due to high levels of UV radiation. Many tourists have scoffed at warnings by locals, claiming that they 'don't get sunburned' only to end up red raw within a couple of hours of exposure. The lobster look has never been in vogue – unless it's on a plate with a glass of Sauvignon Blanc.

WINE TOURISM

Wine, along with lamb, the All Blacks and *The Lord of the Rings* films, is one of New Zealand's successful exports. Shipped to more than ninety countries around the globe, it is no surprise that some of the 3.6 million tourists visiting New Zealand want to enjoy a glass of its famous wines *in situ*. New Zealand wineries are delighted to welcome holidaymakers through their doors with approximately 250 cellar doors nationwide and around seventy-five winery restaurants. Of the 3.2 million international visitors who made the trip to New Zealand in 2017, 22 per cent – more than 700,000 – visited a cellar door during their trip.

There's a small fee at more than half of the cellar doors, according to research by the national wine association New Zealand Winegrowers, a fee which is usually – but not always – refunded if you buy a bottle of wine. Most wineries offer international shipping options so you can send wines you discover in New Zealand to your home. Opening times vary: some open only during the summer months and at the weekend; others are open seven days a week all year round. Check the producers' websites before visiting. You must be eighteen to drink wine in New Zealand and the drink driving laws are stringent: the legal drink drive limit for drivers under twenty is zero; it is 50 mg of alcohol per 100 ml of blood for those aged twenty and over. There are many tour operators in the wine regions who are happy to transport you from winery to winery.

From north to south, New Zealand's wine regions offer beauty and deliciousness in equal measure. In addition to cellar doors suggested in each regional chapter, there's more inspiration for planning a trip to wine country. The website of New Zealand Winegrowers (nzwine.com) and the official travel website (newzealand.com) are also invaluable tools for visitors.

Northland

New Zealand's winterless north is a few hours' drive from Auckland. The time poor should take a flight to Kerikeri but if you hit the (mostly one-lane) road, you can take in Matakana en route, go kayaking and diving on the Tutukaka coast, or try a diversion to the west coast and visit New Zealand's largest kauri tree in Waipoua forest. There are also the Hundertwasser toilets in Kawakawa, where cistern meets modern art. Designed by a reclusive Austrian artist who lived out his days in this small coastal town, this is one of the few public conveniences in the world that doubles as a tourist attraction. Unlike other New Zealand wine regions, the wineries of Northland are spread over a vast distance: the drive from Mangawhai in the south to the Karikari Peninsula in the north is 250 kilometres. For this reason, wine lovers should visit Northland for a relaxing holiday with beaches, boats, bush and a little bit of wine splashed in rather than an immersive wine trip.

Northland is home to the Bay of Islands, a sailing mecca comprising 144 islands. The most popular spots for dropping anchor include the Waitangi Treaty grounds, where Māori chiefs signed a formal agreement with the British crown; while it remains controversial to this day, it is considered the country's founding document. For wine lovers, the grounds take on extra significance: as previously noted, this was the site of James Busby's home and vineyard. In 1840, a white wine was deemed 'delicious' by French naval officer Jules Dumont d'Urville when he rowed ashore from his ship *Astrolabe*, which had been exploring Antarctic waters. It is also worth stopping off in the quaint village of Russell. Once called the hell-hole of the Pacific, it is now a popular tourist spot. Enjoy lunch on the waterfront at New Zealand's oldest licensed premises, the Duke of Marlborough Hotel, which has an interesting selection of Northland wines. Walk off your lunch on the Russell to Okiato walkway, which can be done in sections or a half day. Winery Omata Estate (omata.co.nz) is about two hours' walk from Russell and has a cellar door and cafe. Alternatively, you can kayak to the winery with a local guide.

You might like
- Paroa Bay. Drive the short but winding journey from Russell to Paroa Bay. It opened a cellar door and Italian-inspired restaurant – Sage – in 2017 overlooking the sparkling blue waters of the Bay of Islands. Sit on the terrace or gaze out of the floor-to-ceiling glass windows toward Roberton Island with its two natural lagoons. It is open for lunch and dinner Wednesday to Sunday. Paroa Bay also offers several accommodation options including Tarapunga, a luxury villa complete with 17-metre infinity pool, gym, tennis courts, pétanque area, putting green, home theatre and a private deep-water boat to whisk you off to the best fishing spots and dolphin watching areas (paroabay.com).
- The Landing is an exclusive luxury retreat about half an hour's drive from Kerikeri down an unsealed road. This hideaway with four private villas caters to your every whim complete with staff on hand to cook, clean, arrange massages and helicopter rides to the exclusive Kauri Cliffs golf resort. There's also a boat on hand to help you discover some of the area's unspoiled islands. But you might not want to leave this sanctuary with its natural beauty and, for those who like to actively relax, a tennis court, gym and the sea on your doorstep (thelandingnz.com).
- Te Whai Bay Wines. In the south of the Northland region, Te Whai Bay Wines is nestled in the Brynderwyn range. On Saturday afternoons in the summer, live music accompanies the wine and tasting platters (tewhaibaywines.co.nz).
- Marsden Estate is just a few minutes outside of Kerikeri, making it popular with locals and visitors. Its charming and unpretentious restaurant and cellar door overlook the vines and a lake, complete with resident ducks for children to feed. It's open seven days a week. Check website for opening times (marsdenestate.co.nz).

- Okahu Estate is a remote outpost of New Zealand wine but for those visiting the far north, including 90-Mile Beach and the northernmost tip of the country, Cape Reinga, this is a lovely winery with a history dating back to 1984 (okahuestate.co.nz).
- Northland Winegrowers has a wine trail map, which can be downloaded from its website (northlandwinegrowers.co.nz).

Auckland

New Zealand's largest city might not be the first place you think of basing yourself for vineyard tours but it has three distinctive sub-regions, each less than an hour's journey from the CBD.

Matakana

Matakana is around an hour's drive north of Auckland, depending on the city's dreadful traffic. It is a region known for high-quality produce, galleries and beaches, making it popular with weekending Aucklanders. Saturday morning plays host to the Matakana farmers' market where you can get your coffee fix and stock up on fresh produce for the days ahead while being serenaded by local musicians. Grab a picnic on a beautiful day and head out to the golden sands and calm waters of Tawharanui Peninsula, buying a bottle en route from Hyperion Wine (hyperionwines.co.nz) or Takatu Lodge & Vineyard (takatulodge.co.nz).

Art goes hand in hand with wine in Matakana. Two vineyards – Brick Bay (brickbay.co.nz) and Sculptureum (sculptureum.co.nz) blend vineyards, gardens and art installations across their delectable properties. The Brick Bay Sculpture Trail is a 2-kilometre stroll through its grounds, passing an ever-changing exhibition of contemporary sculptures by New Zealand artists in the idyllic vineyard setting overlooking the coast. The walk starts and ends at the Glass House, where you can taste the estate's wines and enjoy lunch. In 2017, another ambitious sculpture park-cum-winery was opened by two Auckland lawyers, married couple Anthony and Sandra Grant. The $10 million Sculptureum project brings together an outdoor sculpture park and galleries housing their private collection with works by Matisse, Cézanne and Picasso – plus a bar and restaurant, named Rothko. If you fancy swapping the grape for the grain, Sawmill Brewery (sawmillbrewery.co.nz) offers welcome relief, four minutes' drive from the centre of Matakana. There are tours on a Saturday morning, which include tastings.

You might like

- Runner Duck Estate and Plume Restaurant. Mumbai couple Clyde and Farida Cooper left India behind for Matakana and bought a vineyard and later invested in Plume, a restaurant with a small parcel of Sangiovese, which is now home to the Runner Duck cellar door. The menu is French inspired but, reflecting the heritage of its owners, there are also a few curries that sneak on to the selection (runnerduck. co.nz).
- The Vintry. In the heart of Matakana village, this 'wine centre and lounge bar' offers Matakana wine tastings and an impressive area of local wines by the glass and bottle (thevintry.co.nz).
- Takatu Lodge and Vineyard. Four modern and luxurious suites perched on the top of a rolling vineyard with views to the ocean are perfectly positioned for exploring the area in style (takatulodge. co.nz).
- Matakana Lodge. Originally a contemporary Tuscan-style private dwelling, this is a luxury four-bed property with indoor pool, spa room, home theatre, private cellar and in-lodge chef (matakanaestate. co.nz).
- Download a map of Matakana and its wineries, find out about events and wine tours through the website matakanawine.co.nz.

West Auckland

The rolling hills of west Auckland provided the backdrop for many of the earliest vineyards of New Zealand. While many have since closed their doors or transferred their operations to Marlborough, west Auckland remains home to some superb wineries and stunning black-sand surf beaches. Spend a day touring the area visiting Bethells, Karekare and Piha beaches, and between August and March visit the gannet colony at Muriwai beach. Remember not to go barefoot on a hot day or you will burn your soles on the blistering sands. The fertile soils of west Auckland are also home to fresh produce including strawberries, making it one of the best places to stop for real fruit ice cream in the summer months.

You might like

- Kumeu River: Just thirty minutes from Auckland city centre, it would be crazy not to visit the Brajkovich family's cellar door and winery, home to what are arguably New Zealand's finest Chardonnays. Open six days a week, there is little excuse for not making the journey (kumeuriver.co.nz).

- Coopers Creek. On the road out of Kumeu toward the village of Huapai – and great mountain biking trails at Woodhill Forest – lies Coopers Creek winery. While Auckland fruit makes up a tiny proportion of its wines, this is a family-friendly cellar door: there's a playground, giant chess set and you can bring your own picnic to enjoy with a glass of wine. The winery has become known for its free Sunday jazz sessions in summer (cooperscreek.co.nz). Giving you even more reason to visit, try neighbouring restaurant The Tasting Shed (thetastingshed.co.nz) to taste some of the most thoughtful and exciting food in Auckland.
- Babich Wines. West Auckland is thick with Croatian names and the Babich family is one of its success stories. While the vineyard that surrounds its Auckland winery represents a tiny dribble of its total wine production today, this is home to its cellar door. Historic displays offer a wonderful glimpse of its heritage (babichwines.com).
- The Hunting Lodge. On the site of the former Matua Valley winery site, the new owners of this 32-hectare estate and winemaking facility have given the tourism offering a new lease of life. There are now tours and blending sessions, and celebrated Auckland chef Des Harris (ex-Clooney) has been drafted in to help elevate the food beyond the usual platter fare. Kids are welcome to roam the grounds, play pétanque and picnic on the lawns with a bottle plucked from the cellar door (thehuntinglodge.com).
- The websites westauckland.net.nz and kumeuwinecountry.co.nz are good places to start planning your visit out west.

Waiheke Island

Jump on the ferry from downtown Auckland and you'll soon be deposited on the laid-back island of Waiheke. From the ferry terminal, hop on the local bus, hire a scooter or join an organized tour to sample the wineries dotted the length of the island. The rolling landscape, series of sheltered bays and sandy beaches make this a place to escape the madding crowd – although in the height of summer it feels like most of Auckland has had the same idea (if you're going to Waiheke for a day trip in peak season, you may need to queue for ferries back to the mainland, so arrive well in advance of departure time). Waiheke also prides itself on its fine-dining establishments and luxury accommodation, offering breathtaking views and impeccably designed interiors.

You might like

- A little-known walking path in the Onetangi Valley takes you through six vineyards: Stonyridge, Te Motu, Wild on Waiheke, Tantalus, Obsidian and Casita Miro. Meander through vineyards and bush before finishing your day at Onetangi beach, where you can soak your weary feet in the waters of the Hauraki gulf. If you haven't already feasted at the cellar doors, join the locals at Charlie Farley's restaurant and bar for a sundowner and a bowl of 'massive fries'; swimwear, flip-flops ('jandals') and sandy feet are all acceptable here. The walk crosses private land and is thus not widely publicized. If you'd like to take part, visit one of the wineries on the route to receive directions.
- Zip, wine and dine experience. The local ferry company, Fullers, runs a tour of Waiheke Island, which includes whizzing down three separate ziplines over native forest and vineyards before visiting several wineries for tastings and lunch. If you are an adrenaline junkie, this might be the wine tour for you. Visit ecozipadventures.co.nz.
- Wine-loving parents can enjoy five minutes' peace at Wild on Waiheke (wildonwaiheke.co.nz). A play area, sandpit, trampoline and giant chess set are all part of the distractions for children while you sample the beers and wines surrounded by vines. Adults can also try their hand at archery, clay pigeon shooting and pétanque.
- A number of Waiheke's finest restaurants can be found at wineries including Mudbrick Vineyard and Spanish-inspired Casita Miro, just a few minutes' walk from Onetangi beach. In a remote spot at the eastern end of the island lies Poderi Crisci (podericrisci.co.nz). Run by Italian-born Auckland hospitality doyen Antonio Crisci, its long lunches are legendary.
- Tantalus Estate. Opened in 2016, Tantalus is a vineyard and winery, a sleek, modern restaurant and a craft brewery rolled into one polished experience (tantalus.co.nz).
- Man O'War. A strong contender for the most idyllic setting for a cellar door and winery, Man O'War Bay is tucked away in the far east of Waiheke Island. While away a lazy afternoon on the lawn at

Man O'War, and cool off in the clear waters. Access for vehicles is via a winding dusty track while boat owners drop anchor and row into shore – or arrive in style in a seaplane (manowarvineyards.co.nz and aucklandseaplanes.com/dine.php).
- Wine lovers can obtain more information on cellar doors, vineyard restaurants and accommodation on the island, as well as transport options and a wine map on the website waihekewine.co.nz.

Auckland – east and south
You might like
- Villa Maria. If you have a few hours to kill at Auckland airport or arrive early for your flight, head to Villa Maria HQ for a wine tasting and lunch among the vines (food is served between 11 a.m. and 3 p.m.). Schedule your lunch accordingly and you can join the 11 a.m. or 2 p.m. daily tour of the winery ($5 fee per person).

Gisborne

Gisborne, says Villa Maria viticulturist Tony Green, is 'New Zealand like it used to be'. Come to Gisborne to relax and get back to the simpler pleasures in life. Fly fishing for trout on local rivers is popular, and out on the ocean waves, tuna, marlin, snapper and kingfish are common catches. Instead of catching fish to eat, you can feed the fish in Gisborne. Pull on a pair of waders and walk across a reef at low tide to feed wild stingrays (divetatapouri.com). Daring locals also like to head to the Rere Rock Slide where they jump on a boogie board, lilo or inner tube and slide down a 60-metre long natural water slide. Broken bones are not uncommon, so you might prefer to watch.

Gisborne's wineries are all within a fifteen-minute drive of the city centre and airport, meaning you can visit most cellar doors over the course of a leisurely weekend.

You might like
- The Gisborne Wine Centre, located in central Gisborne overlooking the harbour, showcases local wines in its tasting room, and in the on-site restaurant and bar Crawford Road Kitchen (gisbornewinecentre. co.nz).
- Millton Vineyards and Winery. Enjoy a personal tasting at the cellar

door of this biodynamic estate before taking a seat under the shade of an umbrella, enjoying a glass of Chenin Blanc and watching the native tui dance around the garden that has been lovingly nurtured by co-founder Annie Millton (millton.co.nz). (See Chapter 6 for more information on cellar door visits at other Gisborne wineries.)

- The Chardonnay Express. A group of Gisborne Chardonnay makers launched a wine-tasting event in 2017 that is expected to become regular. On a return journey from Gisborne railway station, passengers board a steam locomotive, sip barrel-fermented Chardonnays and eat matched canapés produced by members of Gisborne Classic Chardonnay (gisbornechardonnay.co.nz).
- Nisbet Smith is a fount of Gisborne knowledge and his company Gisborne Tours will guide you around the region. Whether you want to learn about the history of the east coast or whizz around the wineries, he is your man (gisbornetours.nz).
- For those looking to enjoy Gisborne in style, The Blackhouse on Wainui beach is a luxury retreat for up to ten people. Sitting 6 kilometres from Gisborne centre, it is the perfect place to unwind after a day's tasting with uninterrupted views over the ocean (blackhousewainui.co.nz).
- Plan your visit to the region using the website tairawhitigisborne. co.nz.

Hawke's Bay

New Zealand's Art Deco capital, Hawke's Bay, has gained a reputation for excellent Chardonnay, Bordeaux blends and Syrah in recent times. It has a shaky past however: destroyed by an earthquake in 1931, the rebuilding of Napier was inspired by the European art movement, and the city celebrates its distinctive style in a 1930s-inspired weekend every February. Embrace the Art Deco theme any time of the year by hiring a classic car and driving out to Cape Kidnappers to visit the gannet colony.

The temperate maritime climate means that Hawke's Bay is a wonderful place to explore the outdoors: hire a bike and cycle the wine trails, take a hike up Te Mata Peak, dive under the waves at Waimarama beach or get your adrenaline fix white-water rafting along the Mohaka river. The region is also home to a prestigious golf course (see below) and some of the country's best trout fishing.

From the coast to the plains and into the hills, Hawke's Bay has a wealth of excellent winery restaurants, friendly cellar doors and a growing number of luxury accommodation options.

You might like

- A day exploring the coastline, visiting Te Awanga Estate, Clearview Estate, Beach House Wines, and Elephant Hill after a morning of exploring the dramatic Cape Kidnappers peninsula on foot (or by helicopter) and visiting the gannet colony.
- Explore the history of New Zealand's oldest winery at Mission Estate. Founded by French missionaries in 1851, the property has had its fair share of challenges from floods, fires and earthquakes to a Rod Stewart concert. The plane tree-lined driveway was first planted in 1911 and, as you approach the estate, look out for a single row of Muscat vines that have been grafted over the years from the original stock brought from France in the nineteenth century (missionestate.co.nz).
- The Farm at Cape Kidnappers is an elegant lodge sitting atop cliffs that plunge nearly 250 metres to the crashing waves of the Pacific. Not only is this secluded luxury retreat home to one of the country's finest golf courses, the cellar is one of the most comprehensive in the country, offering mature vintages of fine wines from Hawke's Bay and beyond (capekidnappers.com).
- There are close to 200 kilometres of dedicated cycle paths in Hawke's Bay from half-hour cycles to four-day adventures. Combine your love of wine and cycling on the wineries ride, passing ten cellar doors.
- Black Barn Vineyards. On the outskirts of Havelock North, this winery has also become a hive of community activity with a farmers' market every Saturday morning in summer, an amphitheatre that hosts regular music concerts and a bistro open year round. There is also a range of accommodation options in the vineyard and across Hawke's Bay (blackbarn.com).
- Nestled under Te Mata Peak, Craggy Range offers a wide range of tastings at its swish cellar door, a fine-dining restaurant, and accommodation at its Giants winery, including a sumptuous private lodge which offers gourmet feasts, winemaker-led tastings and personalized itineraries for even the most demanding guests (craggyrange.com).

- Hawke's Bay hosts the Food and Wine Classic (FAWC) twice a year, offering ten-day programmes of food and wine events across the region (fawc.co.nz).
- Since 1991, Hawke's Bay has run the New Zealand equivalent of the Hospices de Beaune auction. In aid of a local hospice, the November event is an opportunity to understand the region's laid-back attitude – no shirt and tie needed here – as well as to buy rare parcels of wine. (hawkesbaywineauction.co.nz).
- The Hawke's Bay tourism website (hawkesbaynz.com) is packed with information on visiting the region, while hawkesbaywine.co.nz offers the wine lover information on the vineyards, wine trails and upcoming events.

Wairarapa

Before journeying to Wairarapa, spend a day in Wellington, starting with a flat white – this city does coffee that Robert Parker would rate 100 points. Take a stroll along the waterfront, wander the exhibitions at New Zealand's inspiring national museum Te Papa, take a ride from the city to the Botanic Gardens on the funicular railway and spot a kiwi at Zealandia, the city's eco-sanctuary, before finishing with a cocktail in one of the city's bars (ask a local as the best bars are so positioned that they are wonderfully tricky to find).

A scenic train ride will transport you from the city lights to rural wine country. Alternatively, the car journey takes around an hour but be warned that the hairpin bends can leave you feeling green by the time you arrive in Martinborough, the most prestigious wine village in Wairarapa. Home to some of the country's finest Pinot Noir producers including Ata Rangi, Dry River and Escarpment, wine has put this tiny town on the wine world's map. Don't blink if you pass through Martinborough or you'll miss it: the population is just 1,300 but it has three hairdressers, a cinema, an underwear producer, and more antique shops than the permanent population can sustain.

It's easy to spend a weekend in Martinborough wine touring. The vineyards and wineries are within walking – or cycling – distance of the town centre. And even better, it's flat so you won't be hot and sweaty when you arrive for a tasting. The producers here are small and it is more than likely you'll chat to an owner, winemaker or viticulturist while tasting at the country casual cellar doors. From having no suitable accommodation to house an American wine writer in 1991, Wairarapa now has a wealth of bed and breakfasts, vineyard cottages and luxury lodges although evening dining options are still rather limited.

You might like

- Toast Martinborough. Since 1991, Martinborough's 1,300 residents have prepared for an annual 8,000-strong crowd descending on its wineries every November to taste Riesling, Pinot Noir and Syrah followed by some wine-fuelled dancing. It is not uncommon for tickets for Toast Martinborough to sell out in fifteen minutes (toastmartinborough.co.nz).
- There are several cycle-hire companies eager to get you on two wheels in Martinborough but for those particularly fond of their bouffant hairstyle, be warned: it is compulsory to wear bike helmets in New Zealand. Visit wairarapanz.com for more information on the region and cycle hire options.
- Popular cellar-door-cum-lunch spots in Martinborough include Poppies (poppiesmartinborough.co.nz), Tirohana Estate (tirohanaestate.com), Margrain Vineyard (thevineyardcafe.co.nz) and Palliser (palliser.co.nz) which also has a cooking school. Te Kairanga also runs a farmers' market on the first Sunday of every month through spring and summer. Visit Chapter 8 for more information on wineries to visit.
- There are many vineyards in Wairarapa which offer accommodation on site including Gladstone Vineyard (gladstonevineyard.co.nz), Luna Estate (lunaestate.co.nz), and Porters (porterspinot.co.nz) which also rents one of Martinborough's original homesteads in the centre of the town.
- Owned by Bill Foley, an American businessman and wine lover with brands from New Zealand to Napa Valley, Wharekauhau Lodge offers the beauty of Edwardian architecture with modern Kiwi hospitality. The spectacular country estate spans 2,225 hectares and guests can explore native forest, farmland, gardens and orchards and can even participate on the farm if they're looking for the ultimate Kiwi experience (wharekauhau.co.nz).
- From Martinborough, it's an hour's drive to Cape Palliser, where you'll find a seal colony, stunning sea views and a 250-odd step climb

to the late-nineteenth century lighthouse. It's also worth making a visit to the Putangirua Pinnacles, a strange rock formation that was a location in *The Lord of the Rings*.
- The websites wellingtonnz.com, wairarapanz.com and wairarapawinegrowers.co.nz are all useful resources for planning your visit.

Nelson

Home to three national parks, two of New Zealand's great walks and one wine region, Nelson is a place to relax and enjoy what nature has to offer. You are never far from water in Nelson and locals spend their weekends on the beach, sailing, kayaking, diving or fishing. In winter, it is an easy drive to the ski fields where Nelson wine pioneer Hermann Seifried met his wife Agnes more than forty years ago.

Nelson attracts alternative types: hippies and naturists are at home in Nelson with its sunny climate and its laid-back vibe. Artists and artisans thrive here; gallery goers will be spoiled for choice; hops are as prolific as vines in Nelson meaning craft brewing sits alongside winemaking while local produce – including berries, kiwi fruit, nuts and cheese – makes the Wednesday farmers' market a gourmet extravaganza.

You might like
- In the village of Upper Moutere, not only will you find wineries including Neudorf Vineyards making superlative Chardonnay, but also New Zealand's oldest pub, Moutere Inn (established 1850), a sheep's milk cheesemaker (thorvald.co.nz), an olive grove, a cider maker and a handful of galleries (moutereartisans.co.nz).
- Visit Nelson's oldest winery Seifried (seifried.co.nz) with its child-friendly cellar door before spending the rest of your day on nearby Rabbit Island. The sandy beach and shallow water make this perfect for little ones; there is also a network of mountain bike trails.
- Beyond the wineries of the Waimea Plains and Moutere Hills lies the Abel Tasman National Park. Kayak and walk the coastal track, mixing hiking with sunbathing on the golden beaches and swimming in the warm waters. Visit the Department of Conservation website (doc.govt.nz) for more details.
- The regional websites nelsontasman.nz and winenelson.co.nz are useful for planning your stay in Nelson.

Marlborough

A trip to Marlborough is about its land, its waters and nature's bounty. The stunning gateway to the region is the Marlborough Sounds, home to oysters, mussels and salmon. Life doesn't get much better than a freshly shucked oyster plucked out of the clear waters of the Sounds, served with a cool glass of Sauvignon Blanc.

It is a magnificent, albeit slightly rough, journey across the Cook Strait and through the Marlborough Sounds from Wellington on the North Island to Picton on the South Island aboard the Interislander ferry. The gateway to Marlborough's wine region is a natural playground for active winemakers, who spend their days off in the Sounds, sailing, kayaking, walking and cycling.

Marlborough's main town Blenheim, nicknamed Beaverton in the early days of settlement because it was so flood prone, is no architectural beauty. Nor is it a fine-dining mecca, so stick to the vineyards. Get your bearings by taking a hike – or bike – in the Wither Hills, giving you views out to Cloudy Bay and across the Wairau Valley.

You might like
- Get to grips with the history of wine in Marlborough at the Marlborough Museum (marlboroughmuseum.org.nz) and pay a visit to Auntsfield (auntsfield.co.nz). In 1873, Scottish immigrant David Herd planted the first vines in Marlborough on the Auntsfield Estate while everyone else was farming sheep. It would be another century before wine was taken seriously by locals but his original winery has been restored and can be visited before tasting at the somewhat more modern cellar door. If you arrive via Blenheim airport, look left as you exit the terminal and you'll see a statue of Herd greeting new arrivals.
- Continuing on the theme of history, a steam locomotive runs from Picton to Blenheim (marlboroughflyer.co.nz). Blenheim railway station's 1913 heritage building is also home to The Wine Station (thewinestation.co.nz), a tasting centre and shop, which offers up to eighty different Marlborough wines by the glass via Enomatic wine machines. Load up a card with credit and get tasting.
- Johanneshof Cellars is home to New Zealand's first underground rock cellar. Lying 20 metres below a precipitous hill that climbs above

the camper van-filled road on the way from Blenheim to Picton, it's worth booking ahead for a tour of this unique cellar. Its co-founder is German and in Marlborough's cool climate, it's no surprise the winery excels at aromatic white varieties (johanneshof.co.nz).

- There are more than thirty cellar doors in Marlborough with favourites including Hans Herzog, Fromm, Nautilus, Framingham and more. Brancott Estate's cellar door and restaurant is an impressive glass construction perched above the first block of Sauvignon Blanc vines planted in the region. It affords expansive views over the Brancott Valley and beyond. In addition to the cellar door and restaurant, the winery has an ongoing partnership with Marlborough Heritage Falcon Trust and visitors can watch daily displays of native birds of prey in full flight.

- Jacksons Road is just a few minutes' drive from Blenheim airport, and will keep wine lovers entertained all day. Start at Allan Scott where tours run daily at 11 a.m. (allanscott.com) before crossing the road to visit Cloudy Bay. The cellar door comes alive in summer when the comfy chairs that make up the outdoor lounge are dusted off and the croquet and pétanque sets come out. If you're looking for a more bespoke experience beyond a glass of this iconic Sauvignon Blanc and freshly shucked oysters (and money is no object), book a vineyard tour by car or helicopter followed by a tutored tasting or a day's sailing on a 16-metre yacht on the Marlborough Sounds (cloudybay.co.nz). Rather more affordable is a visit to Jackson Estate's 1850s-style bush hut (jacksonestate.co.nz). And when your palate has had enough wine for one day, Moa Brewing Co – founded by Allan Scott's son Josh – has a cellar door that also lies on this narrow strip of deliciousness.

- Built as a convent in 1901, The Marlborough Lodge is an elegant timber-framed hotel, which has since been moved ten minutes' drive from its original home in Blenheim and now sits in 6.5 hectares of private parkland. Take in the views of the grounds from the balcony of your suite, explore at your own pace or join the head gardener on a daily tour of the gardens and vineyard followed by a glass of Sauvignon Blanc (themarlboroughlodge.co.nz).

- Want to stay on a vineyard? The country casual Hans Herzog cottage (hansherzog.co.nz) is highly recommended (see Chapter 9), The

Bell Tower offers luxury bed and breakfast accommodation at Dog Point vineyard (dogpoint.co.nz) and St Leonards has a number of restored cottages with little extras including a swimming pool, grass tennis court, bicycles, and chickens laying fresh eggs for breakfast (stleonards.co.nz).

• If you have the time and your car insurance allows you to go on the road less travelled, drive from the Wairau Valley to the Awatere Valley via Taylor's Pass. The unsealed road makes for a slow but dramatic journey. Once in the Awatere Valley, pay a visit to Yealands' cellar door. Collect a map or download the app on your phone and take a forty-minute self-guided tour through the vineyards before heading back to the cellar to taste through the wines. You might meet some chickens or sheep, and on a clear day, you will be able to see the North Island (yealands.co.nz).

• The websites marlboroughnz.com and wine-marlborough.co.nz offer the visitor more ideas for upcoming trips to the region.

Canterbury and North Canterbury

Akaroa retains its French flair on Banks Peninsula with French street names, colonial architecture and croissants aplenty. Visit the tourist information centre on the corners of Rue Lavaud and Rue Balguerie before exploring the town settled by both British and French settlers in the mid-nineteenth century. The first French settlers planted vines but their vineyards disappeared with the next generation. However, there has been a small wine renaissance in the area. French vigneron Renan Cataliotti farms the vineyards of French Peak Wines biodynami-cally (frenchpeakwines.com) while Akaroa Wines and Takamatua Valley Vineyards (takamatuavalley.com) are both organic producers sitting on the volcanic slopes above the historic village. Pay them a visit after a morning in the harbour swimming with Hector's dolphins. The website akaroa.com is a useful source of information for visitors.

Less than an hour's drive from Christchurch lies the Waipara Valley, which forms the heart – and soul – of the North Canterbury wine region. It is a compact area, meaning you can cover this little region's biggest names on a day trip from Christchurch or en route to Hanmer Springs – an Alpine resort village with thermal pools.

You might like

- The Waipara Valley offers two of the finest winery restaurants in the land: Black Estate (blackestate.co.nz) and Pegasus Bay (pegasusbay.com) are both winners of the *Cuisine* magazine winery restaurant of the year. Open for lunch only; you'll have to travel to the small town of Amberley if you want to eat after dark.
- A vineyard cycle trail, which can also be undertaken on foot, connects a number of the region's cellar doors. The trail is unsealed and mountain bikes are recommended (hurunuitrails.co.nz).
- Stay the night at Purepod at Greystone (purepods.com), a glass eco-cabin set above the vineyard. Black Estate also offers a modern apartment at the top of its home block while the Old Glenmark Vicarage offers self-contained accommodation as well as bed and breakfast in this historic home, a former vicarage built in 1907.
- Get active and explore the hills, native bush and beaches of the area: pull on your hiking boots and enjoy the three-hour Tiromoana Bush walk, which leads you through wetlands and forest, along coastal cliffs and down to the waters of Pegasus Bay.
- Saturday morning is market day in the local town of Amberley. Pick up locally grown produce, olive oils, lavender, meat and seafood.
- Ride through the limestone-rich Weka Pass on a steam train from Waipara to Waikari (wekapassrailway.co.nz). It is a short drive from Waikari station to Bell Hill and Pyramid Valley vineyards.
- The website visithurunui.co.nz has a wealth of information on tourism options in the North Canterbury area.

Central Otago

Craggy mountain peaks capped with snow, even in the heat of summer, perch majestically above sparkling lakes, bordered by lush cherry orchards and verdant vineyards. The crystal clear air, piercing blue skies and starry nights seem almost unreal in their clarity. It's no wonder that two in three international visitors head to Otago to soak up its unrivalled beauty.

The region is the adventure capital of New Zealand and, between winery visits, you can throw yourself off a bridge, preferably with a bungee rope attached, or jetboat down an impossibly narrow gorge. Queenstown is the tourist capital of the region, and the centre for partying backpackers and adrenaline junkies. It's also a beautiful town with high-end hotels and more sedate activities for grown ups and families. For those looking for quieter places with a high standard of accommodation, restaurants and wineries, Arrowtown and Wanaka are picture-postcard settlements offering a more tranquil experience.

Central Otago is an all-year destination. It has an extreme semi-continental climate with hot, dry summers. The sky is a vivid shade of blue and the seemingly endless days at this latitude bring hikers, bikers and watersport lovers in their droves. Winter means snow, attracting ski bunnies from June until October in the best years. There isn't a time not to come to Central Otago, with autumn turning leaves to vivid rusty reds and golden tones. The days are warm and the nights are cool, the wine industry is in full flow, and the smell of fermenting juice fills the air.

You might like
- Cellar doors pepper the region's landscapes. There are more than thirty to choose from, offering a variety of experiences. Amisfield and Gibbston Valley Winery (see Chapter 13) are two of the closest cellar doors to Queenstown and both offer restaurants. Gibbston Valley also offers tours of its wine cellar hewn from the mountainside, a cheesery and bike hire.
- The 4 Barrels Walking Trail is an 8-kilometre circular walk connecting Misha's Vineyard, Aurum Wines, Scott Base and Wooing Tree Vineyard in Cromwell. The route takes you through orchards, around Lake Dunstan and to cellar doors. Maps can be collected from the Cromwell iSite on Murray Terrace and participating wineries.
- Kinross is the 'cellar door' for five of the region's wineries (Coal Pit, Domaine Thomson, Hawkshead, Valli and Wild Irishman). Based in Gibbston, around twenty-five minutes' drive from Queenstown, it also has a bistro and cottages among the vines (kinrosscottages.co.nz).
- Former sea-urchin diver Quintin Quider is the man behind Wild Earth. Located at the Goldfields Mining Centre close to Cromwell, it serves wild food sourced locally, cooked in 'retired' wine barrels, and served on former barrel staves (wildearthwines.co.nz).
- Wineries in Alexandra welcome riders on the Otago Rail Trail cycle: after a day in the saddle, a glass of Pinot Noir is just the ticket. Hawkdun Rise Vineyard and Judge Rock also offer vineyard accommodation.

- Felton Road isn't only home to the who's who of Central Otago wineries. It is the site of the Bannockburn Sluicings, a strange desert landscape that has been carved by miners hunting for gold. A loop track can be accessed from a car park on Felton Road and provides a slice of history between glasses of Pinot Noir.
- Boaters, skiers and wedding parties are lured year-round to Wanaka with its stunning lake and mountain vistas. Vines cascade to the water's edge at Rippon, making it the most photographed vineyard in the country, if not the world. But there's more to Rippon than its looks: its mature vine Pinot Noirs are as impressive as the view (rippon.co.nz).
- Visit centralotagonz.com for more inspiration and information on the region.

Waitaki

The remote Waitaki region has been given a new lease of life with the opening of the Alps 2 Ocean cycle trail (alps2ocean.com). Starting from Aoraki (Mount Cook), it winds its way down through Omarama, past lake after lake to the village of Kurow, the heart of the Waitaki wine area and onward to the finish at Oamaru, the home of a blue penguin colony. It is 301 kilometres, and you are advised to take between four and six days to complete it. The distance is certainly not putting people off, as it is attracting an estimated 18,500 visitors to the area annually.

You might like
- A few kilometres from Duntroon lie the Elephant Rocks. Once the film set for *The Lion, the Witch and the Wardrobe*, there is no charge to wander around these enormous, oddly shaped limestone boulders.
- On Kurow's main street lies the 1930s post office, now home to Ostler Wines' cellar door and offices. Known as The Vintner's Drop, it is open weekdays and, during the summer, it is also opened at the weekend. There are simple tasting plates as well as wine and they also have a local craft beer on top to cleanse your wine-weary palate. Consult the website for opening times and more information (ostlerwine.co.nz).
- River T runs a cellar door on the road between Kurow and Duntroon, showing its Waitaki wines, offering self-guided tours and platters. Open seven days a week from September to May (rivertestate.co.nz).

- Ask a local vintner where to eat, drink and stay in the area and they will all respond 'Waitaki Braids Lodge'. The wine and beer list – and the food – supports local producers and the accommodation has a modern country feel. It is the perfect place to relax after a day's biking, fishing or tasting wine (waitakibraids.com).
- Waitaki Wine Tours offers visitors a personalized and comprehensive tour of this small region. Departing from Oamaru on a daily basis, there are opportunities to taste the wines of local labels that don't have cellar doors in the area (waitakiwinetours.oamaru.net.nz).
- For more information, visit Tourism Waitaki's website (tourwaitakinz. com).

APPENDIX: STATISTICS

Table 1: The growth of the New Zealand wine industry, 1981 to 2017

Year	Total vineyard (ha)	No. of wineries	Total production (m litres)	Exports volume (m litres)	Export value (NZ$m)
1981	5,417	N/A	44.0	0.6	1.1
1990	5,800	131	54.4	4.0	18.4
2000	10,197	358	60.1	19.2	168.6
2010	33,200	672	190.0	142.0	1.04 bn
2017	37,129	677	285.1	253.0	1.66 bn

Source: New Zealand Winegrowers annual reports

Table 2: Climatic comparisons between New Zealand and other classic wine regions around the world[1]

Country/State	Region	Area (km2)	Elevation (m)	GST (°C)	GDD[2]	HI	BEDD
New Zealand	Otago	1,089	340	13.8	805	1,402	841
Germany	Mosel Valley	198	179	14.0	891	1,411	966
Germany	Rheinhessen (Rhine Valley)	327	170	14.1	922	1,473	989
France	Champagne	381	170	14.2	923	1,492	981
Germany	Baden	189	245	14.9	1,056	1,602	1,117
Oregon	Willamette Valley	13,876	122	15.0	1,081	1,748	1,195
New Zealand	Wairau Valley (Marlborough)	611	80	15.1	1,068	1,533	1,094
France	Burgundy	260	264	15.2	1,118	1,648	1,171
New Zealand	Nelson	308	34	15.2	1,101	1,508	1,122
New Zealand	Bay of Plenty	1,821	184	15.8	1,220	1,550	1,203
Italy	Valtellina Superiore	5	476	16.2	1,335	1,880	1,304
New Zealand	Hawkes Bay	599	29	16.3	1,334	1,732	1,358
France	Bordeaux	1,471	50	16.5	1,387	1,890	1,382
New Zealand	Gisborne	228	21	16.6	1,390	1,761	1,411
Spain	Rioja	605	506	16.6	1,410	1,886	1,343
Australia	Yarra Valley	3,120	251	16.6	1,343	1,810	1,179
New Zealand	Kumeu	52	36	16.6	1,401	1,688	1,386
Washington & Oregon	Walla Walla	1,306	317	17.1	1,528	2,296	1,480
France	Côtes du Rhône Méridionales	1,440	174	17.3	1,570	2,067	1,447
Australia	Coonawarra	400	65	17.4	1,511	2,046	1,330

Italy	Barolo	56	314	17.5	1,600	1,960	1,559
Italy	Vino Nobile di Montepulciano	28	307	17.5	1,613	2,057	1,473
Portugal	Vinho Verde	61	190	17.6	1,635	1,987	1,576
New Zealand	Bay of Islands	465	52	17.6	1,606	1,827	1,521
Italy	Chianti Classico	101	321	17.9	1,685	2,112	1,507
Portugal	Porto	807	437	17.9	1,684	2,155	1,489
California	Napa Valley	1,624	248	18.8	1,883	2,504	1,850
California	Paso Robles	2,464	398	18.9	1,903	2,681	2,032
Spain	La Mancha	2,864	689	18.9	1,912	2,417	1,445
Australia	Barossa Valley	590	278	19.0	1,852	2,342	1,489
Australia	Margaret River	2,640	75	19.2	1,887	2,092	1,584
California	Lodi	2,195	24	20.3	2,211	2,797	1,980
Spain	Jerez-Xéres-Sherry	126	57	20.9	2,343	2,441	1,921

Source: Anderson et al. (2012).

1   Area is rounded to the nearest 1 km^2 (100 hectares) and is approximate due to the resolution and precision of the wine region boundary data. Wine producing region total area and spatial median values for elevation and climate indices for Europe over 1950–2000 (Jones et al. 2009), Australia for 1971–2000 (Hall & Jones 2010), the western United States for 1971–2000 (Jones et al. 2010), and selected New Zealand wine regions. Climate indices are growing season average temperature (GST, °C), growing degree days (GDD, C° units), Huglin Index (HI, C° units), and biologically effective degree-days (BEDD, C° units) sorted by GST.

2   Note that the GDDs cited in this table differ slightly to the GDDs provided in the Applicants' Evidence in support of an application to register a Geographical Indication to the New Zealand Intellectual Property Office (iponz.gov.nz).

BIBLIOGRAPHY

Allan, R. M. (1965) *Nelson: a History of Early Settlement*. Wellington, N.Z.: Reed.

Anderson, J. D., Jones, G. V., Tait, A., Hall, A., & Trought, M. C. T. (2012) 'Analysis of viticulture region climate structure and suitability in New Zealand.' *Journal International Des Sciences De La Vigne Et Du Vin*, 46(3), 149–165.

Anon. (2005) 'Pioneering spirit puts Wellsford family into hall of fame.' *The Rodney Times*, 21 April, p. 5.

Atkinson, G. (2016) '"Hermitage" in New Zealand: the Origins and Development of the Te Kauwhata "Hermitage" Syrah.' https://stonecroft.co.nz/history/

Bassett, M., & Bassett, J. (2015) *The Next Vintage: the Babich family and 100 years of New Zealand Wine*. Auckland, N.Z.: David Ling Publishing Limited.

Bell, V. A. (2015) 'An integrated strategy for managing grapevine leafroll-associated virus 3 in red berry cultivars in New Zealand vineyards (thesis).' Victoria University of Wellington. http://researcharchive.vuw.ac.nz

Beresford, R. M., Mundy, D. C., & Wood, P. N. (2013) 'Understanding causes of slip skin: final report.' *New Zealand Winegrowers*.

Bloomfield, G. T. (2015) 'Alcohol consumption, 1920–60.' https://teara.govt.nz

Bollinger, C. (1959) *Grog's Own Country; The History of Liquor Licensing in New Zealand*. 2d. rev. ed. Auckland, N.Z.: Price Milburn.

Brady, A. (2010) *Pinot Central: A Winemaker's Story*. North Shore, N.Z.: Penguin.

Bragato, R. (1895) *Report on the Prospects of Viticulture in New Zealand: Together with Instructions for Planting and Pruning.* Wellington, N.Z.: S. Costall.

Brien, B. (2003) *100 Years of Hospitality in New Zealand: the People, the Politics, the Passion.* Wellington Museums Trust in association with the Hospitality Association of N.Z.

Busby, J. (1833) *Journal of a Tour through some of the Vineyards of Spain and France.* Sydney, Australia: Stephens & Stokes.

Busby, J. (1866) *Our Colonial Empire and the Case of New Zealand.* London, UK: Williams and Norgate.

Caldwell, A. (2010) 'The island of the day before …' *New Zealand Geographic.* https://www.nzgeo.com

Campbell, B. (2002) 'Phylloxera hits New Zealand's fastest-growing wine region.' *Wine Spectator.* http://www.winespectator.com

Carpenter, L. (2016) 'The use of Gold Rush nostalgia on wine labels: brief history of New Zealand's Central Otago wine region,' in G. Muratovski (ed.), *Consumer Culture: Selected Essays.* Bristol, UK: Intellect.

Cheeseman, L., Henderson, D., Atkinson, B., & Gherman, M. (2007) *A Love Affair with Wine.* Auckland, N.Z.: Random House.

Clark, O. (2002) *Oz Clarke Wine Atlas: Wines and Regions of the World.* 2nd ed. New York: Little Brown & Co.

Cocker, J., & Murray, J. M. (1930) *Temperance and Prohibition in New Zealand, comp. and issued under the auspices of the New Zealand Alliance for the Abolition of the Liquor Traffic.* London, UK: Epworth Press (J.A. Sharp).

Cooper, M. (1998) 'Wohnsiedler, Friedrich', in *Te Ara – the Encyclopedia of New Zealand, Dictionary of New Zealand Biography.* https://teara.govt.nz

Cooper, M., & Morrison, R. (1988) *The Wines and Vineyards of New Zealand.* Auckland, N.Z.: Hodder and Stoughton.

Cowen, T. (2017) 'Feisty, protectionist populism? New Zealand tried that.' *Bloomberg.* https://www.bloomberg.com/

Dalley, B. (2012) 'Migrant groups and the wine industry.' https://www.teara.govt.nz/en/wine/page-2

Farm Editor. (1984) 'Dreaded pest found in local vineyard.' *The Marlborough Express*, 9 January.

Franson, P. (2015) 'How New Zealand controls leafroll virus.' *Wines & Vines*. https://www.winesandvines.com

Gasteiger, F. (2008) *Marlborough Wine: Stories from New Zealand's Premier Wine Region*. Blenheim, N.Z.: Oriel Design & Pub.

Goldwater, K. (2013) *Vineyard Virgins*. Auckland, N.Z.: Putiki Press Ltd.

Goode, J. (2005) *The Science of Wine: from Vine to Glass*. Berkeley, CA: University of California Press.

Goode, J. (2007) 'The David Hohnen interview: The man behind Cloudy Bay and Cape Mentelle makes a fresh start.' *Wine Anorak*. http://www.wineanorak.com

Goode, J. (2012) *The Science of Sauvignon Blanc*. London: Flavour Press.

Grahm, R. (2012) *Been Doon So Long: a Randall Grahm Vinthology*. Berkeley, CA: University of California Press.

Green, J. A., Parr, W. V., Breitmeyer, J., Valentin, D., & Sherlock, R. (2011) 'Sensory and chemical characterisation of Sauvignon Blanc wine: influence of source of origin.' *Food Research International*, 44(9), 2788–2797.

Gustafson, B., & Smith, M. (2009) *His Way: a Biography of Robert Muldoon*. Auckland, N.Z.: Auckland University Press.

Hall, A. and Jones, G.V. (2010) 'Spatial analysis of climate in winegrape-growing regions in Australia.' *Australian Journal of Grape and Wine Research*, 16(3), 389–404.

Hamilton, P., & Shopes, L. (2008) *Oral History and Public Memories*. Philadelphia: Temple University Press.

Hay, C. (2014) *New Zealand Wine Guide: An Introduction to the Wine Styles & Regions of New Zealand*. Auckland, N.Z.: Hay Publishing.

Haydn, J. (1997) 'Our love affair with wine.' *New Zealand Geographic*, 35, 18–42.

IFOAM – Organics International, F. I. B. L. (2017) *The World of Organic Agriculture – Statistics and Emerging Trends, 2017*. https://shop.fibl.org/

Intellectual Property Office of New Zealand (2018) Geographical indications register. https://www.iponz.govt.nz

Jackson, R. S. (2014) *Wine Science: Principles and Applications*. London: Elsevier/Academic Press.

Johnson, H. (2006) *Wine: A Life Uncorked*. Berkeley, CA: University of California Press.

Jones, G., & Grandjean, E. (2017) 'Creating the market for organic wine: sulfites, certification, and green values (working paper).' *Harvard Business School.* http://www.hbs.edu/

Jones, G., & Mowatt, S. (2016) 'National image as a competitive disadvantage: the case of the New Zealand organic food industry.' *Business History*, 58(8), 1262–1288.

Jones, G.V., Moriondo, M., Bois, B., Hall, A. and Duff, A. (2009) 'Analysis of the spatial climate structure in viticulture regions worldwide.' *Bull. OIV*, 82(944), 507–518.

Jones, G.V., Duff, A.A., Hall, A. and Myers J.W. (2010) 'Spatial analysis of climate in winegrape growing regions in the western United States.' *Am. J. Enology Vitic.*, 61(3), 313–326

Jouanneau, S., Weaver, R., Nicolau, L., Herbst-Johnstone, M., Benkwitz, F., & Kilmartin, P. (2012) 'Subregional survey of aroma compounds in Marlborough Sauvignon Blanc wines.' *Australian Journal of Grape and Wine Research*, 18(3), 329–343.

Kemp, B. (2010) 'The effect of the timing of leaf removal on berry ripening, flavour and aroma compounds in Pinot Noir wine (thesis).' *Lincoln University Research Archive.* https://researcharchive.lincoln. ac.nz/

King, M. (2003) *The Penguin History of New Zealand.* Auckland, N.Z.: Viking.

King, P. D., Meekings, J. S., & Smith, S. M. (1982) 'Studies of the resistance of grapes (*Vitis spp.*) to phylloxera (*Daktulosphaira vitifoliae*).' *New Zealand Journal of Experimental Agriculture*, 10(3), 337–344.

Knight, S., Klaere, S., Fedrizzi, B., & Goddard, M. R. (2015) 'Regional microbial signatures positively correlate with differential wine phenotypes: evidence for a microbial aspect to terroir.' *Scientific Reports*, 5:14233.

Lewis, N. (2014) 'Beyond the flawed narratives of a crisis of over-supply: a conceptual fix for New Zealand wine.' In *Social, Cultural and Economic Impacts of Wine in New Zealand* (pp. 86–102). Abingdon, UK: Routledge.

Logan, G. A. (2015). 'Rotundone in New Zealand *Vitis vinifera* (thesis).' *The University of Auckland.* Retrieved from https://researchspace. auckland.ac.nz/

Lund, C. M., Thompson, M. K., Benkwitz, F., Triggs, C. M., Gardner, R., Heymann, H., & Nicolau, L. (2009) 'New Zealand Sauvignon Blanc distinct flavor characteristics: sensory, chemical, and consumer aspects.' *American Journal of Enology and Viticulture*, 60(1), 1–12.

Macara, G. R. (2016). *The Climate and Weather of Nelson and Tasman District.* https://www.niwa.co.nz/node/110338

MacGibbon, J., & Higginson, M. (2017) *The Look of Martinborough: Rural Servicing, Wine Village, Tourist Destination 1870–2017.* Masterton, N.Z.: Fraser Books.

Mackay, J. A. (1949) 'Historic Poverty Bay and the East Coast.' *New Zealand Electronic Text Centre.* http://nzetc.victoria.ac.nz

McLean, G. (2015) *Robert Muldoon.* https://nzhistory.govt.nz/people/

McLintock, A. H. (1966) *An Encyclopaedia of New Zealand.* Wellington, N.Z.: Govt. Printer.

Moran, W., & Drecki, I. (2016) *New Zealand Wine: the Land, the Vines, the People.* Auckland, N.Z.: Auckland University Press.

New Zealand Winegrowers https://www.nzwine.com/en/

Nicholson, T., Martin, D., & Plant & Food Research. (2016) 'Protecting grapes from UVs.' *New Zealand Winegrower.* https://www.ruralnewsgroup.co.nz/

Orange, C. (1990) 'James Busby.' *Dictionary of New Zealand Biography.* Te Ara: The Encyclopedia of New Zealand. https://teara.govt.nz/en/biographies/

Parr, W. V., & Green, J. A. (2007) 'What is a typical Marlborough Savvy?' *New Zealand Winegrower*, 10(6), 70–73.

Parr, W. V., Frost, A., White, K. G., & Marfell, J. (2004) 'Sensory evaluation of wine: deconstructing the concept of Marlborough Sauvignon Blanc.' *The Australian & New Zealand Grapegrower & Winemaker.* 32nd Annual Technical Issue, 63–69.

Parr, W. V., Valentin, D., Green, J. A., & Dacremont, C. (2010) 'Evaluation of French and New Zealand Sauvignon wines by experienced French wine assessors.' *Food Quality and Preference*, 21(1), 56–64.

Perriam, J. (2009). *Dust to Gold: the Inspiring Story of Bendigo Station.* Auckland, N.Z.: Random House.

Prial, F. J. (1995) 'Wine talk.' *New York Times*, 30 August, p. 4.

Rawson Elder, J. (ed) (1932) *The Letters and Journals of Samuel Marsden.* Dunedin, N.Z.: Coulls, Somerville, Wilkie Limited.

Rice, G. W. (1992) *The Oxford History of New Zealand.* 2nd edn Oxford, UK: Oxford University Press.

Rice, G. W. (2002) *The Oxford History of New Zealand.* South Melbourne, Australia: Oxford University Press.

Robinson, J. (2015) 'The man who dreamt up Cloudy Bay.' 1 October, www.jancisrobinson.com.

Robinson, J., Harding, J., & Vouillamoz, J. F. (2012) *Wine Grapes: A Complete Guide to 1,380 Vine Varieties, Including their Origins and Flavors.* New York: Ecco/HarperCollins.

Rolland, F. (1872) 'Fr. Rolland to Fr. Favre.' https://mariststudies.org/docs/Clisby211

Rosenman, H., & d'Urville, J. D. (1988) *An Account in Two Volumes of Two Voyages to the South Seas by Captain (later Rear-Admiral) Jules S-C Dumont d'Urville of the French Navy to Australia, New Zealand, Oceania, 1826–1829 in the Corvette* Astrolabe *and to the Straits of Magellan, Chile, Oceania, South East Asia, Australia, Antarctica, New Zealand, and Torres Strait, 1837–1840 in the Corvettes* Astrolabe *and* Zélée. Honolulu, HI: University of Hawaii Press.

Schuster, D., Jackson, D., & Tipples, R. (2002) *Canterbury Grapes & Wines 1840–2002.* Christchurch, N.Z.: Shoal Bay Press.

Scott, D., & Friedlander, M. (2002) *Pioneers of New Zealand Wine.* Auckland, N.Z.: Reed.

Scott, D., & Keats, A. C. (2014) *A Stake in the Country: Assid Abraham Corban and his Family, 1892–1977.* Auckland, N.Z.: Royal New Zealand Foundation of the Blind.

Smart, R. (2017) 'Save your vineyard from trunk diseases.' *New Zealand Winegrower,* June/July (104), 16–17.

Smith, D. (1946) *Report of the Royal Commission on Licensing.* Wellington, N.Z.: E.V. Paul.

Song, M., Fuentes, C., Loos, A., & Tomasino, E. (2018) 'Free monoterpene isomer profiles of *Vitis vinifera* L. cv. white wines.' *Foods,* 7(2), 27.

Spence, R. (2017) 'The history of Sauvignon Blanc.' *New Zealand Winegrower.* https://www.ruralnewsgroup.co.nz/

Stewart, K. (1997) *Te Mata: the First 100 Years*. Auckland, N.Z.: Godwit.

Stewart, K. (2010) *Chancers and Visionaries: a History of Wine in New Zealand*. Auckland, N.Z.: Godwit.

Sweet, M., Cowley, P., & Whittaker, T. (2015) *Wine Stories from Hawke's Bay*. Havelock North, Hawke's Bay, N.Z.: BayBuzz.

Taber, G. M. (2007) *To Cork or not to Cork: Tradition, Romance, Science, and the Battle for the Wine Bottle*. New York: Scribner.

Thorpy, F. (1976) *New Zealand Wine Guide*. Sydney, Australia and Auckland, N.Z.: Books for Pleasure.

Tonietto, J., & Carbonneau, A. (2004) 'A multicriteria climatic classification system for grape-growing regions worldwide.' *Agricultural and Forest Meteorology*, 124(1–2), 81–97.

Tonkin, P., Webb, T., Almond, P., Creasy, G., Harrison, R., Hassall, L., & Smith, C. (2015) 'Geology, landforms and soils of the Waipara and Waikari regions of North Canterbury with an emphasis on lands used for viticulture.' *Lincoln University and Landcare Research*, New Zealand. Retrieved from https://hdl.handle.net/10182/7350

Trought, M. C., Agnew, R. A., Bennett, J., Stronge, K., Parr, W., & Greven, M. (2010) 'Soils, climate and vine management: their influence on Marlborough Sauvignon Blanc wine style.' *VIII International Terroir Congress*. Soave, Italy: ResearchGate. https://www.researchgate.net

Tyack, K. (2012) *The winemaker: George Fistonich and the Villa Maria story*. Auckland, N.Z.: Random House New Zealand

Walker, S. (1992) 'Obituary: Sir Robert Muldoon.' *Independent*. www.independent.co.uk

Woodfield, P., & Husted, K. (2017) 'Intergenerational knowledge sharing in family firms: case-based evidence from the New Zealand wine industry.' *Journal of Family Business Strategy*, 8(1), 57–69.

Worrall, R. (1995) 'The new lake.' *New Zealand Geographic*, January – March 1995. www.nzgeo.com/stories/the-new-lake

Young, A. (2000) 'Tyre let down so drunk PM could not drive car.' *The New Zealand Herald*, 30 June 2000, www.nzherald.co.nz

INDEX